VOLTAGE VALLEY REVOLUTION
POWER, POLITICS, AND TECHNOLOGY

AI

The next **industrial revolution** built in America, told by Appalachia in 25 unforgettable stories.

DR. WILLIAM PAOLILLO

Copyright © 2025 by Dr. William Paolillo

ALL RIGHTS RESERVED.

NO part of this book may be reproduced or transmitted in any form by any means, electronic or mechanical, including photocopying and recording, or by any information storage and retrieval system, except as may be expressly permitted in writing from the author.

To my children

Michael & Laura, Gabrielle & Peter, Isabelle, and James

You are amazing people –Those who do good, do well.

Dream Big…….

To my Grandchildren Lucia, Lilia, Leonardo, and Lennon you are our inspiration, because every revolution needs a next generation.

Love, Papi

To All the chapter participants - without you, this would not be possible - thank you.

Acknowledgment

This book was shaped *in quiet corners and open kitchens, through **long conversations** and **brief moments of grace -around the world**. Whether you **provided a place to write, offered thoughtful suggestions, challenged me to go deeper**, or simply **listened with care**—please know that **you were an important part of this journey**.* To those who shared their stories – thank you.

Every story here carries the imprint *of those who believed in its purpose, even when the path was uncertain. **Although your names are not listed**, your presence is **felt in every chapter**.*

This revolution is **not mine alone**; it belongs to all who helped bring these pages to life.

From the bottom of my heart, much love and thank you.

Table of Contents

About the Cover 8

True Stories from Appalachia: The Human Face of America's Next Industrial Revolution ... 9

Historical Foundation and Background 10

Voltage Valley Industrial Revolution 12

    Industrial Revolutions in America: 1945–2025 13

    Digital Revolution (Late 1990s–2020) 14

    Voltage Valley Revolution™:(2020 and beyond) 14

Section & Pages 17

    Support for Appalachian Youth Charities 18

        Including the Dolly Parton Imagination Library 18

    Foreword By Dr. Benjamin Cross 19

    Chapter 1 Author's Note 20

        Why This Matters to Me 21

        Walking the Path Together 22

    Chapter 2 How to Read This Book 23

        How to Read This Book 23

Section 1: Greatest Generation 24

    "The Greatest Generation" 25

    Chapter 3 Uncle Bill: The Fight to Stand Again w/ Dean Smith 27

    Chapter 4 The Power of the Journey w/Stephen Dean 31

Section 2: Tipping Point 36

    Chapter 5 The Human Factor in the Voltage Valley Revolution™ 37

    Chapter 6 Coal Miner Son Finds His Place in the World w/Michael Armour 48

        Appalachia's first Industrial Revolution was powered by the People of Appalachia and Coal. 48

        Michaels Story 48

    Chapter 7 From Politics to Purpose w/David Wilhelm 52

    Chapter 8 Make It, Break It, Make It Better w/ Dr. Benjamin Cross 56

        Appendix 58

    Chapter 9 Love, Resilience, and Community w/Gayle Manchin 60

        A Vision Rooted in Education, Family, and Community 61

- Appendix 62
- Chapter 10 A Mother's Love w/Arria Hines 63
  - Appendix – Technical Facts 65
- Chapter 11 Smart Enough to Try w/Dr. Benjamin Cross 67
- Chapter 12 Forging a Path forward w/Don Wingate 70
  - Appendix Digital Twin Technology – Technical Talk 73
- Chapter 13 Powering Possibilities w/Samantha Childress 75
- Chapter 14 A Child Breaks Through the Cycle of Poverty w/Amanda Woodrum .. 79
- Chapter 15 The New –Collar Revolution w/Jennifer Oddo 82
  - The Great Recession: Losing It All—Again 83
  - Reinvention at IBM: Creating Pathways for the Underserved 83
  - The Voltage Valley Revolution™: Returning to Appalachia 84
  - Appendix 86
- Chapter 16 Courage Forged in Steel w/Rick Stockburger 87
  - A Family's Struggle 87
  - Learning to Lead in the Army 88
  - Finding Purpose Back Home 89
  - The Power of Connection 89
  - A Best Day at Work 90
  - The Heart of the Voltage Valley Revolution™ 91
  - Appendix 91
- Chapter 17 The Heart of Voltage Valley™ w/Tim Petrey 92
- Chapter 18 A Fathers Dream w/John Holbrook 96
- Chapter 19 Celebrating Loving Day w/Kevin Schwab 99
- Chapter 20 Figuring it Out w/ Chris Montgomery 102
  - Key Features of the Pathways to Apprenticeship Program: 103
- Chapter 21 Catalyst for Change w/ Petra Mitchell 105
  - Appendix: Catalyst Connection 107
- Chapter 22 Building More Than Walls w/ Bhavin "B." Patel 109
  - Green Harvest Capital (GHC) 112

Hydrogen Posse Section 113
- Chapter 23 Hydrogen Scientist w/Zane Rhodes 114
  - Appendix: Reimagining the A-Plant in Piketon, Ohio 116
- Chapter 24 The Rhodes Brothers' Journey – Vision to Reality w/Zane & Wiley Rhodes 118

If— 119

Chapter 25 Hydrogen Cowboy w/ Wiley Rhodes 120

Chapter 26 Little Red Heifer w/ Carrie and Tony Montgomery 123

    Tony Montgomery Pike County Commissioner 124

Chapter 27 Community, Family, and Clean Energy w/Caitlin Holley 126

Chapter 28 Finding Purpose in the Pandemic w/Chris Guerri 129

Chapter 29 Energy, Resilience, and the Power to Transform w/ Charles Johnson 132

Section – Forging A Path Forward 135

Chapter 30 A Mother's Vision, A Nation's Power w/ Caroline Cochran PhD 136

Chapter 31 Bridging Worlds: The Diplomat and the Nuclear Fusion Scientist w/Matthew Smith 139

Chapter 32 Rooted to Rise: Microgreens, Medicine, and a New Appalachian Power /James Valencia 143

Conclusion 148

Final Reflection 153

    Every Revolution Asks Something of Us .... **Error! Bookmark not defined.**

    Part I: Tariffs, Whiskey, and the Taxes That Bind a Nation .. **Error! Bookmark not defined.**

    Part II: The Medici, the Black Plague, and Civilized Capitalism .... **Error! Bookmark not defined.**

    Part III: Moore's Law, Chips, and the Power of Less .... **Error! Bookmark not defined.**

    Part IV: Hemingway's Lost Generation vs. Life of Integrity **Error! Bookmark not defined.**

    Part V: Clean-Innovation Ecosystems, Universal Income, and the Future of Care .... **Error! Bookmark not defined.**

    Part VI: Poverty, Orphans, and the Call of Community .... **Error! Bookmark not defined.**

    Pulling It All Together: People, Technology and Renewal .... **Error! Bookmark not defined.**

Epilogue A Benediction for Appalachia And Beyond 161

Appendix 162

Chapter 33 The Academic Article That Inspired This Book 162

    Clean Innovation Ecosystems: Lifting Distressed Communities in Appalachia with Clean Energy 162

    Summary of the remaining article 165

    Results 167

    Universities, Trade Organizations, and Local Models 169

    From Silicon Valley to Voltage Valley 169

Chapter 34 **AI-Powered Digital Spatial Intelligence**: Empowering Asset Owners in Architecture, Engineering, and Construction to Maximize Operational Efficiency, Sustainability, and Lifecycle Value 172

    Abstract 172

    1. Introduction: The Dawn of Digital Spatial Intelligence in the Built Environment 172

    2. Literature Review and Epistemological Framework 174

    3. Methodology 177

    4. Findings and Analysis 177

    5. Discussion: Operationalizing Digital Spatial Intelligence (DSI) 179

    6. Conclusion 182

Chapter 35 Unlocking the Future of Clean Energy: DOE Programs 184

    The Loan Programs Office: Financing the Next Industrial Revolution 184

    The Impact of the Inflation Reduction Act 186

    Navigating the Application Process 186

    The Road Ahead: Building the Future with LPO and IRA 187

About the Cover

The cover of *Voltage Valley Revolution*™ draws from the visual storytelling of artist Donna Spatidol, known for capturing cycles of nature, resilience, and transformation. Her influence runs through every part of this design.

At the center stands the **Digital Sycamore**—a living circuit rooted in Appalachian soil and wired to the future. Its branches form two human profiles, facing each other, not in conflict but in recognition. Intelligence flows between them, not as a command but as a connection. At the base, a chip marked **"AI"** feeds into the roots: a fusion of memory and machine.

This isn't a metaphor. It's the blueprint. A new economy is growing—circular, intentional, built by people who know the cost of power and the value of community.

To the left, a **great blue heron** rises from the industrial shadow. Common to Appalachian waterways, the heron is presence, patience, and return. It watches, adapts, survives—just like the people in these pages.

Across the horizon, rusting infrastructure—factories, towers, rail—doesn't signal decay. It marks **transformation**. What was once extracted now regenerates. What was left behind is being reimagined. **Stewardship replaces sprawl.**

To the right, a **human silhouette** glows from the circuit, a reminder that none of this happens without people: the builders, the thinkers, and the families who stayed and shaped what comes next. In this future, **technology serves humanity**, not the other way around.

Above all, a **recycling symbol** hovers—not just for materials but also for systems, mindsets, and values. Appalachia isn't catching up. It's carving a path. What the coasts call disruption, Appalachia calls **resilience**. This revolution isn't just electric. It's emotional. It's cultural. It remembers—and it builds.

The heron lifts. The sycamore stands.

This time, we build to last.

True Stories from Appalachia: The Human Face of America's Next Industrial Revolution

25 True Stories from Appalachia: The Human Face of America's Next Industrial Revolution

"The most important shift you haven't heard about." Inspired by Malcolm Gladwell

"If you want the rainbow, you gotta put up with the rain." —Dolly Parton

Inspired by Malcolm Gladwell's The Tipping Point, this book captures Appalachia at its second tipping point—not collapse, but a comeback. As coal declined, factories closed, and opioids crept in, a new story quietly took root: resilience, reshoring, and a revolutionary change.

Told in their own words, these 25 raw and deeply human accounts reveal what happens after life knocks you down—diagnosis, deployment, divorce, addiction—and what it means to rise again. From a mom of four leading a billion-dollar manufacturing hub; to a NASCAR legend turning race tech into clean transportation, these are the people leading America's next industrial era.

This story is personal for Dr. William Paolillo. A sustainability professor and former clean tech executive, he spent childhood summers on his grandfather's Appalachian dairy farm. Those early experiences shaped a lifelong belief: the soul of America lives in its overlooked regions—and its future depends on them.

Voltage Valley Revolution ™ connects past struggle to future strength—reshoring American manufacturing: AI- jobs, scaling clean energy, and bringing dignity back to work. This is economic renewal rooted in people, not platforms.

For readers of Hillbilly Elegy, The Tipping Point, Evicted, and Foxfire—this is what's next and going right.

10% of the royalties from this book will go to support Appalachian youth Charities—because every revolution needs its next generation.

VOLTAGE VALLEY REVOLUTION™

Historical Foundation and Background

"What counts is not the mere fact that we have lived. It is what difference we have made to the lives of others that will determine the significance of the life we lead." Nelson Mandela

The United States has long been shaped by moments of collective sacrifice. The Greatest Generation—those who endured the Great Depression and fought in World War II—did more than win a war. They returned home and helped build one of the most productive industrial economies the world had ever seen. Their grit and discipline laid the foundation for the American Century.

This postwar boom gave rise to the idea of **American exceptionalism**—the belief that the U.S. has a unique role in promoting democracy, freedom, and innovation. In *Democracy in America*, Alexis de Tocqueville first observed the remarkable spirit and structure of American life. That spirit fueled economic growth and a sense of national mission: doing good could also meant doing well.

In the decades following WWII, Appalachia became a critical engine of national power. The coalfields of Kentucky, Ohio, West Virginia, and Pennsylvania kept the lights on, and the uranium enrichment plants in Piketon, Ohio, and Paducah, Kentucky, became central to Cold War security.

The **Portsmouth Gaseous Diffusion Plant** in Piketon once used nearly 5% of America's electricity to enrich uranium. Its workers—nicknamed *Cold War Warriors*, helped maintain national security just as earlier generations had secured victory overseas.

U.S. industrial expansion cam with steep price: black lung, environmental destruction, and radioactive waste. The sacrifices of Appalachian communities powered the nation, but they also carried the consequences. Strip mining scarred the Appalachian landscape, mountaintop removal erased ecosystems, and radioactive contamination still lingers in places like Piketon, where the cleanup continues today.

Yet, these communities never stopped showing up. They've endured economic collapse, environmental damage, and public health crises but never lost their resilience.

Now, Appalachia stands on the brink of a new era.

The **Voltage Valley Revolution**™ is not just a rebound, it's a redefinition. It's a second industrial revolution rooted not in extraction but in **innovation**: advanced manufacturing, clean energy, digital infrastructure, material science, and sustainable industry.

In Piketon, Ohio, and its sister site in Paducah, Kentucky—once home to uranium enrichment for the Department of Energy—these Appalachian-edge towns are being reimagined as centers for Clean Energy, Data Centers, Battery Innovation, and Advanced Nuclear Technologies. In Youngstown, Ohio, the echo of steel mills is giving way to battery manufacturing lines. And in

Syracuse, New York, far from the coal seams but still part of the region's industrial fabric, a semiconductor hub is rising—driven by clean energy and smart public policy.

This revolution is learning from the last one.

It's not just about GDP. It's about dignity.

Not just markets. But meaning.

Not just capital. But **people**.

Because **the one thing every revolution needs is people**—those willing to show up, adapt, and build.

Appalachia's past helped build American power. Its future may help redefine it.

This time, the goal isn't domination—its sustainability, equity, and shared progress.

The **Voltage Valley Revolution**™ is the next chapter. Rooted in resilience. Fueled by innovation. And led by people who still believe in a better future because they've already paid the price of the last one.

Voltage Valley Industrial Revolution

The "Voltage Valley Revolution™" refers to a transformative movement revitalizing the Appalachian region and the United States by fostering clean energy and advanced manufacturing industries. This initiative leverages technologies such as electrification, artificial intelligence, data centers, semiconductors, advanced materials, and the Internet of Things to drive economic growth and sustainability. **Dr. William Paolillo (Crains Business 2022)**

"You need to know where you come from to understand where you're going." Maya Angelou's words strongly connect with Appalachia, a region critical to America's industrial growth and now central to the Voltage Valley Revolution™. This movement is changing the region's future and is known for its hard work, resilience, and innovation. After World War II, Appalachia played a key role in the tremendous economic growth. Industries like automotive, aerospace, and electronics prospered, making the American worker a symbol of creativity and determination, helping the nation move forward. The American Dream—achieving success through hard work and perseverance—began in places like Appalachia.

However, the tides turned as the spotlight shifted westward to Silicon Valley. By 2010, 30% of U.S. venture capital flowed into Silicon Valley, cementing it as a global hub of technological breakthroughs. Companies like Apple and Intel redefined innovation, which came at a cost. While technology boomed, manufacturing jobs critical to regions like Appalachia were outsourced overseas. Unfair trade deals gutted American factories, favoring cheap foreign labor and weakening domestic supply chains. Once central to the industrial expansion that fueled local economies, construction jobs declined as the service-oriented tech economy prioritized digital infrastructure over physical manufacturing facilities. Appalachia's communities depended on industries that have since declined, leading to economic challenges in the region.

The COVID-19 pandemic highlighted weaknesses in this system. Disruptions in the global supply chain showed the risks of relying too much on foreign manufacturing. Essential items like semiconductors and personal protective equipment (PPE) became hard to find. The U.S.'s inability to produce crucial materials in the U.S. is a threat to national security. As the current global relationship risk of technological espionage increases, it is becoming increasingly urgent to regain control over America's industrial base.

The Voltage Valley Revolution™ aims to revive jobs in manufacturing and construction and boost economic growth. This new industrial era focuses on advanced manufacturing and clean energy projects. It addresses two key needs: forming new industries and building the infrastructure to support them. Appalachia is ready to lead again, concentrating on electrification, artificial intelligence, renewable energy, and the Internet of Things (IoT). This movement is not just about reviving old industries; it looks to create a sustainable, high-tech future that boosts our economic independence and strengthens our national defense.

Historic investments like the Inflation Reduction Act aimed to reshape America's energy future. It allocated $400 billion to clean energy, with $8 billion for hydrogen hubs. With budget pressures growing, some funds might face cuts or be redirected. This makes it clear that regions like Appalachia need to find other ways to support change beyond just federal dollars. The Voltage Valley Revolution™ is built on values, not handouts. It's about doing what's right for our communities, workers, and the planet. We're creating a self-sustaining, Clean Innovation Ecosystem. We draw on regional strengths, such as our skilled workforce, industry knowledge, and strong community spirit. This ecosystem unites sustainable technology and local skills. It helps Appalachia achieve energy independence, economic growth, and lasting stability. This stands strong, regardless of what happens in Washington. The concept of business clusters is not new, but it is being reimagined for the Voltage Valley Revolution™. Michael Porter's 1998 paper, "Clusters and the New Economics of Competition," showed that geographic clusters of interlinked firms can boost competition, spark innovation, and drive economic growth. The Voltage Valley Revolution™ will create clusters. They will focus on the needs of clean energy and advanced manufacturing. These clusters will include specialized suppliers, services, infrastructure, and universities. They will work together to push the boundaries of innovation.

Porter identified three ways that clusters enhance competition:

1. Increasing the efficiency of local companies.
2. Driving the pace of innovation is crucial for future productivity.
3. Stimulating the formation of new businesses and expanding existing ones.

These clusters are the key to building strong, sustainable industries. They offer flexibility and create synergies not possible through isolated companies. In the Voltage Valley Revolution™, these clusters will be the heart of the clean innovation ecosystem. They will unite businesses, universities, think tanks, and local governments. Together, they will work toward a shared vision of prosperity, sustainability, and security for the region and the nation alike.

Let's look at how this has worked with past industrial revolutions.

Industrial Revolutions in America: 1945–2025

From 1945 to 2023, the U.S. underwent transformative industrial revolutions that drove technological progress and economic growth. These periods were defined by groundbreaking innovations and the rise of key business clusters, each shaping the nation's economy and labor markets.

Post-World War II Era (Late 1940s–1960s)

- **Focus**: Mass production, automation, and early computing.
- **Highlights**:

- Growth in automotive, aerospace, and electronics industries led by companies like General Motors and Boeing.
- Defense industry expansion during the Cold War spurred advancements in materials science and engineering.

This era established America as a global industrial leader through manufacturing and defense.

Information Age (1970s–Late 1990s)

- **Focus**: Personal computing and digital networking.
- **Highlights**:
  - Silicon Valley became the hub of tech innovation with pioneers like Apple, Intel, and Microsoft.
  - Telecom giants AT&T and Verizon laid the groundwork for digital connectivity.

This shift to knowledge-driven industries set the stage for the digital economy.

Digital Revolution (Late 1990s–2020)

- **Focus**: Internet growth, mobile computing, and social media.
- **Highlights**:
  - E-commerce leaders like Amazon emerged during the dot-com boom.
  - Social media platforms such as Facebook have transformed communication globally.
  - Companies like Netflix have redefined digital entertainment.

This revolution integrated digital technologies into daily life, positioning tech firms as dominant global players.

Each phase of industrial evolution brought distinct business clusters that shaped the economy:

- **Post-WWII**: Focused on manufacturing and defense.
- **Information Age**: Marked by the rise of Silicon Valley and software innovation.
- **Digital Revolution**: Expanded into e-commerce, social media, and digital content.

These revolutions reflect America's journey from an industrial powerhouse to a tech-driven global leader, paving the way for the **Voltage Valley Revolution**™.

Voltage Valley Revolution™ *:(2020 and beyond)*

The fourth Industrial Revolution marks a transformative period focused on electrification, advanced artificial intelligence (AI) and machine learning (ML), and the next generation of integrated circuit (IC) chips. Internet of Things (IoT), renewable energy, advanced nuclear, and advanced manufacturing (including 3D printing). This era is characterized by digital, physical, and biological convergence, driving a sustainable and interconnected world.

Technological Focus

Electrification: A major thrust towards electrifying transportation, infrastructure, and industries, with significant advancements in electric vehicles (EVs), battery storage solutions, and smart grids.

Artificial Intelligence and Machine Learning: Deep integration of AI and ML into everyday life and industries, leading to more efficient data processing, autonomous systems, and personalized technology experiences.

Advanced Integrated Circuits: Development of ultra-efficient, powerful semiconductor chips, enabling more sophisticated computing devices and IoT applications. They support the backbone of AI and ML technologies.

Business Clusters

Electric Vehicle and Battery Manufacturers: Companies like Tesla and Rivian and battery producers such as LG Chem and Panasonic are at the forefront, driving the transition toward a more sustainable transportation system.

AI and ML Innovators: Tech giants like Google, Amazon, and ChatGPT, along with startups, are creating AI solutions for healthcare, finance, and manufacturing. They aim to make AI and ML more accessible and impactful.

Integrated Chip Manufacturers: Firms like Intel, TSMC, Micron, AMD, and NVIDIA are pushing the boundaries of chip technology, focusing on creating more robust, energy-efficient chips critical for everything from consumer electronics to AI computing platforms.

Advanced manufacturing in Voltage Valley Revolution™ goes far beyond 3D printing. It includes modular construction, process intensification, and closed-loop systems. These are meant to speed up production, cut waste, and reach real sustainability. These innovations aren't happening alone. They are part of a bigger ecosystem that includes the Internet of Things (IoT) and renewable energy. Together, these business clusters are reshaping Appalachia's economy. They spark innovation, build strong jobs, and tackle global issues. These include climate change, energy equity, and digital access. This change brings together the digital, physical, and biological worlds. It sets the stage for a more sustainable and connected future.

People, not companies, are leading the Voltage Valley Revolution™. For a firm to succeed, it must know the power of the individual. It must uplift not just its employees but also the community and external stakeholders. Financial results: Profit is not enough: a company's impact on the Planet and People is also measured.

VOLTAGE VALLEY REVOLUTION™

Appalachia's rise in the Voltage Valley Revolution™ is a tale of change. It's also a story of communities uniting to build a better future. The *Voltage Valley Revolution™* is leveraging its natural strengths—its people, resources, and work ethic—to lead this new revolution. The region aims to lead the fourth industrial revolution. It will do this through advanced manufacturing, clean energy, and new tech like AI and IoT. It also seeks to address climate change and supply chain security.

Past industrial revolutions show us that this change won't be easy. From the 1940s to the 1970s, American industry thrived. However, it damaged the environment and worsened social inequality. Coal-fired power plants were important. However, they emitted harmful pollutants that harmed the environment and public health. By the 1970s, many manufacturing jobs began to fade. This led to unemployment and economic struggles in places like Appalachia. Today, the region still struggles with the aftermath. A widespread opioid crisis has devastated communities.

However, the *Voltage Valley Revolution™* offers hope. This new revolution is not just about jobs and the economy. It is about creating industries that work for both people and the planet. This industrial revolution is unlike past ones. They often prioritized profit over the environment and people's well-being. This industrial revolution aims to create a fair, sustainable, and inclusive future. This revolution's success depends on balancing economic growth with protecting the environment and helping people to flourish. The region of Appalachia is uniquely positioned to lead the way.

As we embark on this new chapter in American manufacturing, the *Voltage Valley Revolution™* is not just about technology or economics. It is about people—the constructors, makers, and doers who will shape the future. It is about ensuring that the lessons of the past guide us toward a future that is sustainable, equitable, and innovative. This revolution is more than an industrial shift. It is a movement. It is driven by the same grit, ingenuity, and community spirit that has always defined Appalachia.

The *Voltage Valley Revolution™* is happening now, and its success will depend on the collective efforts of all those involved. From the people who will build the factories and operate the machines to the entrepreneurs, scientists, and policymakers who will drive innovation, this revolution is a testament to the power of community and collaboration. By looking to the past and understanding where we came from, we can forge a future that honors the legacy of the American worker while building a more sustainable and prosperous tomorrow.

Section & Pages

Support for Appalachian Youth Charities

Including the Dolly Parton Imagination Library

This book is not affiliated with, endorsed by, or sponsored by Dolly Parton or the Dolly Parton Imagination Library.

Out of deep respect for the organizations building a brighter future in Appalachia, the author will donate **10% of this book's royalties** to nonprofits serving youth, education, and community development, **including, but not limited to, the Dolly Parton Imagination Library**.

The Imagination Library has delivered over 200 million free books to children around the world, inspiring early literacy and opportunity. Though not affiliated, this book honors its mission to empower children through access to books.

Other potential beneficiaries of these voluntary donations include:

- **Save the Children (Appalachia)**
- **Mission of Hope**
- **Reimagine Appalachia**, which advocates for sustainable jobs and inclusive economic renewal
- **Appalachian Regional Commission Youth Programs**

These contributions are made independently by the author and reflect the spirit of the **Voltage Valley Revolution™**—that real change comes from investing in people and planting seeds for the next generation.

This is a book about renewal, resilience, and rebuilding—and supporting Appalachian youth is one way to live that message.

VOLTAGE VALLEY REVOLUTION™

Foreword

By Dr. Benjamin Cross

I was born in 1954 and lived on a105-acre farm near Cherry Fork, Ohio. Back then, Adams County was one of the poorest in Appalachia, Ohio. Back then, poverty wasn't measured in statistics. It was realized in worn-out jeans, shared bedrooms, and Christmas mornings where a single apple and new underwear were gifts enough. But we didn't feel poor. We felt proud. We had our land, our family, and belief. If you were smart enough to find solutions and just brave enough to ignore those who said it couldn't be done, you could achieve something great.

Primarily, I worked on nuclear energy systems. including fusion energy. Fusion isn't just science fiction anymore—it's a frontier that could power a clean and abundant future if we get it right. Dr. Stephen Dean, a leader in the field, shared a key truth: "Success is the journey and what you learn along the way—not the destination." This idea has shaped my career and I believe it will shape the Voltage Valley Revolution™.

This book, Stories of the Voltage Valley Revolution™, is more than personal stories. It is a roadmap for a new kind of industrial revolution—one powered not by extraction but by restoration, not by monopolies but by communities. It shows what happens when the people of Appalachia, often underestimated, choose to stop waiting for someone else to save them.

I've lived long enough to watch our region go from the backbone of American manufacturing to a symbol of its decline. But I've also lived long enough to see its rebirth. On these pages, you'll meet dreamers and doers, engineers and entrepreneurs. You'll find single moms and returning veterans. Their stories reflect the grit of past generations and focus on the future.

Voltage Valley is real. It's being built in places across West Virginia, Ohio, Kentucky, Tennessee and Pennsylvania. It runs on microgrids, cleaner energy, digital twins, and integrated manufacturing. But the actual energy source here is people. People like the ones in this book.

We don't need to chase Silicon Valley. We're not trying to copy it. We're building something better, something rooted in the land, shared sacrifice, neighbors who still look you in the eye and lend a hand when you fall. We show that clean energy and advanced manufacturing can be local, sustainable, and inclusive. As you read these stories, I hope you don't just see what's happening in Appalachia—I hope you know what's possible in your backyard. The revolution doesn't belong to one region. It belongs to everyone bold enough to believe in a future worth building.

And if you ask me why I believe in it? It's simple. Because I came from a place where no one expected much—and I know what can happen when someone dares to dream anyway.

Dr. William Paolillo, the author, is a dreamer. He sees the future clearly and has the heart to help others believe in it, too.

—Dr. Benjamin Cross - Engineer, Farmer's Son, Voltage Valley Revolutionary

Chapter 1
Author's Note

I wrote this book so others could see themselves in these stories—and decide to join the Voltage Valley Revolution™. These thirty-first-person stories all begin the same way:

With a disorienting dilemma: A Cancer diagnosis. Factory layoff. Tour of duty in Iraq, Political defeat, Divorce, Addiction. Plane crash – Death. **Moments that crack life wide open force you to ask:** *What now?*

These are not polished anecdotes. They are lived experiences - raw, often painful, and deeply human. But they don't stop at the fall. They show the rise, how breakdowns become turning points. How real people reimagine what's possible—and get to work.

My own turning point came when I lost my job. No scandal. No drama. Just a quiet leadership change at a Fortune 250 company. One day, I was leading energy projects and building partnerships. Next, I was out.

I had spent years working at the edge of clean energy, construction, and advanced technology. Now, I was asking the same challenging question I would later hear from so many others:

What now?

That moment cracked something open in me. I didn't want to just make a living. I wanted to create something that matters. So, I left corporate life—not in protest, but in pursuit of something more grounded.

And I started listening. I traveled through Appalachia—factory towns, job sites, and small cities. The places that don't make national headlines. What I found wasn't despair. It was momentum.

People who had faced job loss, illness, addiction, and grief were still building. Still moving. Still believing. This book tells their stories.

You've probably heard of *Hillbilly Elegy*. That book painted a picture of the decline in Appalachia.

This book is about what's going right.

I met people leading America's next industrial revolution from the middle out, not the top down.

In Ohio, West Virginia, Pennsylvania, Virginia, Tennessee, and Kentucky, they are:

- Building EV plants, data centers, and looking to build eco-industrial parks.

- Wiring AI into legacy factories
- Mentoring young workers
- Reimagining what small towns can achieve

They're not waiting for permission. They're not asking for a handout. They're doing the work.

✈ **Jack Roush** — Crashed a plane two times. Left for dead once. Now, turning NASCAR tech into clean transportation breakthroughs.

● **Caitlin Holley** — The mother of four children (plus alpacas). Leading a Billion-dollar advanced manufacturing project in Appalachia.

🏛 **David Wilhelm** — Got a U.S. president elected. Then he came home to invest in the towns D.C. forgot.

These aren't survival stories. They're blueprints. And if you've ever faced your own disorienting dilemma—If you've ever asked *What now?* - you may find part of your answer here.

Why This Matters to Me?

My roots stretch from New York City to the foothills of the Appalachians.

My grandfather delivered coal and ice up tenement stairs in Brooklyn. He saved enough to buy a dairy farm in Delhi, New York.

My grandmother, Carmela, was the first of twenty-one children. She taught me that **reinvention is survival**.

I also learned a lot behind the wheel of a cab. I drove long shifts to help pay for college. Picked up factory workers, night-shift crews, business owners, and families doing their best to get by. Some talked. Some didn't. I listened. And I saw that everyone – everywhere - is just trying to figure out the next step.

After years in business, publishing, and energy, I left corporate life. Not out of anger. Out of hunger. For something more connected. More grounded. So, I started writing.

What I found were stories of work, resilience, and belief—people doing the hard, hopeful work of building futures they could stand behind.

That led to this book. And it brought me back to a simple idea that's guided me for years:

Dream Big. Do Good.

That's what I wrote to my children in the dedication of my first book. Not just advice, a calling.

My daughter believed it so profoundly that she tattooed those words on her hip. A reminder—for both of us - to live with purpose and act with intention.

Walking the Path Together

History shows that movements don't start in boardrooms. They begin in garages, classrooms, kitchens, and union halls. That's the spirit of the Voltage Valley Revolution™.

It's not flashy. It's not a trend. It's people helping people, community by community, job by job.

One night, I was tucking in my granddaughter Lucia. She quietly said the Lord's Prayer. When she got to the line: *"Thy will be done on earth as it is in heaven."*

I heard it differently. That's the work we're called to do. To bring something good and lasting into the world. This region of America isn't just about jobs.

It's about **purpose**.

It's about **dignity**.

It's about **building something better together**.

Because here's the truth: no revolution happens without people. Not slogans. Not policy memos.

People who care. People who show up. People who build.

If you're wondering where opportunity lives, it might be closer than you think.

I began this book looking for answers. What I found was this:

The people—maybe people like you—were the answer.

This region is lifting itself with vision, grit, and belief.

And I wrote this book so others could see themselves in these stories—

and choose to join the Voltage Valley Revolution™.

Chapter 2
How to Read This Book

How to Read This Book?

You don't have to read it cover to cover. In fact, we hope you don't.

You can open this book anywhere. It's a collection of 25 first-person stories, each one a self-contained spark. They take 5 to 10 minutes to read.

Start with a name that draws you in. A job you recognize. A struggle you've faced. A place that feels like home—or a future you haven't imagined yet.

These are stories of builders: Mothers. Veterans. Tradespeople. Entrepreneurs. People who've faced real loss—of work, of health, of loved ones. Cancer. Addiction. Grief. Bankruptcy. They didn't bounce back. They rebuilt—piece by piece, block by block, business by business.

Why Appalachia? Because something powerful is rising here. In smart factories, data centers, clean energy startups, and welding schools. In electricians wiring data centers. In union, crews rebuild what others abandoned. This isn't just about clean energy or advanced tech. It's about power - economic, emotional, and personal - being reclaimed.

There's a quote by Theodore Roosevelt that captures the spirit of this book:

"The credit belongs to the man or women who is actually in the arena, whose face is marred by dust and sweat and blood... who strives valiantly... who errs... and who, at the worst, if he or she fails, at least they fail while daring greatly." This book is about those people.

So start anywhere. And if you see yourself on these pages - maybe you're already in the arena, too.

Section 1:
Greatest Generation

"The Greatest Generation"

"What counts is not the mere fact that we have lived. It is what difference we have made to the lives of others that will determine the significance of the life we lead." Nelson Mandela

As Tom Brokaw described, **"the greatest generation any society has ever produced."** Private William F. Stair (my uncle) and Dr, Stephen Dean (Fusion Leader) were part of the Greatest Generation. Uncle Bill came of age during the **Great Depression** and fought in **World War II**. Stephen was born in **1936** and was too young to serve in the war. Yet, he grew up surrounded by its impact. The **sacrifices of those who fought and those who built** the wartime economy shaped their lives.

Their **selfless service and their families' support** helped spark an **industrial revolution** after the war. This put "American Exceptionalism" on display for the world.

American exceptionalism is the idea that the **United States is exceptional**, with a mission to spread **democracy and freedom**. The idea comes from Alexis de Tocqueville's "Democracy in America" (1835). He pointed out the unique traits of American society and the power of its democratic institutions. American Exceptionalism shows that doing good leads to doing well. This is one reason why the United States is among the wealthiest countries in the world.

For men like Uncle Bill and Stephen Dean, American exceptionalism was more than an idea. It was a duty. They had **faith in their country's promise**. It wasn't perfect, but they were determined to make it better. **When the time came, they answered the call**.

Uncle Bill fought overseas in WWII, one of the millions who stood against **Hitler and tyranny**. That generation didn't quit when the war ended. They came back and rebuilt America. This sparked an era of industrial growth and new technology.

Stephen Dean followed that path in his own way. **Driven by purpose** and a legacy of service, he became a **nuclear fusion scientist**. His generation **turned our victory in WWII into scientific progress**. Uncle Bill carried a rifle. Stephen worked in labs and research centers. Stephen Dean was advancing one of the most ambitious energy projects of our time. **Fusion** is the process that fuels the sun. It holds the promise of clean, unlimited energy. Stephen Dean devoted his career to chasing that dream.

Work in nuclear fusion demonstrates how meaningful progress often unfolds over decades. Fusion research pushed the boundaries of plasma physics, driving breakthroughs in semiconductor technology for example. Just this one advancement has allowed the creation of smaller, faster microchips, which in turn accelerated the development of highspeed computing, the internet, and artificial intelligence.

This era saw the rise of **facilities like the Oak Ridge plant** in Tennessee, part of the **Manhattan Project**. Later came the **A Plant in Piketon, Ohio**. The **Portsmouth Gaseous Diffusion Plant**, located in **Appalachia**, played a vital role during the **Cold War**. At its peak, it used **5% of the nation's electricity** to enrich uranium for **defense and energy**. People knew the workers there as "**Cold War Warriors.**" They helped **keep America safe**, like the soldiers who won WWII.

Success isn't just about the destination. It's about the journey and the discoveries made along the way. While fusion promises clean energy, it also helped build today's digital world. Without fusion, there would be no Internet or Artificial Intelligence.

The men and women of this era faced **hardship**. They showed **resilience** in **factories**, on **battlefields**, and in **labs**. Their **sense of duty** pushed them forward. They faced the Great Depression as kids. Then, they helped steer the nation through war and recovery.

To them, **the struggle was a challenge to overcome**. They knew **suffering was temporary**, but **perseverance lasted a lifetime**. Greatness isn't handed down; it's something you achieve. You earn it with effort, sacrifice, and faith in the American Dream. They didn't want easy lives. They wanted the **chance to work, build, and leave something better** for those who came next.

American exceptionalism, for them, wasn't about **superiority**. It focused on responsibility. It was about serving, improving, and believing that hard work can create a better future.

When the time came, they answered the call.

Chapter 3
Uncle Bill: The Fight to Stand Again

Dr. William Paolillo w/ Dean Smith

Amid the chaos of war, the boundary between **life and death** becomes blurred. **Survival** was about **avoiding bullets** and **enduring** when all hope seemed lost. **Inspired by William F. Stair**

A Mistaken Death

The air was thick with **gunpowder and blood**. Pvt. **William F. Stair** lay motionless, half-buried in the dirt. The sky overhead was **pale and indifferent**, offering no comfort, no reprieve.

Time had lost all meaning. It could've been **hours or minutes**. Only the **throbbing pain** in his body reminded him he was alive—sharp and unrelenting, threatening to pull him under.

Boots crunched closer—heavy, deliberate. Then came the cold touch of a **toe tag** on his ankle. They thought he was dead.

The Battle of Kasserie Pass

By 1943, Private **William F. Stair** found himself under the **scorching African sun**, part of the **Allied forces** sent to halt **Rommel's Afrika Korps** in Tunisia. The **Battle of Kasserine Pass** was his brutal introduction to combat. The American forces, **green and untested**, were **no match** for Rommel's seasoned troops. **Chaos reigned**, and many soldiers received a **swift and harsh awakening** to the true nature of war.

Bill's unit was **ordered to hold the line.** But **Rommel's tanks ripped through American defenses.** Men **fell all around him**, but Bill **kept his head down**, every movement a **deliberate effort to survive**.

The **desert** was unforgiving - **dusty, jagged, with no cover in sight**. The enemy was close - too close.

Amid the carnage, a fellow soldier, **Private Ryan**, was **hit and fell hard**. Bill saw him lying there, **bleeding out in the open**.

He **knew** he shouldn't move. **Knew** the smart thing was to **stay put**. But **Bill wasn't the kind of man to leave someone behind.**

Not if there was a chance to save him. **Bill rose from cover and sprinted toward Ryan.**

Bullets **whizzed past him**, kicking up dust. He grabbed Ryan by the collar and **started hauling him to safety**. But before he could make it— Something **sharp and searing** tore through Bill's **back**.

The pain **hit him like a wave**, knocking him to the ground beside Ryan. His **body betrayed him**, darkness **creeping into his vision**. The sounds of battle faded, **echoing like a distant storm**. He **drifted unconscious**.

A Mistaken Death

When Bill awoke, it was **night**. He was **still lying in the dirt**, the battle long over.

Medics, combing the battlefield for survivors, **mistook him for dead**. They **tagged his ankle**, preparing to move his body. Only then did they hear a **faint gurgle** from his throat. A barely audible noise.

"This kid's not dead!" one of the medics shouted, **rushing to get him onto a stretcher**.

From Brooklyn to the Battlefield

Bill was born in **Brooklyn, New York**. After **Pearl Harbor**, he enlisted—like so many young men of his generation. It wasn't a decision he **agonized over**. It was a matter of **duty**.

You didn't question **why** or **what it might cost you**. You **went**—because it was the **right thing to do**.

A Long and Painful Recovery

Bill's injuries were **severe**. The **bullet damaged his spine**, and for a time, it seemed he **might never walk again**. The doctors were **honest with him**—they told him he'd be **lucky** if he ever stood up, **let alone walked**. He was shipped back to the U.S. and spent **two years** in a **VA hospital in New York**.

For **months**, Bill lay in a **body cast, immobile**. The doctors told him to **get used to the idea of a wheelchair**. But **Bill wasn't the kind of man to accept that fate**.

Defying the Odds

Bill watched **other men fitted with leg braces** at the VA—a new treatment. The doctors told him it **wouldn't work for him**. His injuries were **too severe**.

But **Bill insisted**. *"You don't know until you try,"* he said, his voice **calm but unwavering**. The **braces hurt**. Every step was **agony**. But Bill **fought through it**.

He had **no choice**. He couldn't see himself as **anything less than whole**. The first steps were **awkward, stiff, unnatural**. He walked **like a marionette**, but he moved. The **doctors were** astonished. To Bill, it wasn't a **miracle**. It was simply **what you did. You got up. You kept moving.**

Life After War

After the war, Bill worked for the **state government**, ensuring **taxpayer money was well spent**.

But the war **never left him**. It **lingered in his bones**, in the **nightmares** that woke him in the middle of the night. On a cold December night, Bill took his **young nephew, Billy**, to a **minor league hockey game** on Long Island.

As they left the rink, the **parking lot was slick with ice**. Bill's **legs gave out**. He **fell hard**. Billy, just **ten years old**, tried to help him up. But Bill was **too big—six foot four, 250 pounds**.

Billy **ran for help**, and soon, a **stranger** came to lift Bill back onto his feet. As they got into the car, **Billy sat beside his uncle, shaken, crying**. *"Why are you crying, kid?"* Bill asked. *"I thought you were hurt,"* Billy replied. Uncle Bill chuckled, his breath **visible in the cold air**.

"This is America, Billy. Greatest country in the world. All you gotta do is ask for help, and someone will give it. You remember that."

That moment stayed with Billy **for the rest of his life**. It was a lesson **beyond war and struggle**— It was about **resilience**. About the **power of community**. About **never being too proud to accept a helping hand**. Bill **never saw himself as unique**. Never wanted to be called a **hero**. But to those who knew him—**he was one**.

A Moment of Recognition – The Army-Navy Game

Years later, Bill attended an **Army-Navy football game** with his nephew, Dean. He didn't go for the fanfare—he went **for the company**. As they sat in the stadium, a **colonel from the Blue Angels** spotted him. The man approached, noticing Bill's **veteran's cap**, and asked where he had served.

When Bill told him **he had fought at Kasserine Pass**, the colonel's **eyes widened in awe**. *"You look at me like I'm a hero,"* the colonel said to the crowd, *"but this man here - Private Bill— is a true American hero."*

Bill, as always, just **shrugged it off**. To him, it wasn't about recognition or the **medals**. It was about **duty, sacrifice, and doing what was right**.

Final Resting Place – Arlington National Cemetery

As the years passed, Bill's body **began to show the wear of time and war**. Despite the **pain and limitations**, he **never let them define him**. When the time finally came to lay Bill to rest, his nephew **Dean made sure** he was buried in a place **worthy of his sacrifice**.

Although Bill had **requested a simple veteran's cemetery**, Dean knew **his legacy deserved more**. Bill was laid to rest in **Arlington National Cemetery**. A fitting place for a **man who had given so much**.

A Story of Resilience—For America and Appalachia

I know all this because I grew up hearing about Uncle Bill. Not from him = he wasn't one to dwell on his own suffering - But from the people who had seen his resilience firsthand.

I **carry his name** as a reminder of what he stood for - his story is also **my inheritance**. William F. Stair was my uncle—I am known as Billy when we are in the same room.

Just like **Appalachia and the Voltage Valley Revolution™**, Uncle Bill's story is one of **resilience and community**. As **Bill refused to stay down**, so too does the **spirit of Appalachia**. The **Voltage Valley Revolution™** offers a chance to **revive the region**. Uncle Bill's legacy lives **on** - In **everyone** who refuses to give up. His story is a **beacon of hope**.

"You don't know until you try." **Uncle Bill**

Chapter 4
The Power of the Journey

Dr. William Paolillo w/Stephen Dean

"Success isn't just about the destination. It's about the journey and the discoveries made along the way." **Inspired by Stephen Dean**

Stephen Dean was born in 1936. This was during the last years of the Great Depression. He entered a divided world. The divides were economic, social, and racial. Stephen Dean's story is one of perseverance, intellect, and a deeply rooted belief in the fundamental equality of all people. His life's work in **fusion energy**, his leadership in **forming collaborations**, and his unwavering **commitment to equality** make him an ideal figure to set the stage for Stories of the Voltage Valley Revolution™. He started his journey in Niagara Falls. There, he dealt with economic hardship and faced racial segregation. Now, he stands at the forefront of nuclear fusion innovation. His story shows how visionaries can change the world. They value scientific progress and human dignity.

Early Life: Lessons in Resilience and Inclusion

Stephen grew up in Niagara Falls, New York, and saw economic instability up close. Both of his parents worked. To help make ends meet, Stephen moved in with his Irish grandmother, Ellen "Nellie." She played a key role in his upbringing. Nellie taught him strong morals and fairness. These lessons shaped Stephen's view of the world for life.

Niagara Falls was a city marked by profound segregation. The neighborhoods had clear ethnic enclaves. Irish, Italian, Polish, and African American communities each lived in their own areas. The Catholic and Protestant populations were also starkly divided. This strict social structure controlled all parts of life. This included relationships, friendships, and dating. Stephen saw firsthand how these divisions were enforced and questioned them early on.

One of the most defining moments of his youth was when a **Black classmate wanted to date his sister**. His father was furious. He did not allow the relationship, reflecting the racial attitudes of the time. Stephen was **deeply influenced by his Catholic upbringing and readings of the Bible**. He could not reconcile these prejudices with the idea that God created all people as equals. He challenged his father. He believed no one should be judged by skin color. Instead, we should judge by character. This belief later influenced his view on global scientific teamwork. He believed no nationality or race was superior, just shared human potential.

Another pivotal moment came on the baseball field. As a child, Stephen loved organizing neighborhood baseball games. **When forming a team to play in a local city league, he included** a girl who was an exceptional first baseman. **The city official objected when he submitted the team roster. He said girls couldn't play.** Stephen, in his characteristic way, pushed back. **"Is there a rule that says girls can't play?"** he asked. When the official admitted there wasn't, Stephen stood firm. The girl played and was one of the best on the team. From a young age, Stephen cared about justice for everyone. This included race, gender, ability, and opportunity.

Education and the Path to Fusion Energy

Despite growing up in a community that did not emphasize high technology or scientific innovation. Stephen's **natural talent for mathematics and English** set him apart. Unsure of his career, he went to Boston College. His passion for numbers and solving problems drew him to physics. He found his calling after stumbling upon a book named **Project Sherwood**. The book discussed nuclear fusion as a potential energy source. The concept that humans could replicate the sun's energy to generate unlimited power was exciting.

He understood that **fusion energy** was more than an engineering challenge. It was also **a way to improve life for everyone.** If it works, this could offer clean and almost endless power. It would also avoid the political conflicts tied to fossil fuels. This was not just about science; it was about securing the future for generations to come.

Stephen also carried forward a deep sense of family. He was named after his father, making him **Stephen Dean Jr.**, and he passed this tradition on to his son and grandson, both named Stephen as well. This generational connection reflects his belief in continuity, legacy, and the responsibility to build a better future for those who come next.

He married **Elizabeth "Betty" Dean**, a brilliant English major and editor of her college newspaper. Together, they built a family while Stephen pursued his groundbreaking work in fusion energy. Betty's intellect and strong sense of purpose complemented Stephen's drive, and she played a critical role in shaping the values of their home. They had **three children**, raising them with the same commitment to learning, fairness, and curiosity that defined Stephen's own upbringing.

A Career in Nuclear Fusion and Inclusion

After getting his master's degree at MIT, Stephen applied to the **Atomic Energy Commission (AEC)**. At the time, this agency was the top U.S. government agency responsible for nuclear research. He received warnings about potential arrogance and condescension from leading scientists, especially those who had worked on secret atomic projects. However, when he arrived, he found something completely different. The scientists at the **AEC welcomed him**. They valued his credentials, but more so, they **admired his heart**. His commitment to inclusion and scientific progress stood out.

He was just 23 when he started reviewing multi-million-dollar proposals from top universities and labs. Despite his youth, the experts he met treated him with respect and valued his insights.

The humility and openness he encountered at the AEC confirmed his belief. **Authentic leadership is about collaboration, not hierarchy**.

A Global Approach to Innovation and the Tokamak

Stephen's work in fusion quickly expanded beyond the United States. He was fascinated by how countries worldwide were also investing in fusion research. He saw scientific discoveries differently than many of his peers. For him, it wasn't a competition between nations. He believed **God distributed intelligence equally among all people. Regardless of nationality or background**. The idea that one country had a monopoly on innovation was absurd to him.

This philosophy led him to become a **pioneer in international collaboration**. He took part in European conferences. He also met with scientists from Russia and Japan. He worked diligently to create connections between countries. While some in Washington viewed foreign scientists as competitors, Stephen saw them as **partners in a shared mission**.

The **Tokamak** is a key breakthrough in fusion research. Soviet scientists invented it in the 1950s. It became the leading design for magnetic confinement fusion. The Tokamak uses strong magnetic fields to hold plasma together. Plasma is made of hot, charged particles. The magnetic fields keep the particles contained long enough for nuclear fusion to happen. Stephen understood this technology had great potential for practical fusion energy. He then focused on improving international cooperation in Tokamak research.

His efforts paid off. By the mid-1980s, global fusion research hit a turning point by the creation of the **ITER (International Thermonuclear Experimental Reactor)** project, the largest fusion collaboration in the world. It came from the vision of people like Stephen. They believed that scientific progress should bring us together, not tear us apart. ITER uses the Tokamak design and is a global project **that includes the U.S., Russia, China, the European Union, Japan, India, and South Korea.** ITER shows the **international teamwork** that Stephen desired. It came from the vision of people like Stephen. They believed that scientific progress should bring us together, not create divisions.

The Impact of Fusion on the Modern World

Stephen recognized that work in fusion created more than just energy. It sparked breakthroughs in **plasma physics.** These breakthroughs helped **advance semiconductors, integrated circuit chips, and even Moore's Law.** Moore's Law says that the number of transistors on a microchip doubles every two years. This has led to rapid growth in computing power. In 1970, we could put 5000 transistors on a circuit chip – today we can put 208 Billion by 2030 some believe a trillion.. Plasma-based etching techniques from fusion research made transistors smaller. This change led to fast growth in computers, the internet, and artificial intelligence (AI).

These discoveries laid the groundwork for today's digital world. **Fusion research gave rise to plasma physics, leading to semiconductor advancements, which enabled the modern**

computing revolution. Without these advancements, integrated circuits for smartphones and supercomputers would not exist. In this way, Stephen's work contributed to clean energy and helped usher in the **age of connectivity and information**.

What began as a quest for limitless energy became a **fundamental driver of the digital revolution**. This highlights that the journey is just as important as the destination. In fact, the journey and the discoveries made along the way can often be more significant than reaching the end goal.

Fusion Power Associates: Advancing Global Collaboration

In 1979, Stephen Dean started Fusion Power Associates (FPA), a nonprofit program that promotes fusion energy research. FPA also works to bring together scientists, policymakers, and industry leaders. Unlike bureaucratic institutions, **FPA was built on inclusion and cooperation**. Stephen understood that fusion wasn't just a U.S. effort but a global endeavor.

Under his leadership, FPA became a key link between labs, organizations, and industries around the world. It made sure knowledge was shared, not kept to themselves. The organization has united leading fusion researchers from the **U.S., China, Japan, Europe, South Korea, India, and Russia.** This has led to open discussions and joint projects, bringing fusion energy nearer to reality.

One of FPA's defining missions is its commitment to **mentorship and education**. Stephen knew that fusion is a long-term challenge. It will take many generations of scientists to achieve it. He worked hard to involve young researchers in the field. This way, the spirit of international collaboration would continue.

FPA keeps shaping policy and investment in fusion technology. It pushes for ongoing funding and support for new discoveries and energy solutions. Through its annual conferences, publications, and advisory work, **the organization remains a driving force in the future of fusion energy.**

Lessons for Voltage Valley

Stephen Dean's journey shows that **change comes from people** who reject limits. They look past the barriers of their time and believe in something greater. He believes in science, teamwork, and equality. He thinks big breakthroughs happen when **people work together**. This happens no matter their national, racial, or ideological backgrounds.

As fusion energy and clean technologies advance together, the world stands at another tipping point. Stephen helped start a new era in fusion energy research. Now, the **Voltage Valley Revolution**™ is a new frontier. It **needs visionaries, leaders, and doers who are ready to challenge the status quo and recognize the importance of the journey.**

The spirit of **teamwork, strength, and creativity** that drove Stephen Dean's career is thriving today in Appalachia's energy transformation. The Voltage Valley Revolution™ can draw from the lessons of fusion. This includes **global cooperation, bold experiments, and unwavering perseverance**. These ideas apply to **advanced manufacturing, clean energy development, and AI**.

This belief wasn't just theoretical; it was something he practiced daily. His long-time assistant, **Ruth Watkins**, still worked alongside him for over 50 years, helping to build connections and manage the collaborations that fueled progress in fusion research. Ruth wasn't just administrative support; she was an integral part of ensuring that experts, policymakers, and engineers could focus on the work that mattered most. Together, they embodied a philosophy that groundbreaking science isn't just about brilliant minds - it's about creating the right conditions for those minds to thrive.

Just as Stephen laid the groundwork for a new energy future. **Appalachia now can lead America's new industrial revolution, Voltage Valley Revolution™. Success isn't just about the destination. It's about the journey and the discoveries made along the way.**

Uncle Bill and Stephen Dean represent two generations **driven by duty, resilience, and the belief that America** could always be made better. Whether on the battlefield or in a research lab, their work helped shape a nation - **through war, recovery, and innovation**. Their lives remind us that progress isn't instant. It's built through sacrifice, steady effort, and a commitment to something greater than oneself. As Appalachia steps into a new era of industrial and technological leadership, we carry forward the same values. Their legacy isn't just history. **It's a foundation. And now, it's Appalachia's turn to answer the call.**

The 25 stories in this book show how the spirit of Uncle Bill and Stephen Dean lives in Appalachia and the Voltage Valley Revolution™.

Section 2:
Tipping Point

Chapter 5
The Human Factor in the Voltage Valley Revolution™

The opioid crisis devastated Appalachia, and no one stopped it.

In *The Tipping Point*, Malcolm Gladwell offers a framework for understanding how crises and breakthroughs take hold. Social change doesn't arrive overnight. It builds slowly and surges when the right people, messages, and circumstances align to reach critical mass.

It's a theory that has reached millions—more than 30 million copies of Gladwell's books have been sold worldwide. His ideas have shaped how we think about behavior, influence, and the invisible patterns behind major cultural shifts.

Gladwell's framework feels relevant to what Appalachia lived through during the opioid epidemic.

In Revenge of the Tipping Point: Overstories, Superspreaders and the Rise of Social Engineering, Gladwell revisits the opioid crisis in American life—not to sensationalize it, but to examine how it unfolded. The crisis didn't erupt all at once. It escalated gradually through overprescribing, misinformation, a frayed healthcare system, and corporate overreach. The damage was national, but the toll in Appalachia was intense.

Not because Appalachia didn't care. People showed up. Leaders tried. But too often, they didn't have what they needed. The region lacked what Gladwell calls the three catalytic roles that turn the tide in moments of crisis:

- **Mavens** – the trusted experts who clarify truth from confusion
- **Connectors** – the bridge-builders who link people, institutions, and resources
- **Salesmen** – the persuasive voices who mobilize support and belief

Without that alignment, good intentions weren't enough. Communities were overwhelmed by outside influences, drained by economic decline, and left vulnerable to exploitation. The crisis didn't just harm individuals—it broke connections, trust, and community resilience.

Journalist Sam Quinones illustrates this unraveling in *Dreamland*, a haunting portrait of Portsmouth, Ohio. Once a thriving manufacturing town, Portsmouth became a symbol of how pain, isolation, and lost opportunity created fertile ground for addiction. One story stands out: Matt, a high school football star, prescribed OxyContin for a minor injury and soon found himself in a cycle that ended in heroin and overdose.

Quinones doesn't blame the people of Portsmouth. He mourns with them. He shows how the social fabric—the porches, the parks, the civic institutions—eroded under the weight of something larger. Dreamland, once the name of the town's bustling community pool, becomes a metaphor for what vanished: shared space, shared purpose, shared joy.

That crisis showed us what happens when a region is left to navigate monumental challenges without the full support of coordinated leadership, expertise, and voice.

What we found from talking with the people of Appalachia and in our 25 stories was **a new kind of alignment—between vision and action, local grit and global opportunity, ordinary people and extraordinary change.**

A New Tipping Point: The Voltage Valley Revolution™

Something new is happening in Appalachia—and this time, it's not built on tragedy but on transformation.

The **Voltage Valley Revolution™** reshapes how people live, work, and build in the region. It's about cleaner energy, high-tech jobs, and smarter infrastructure. It's not just rebuilding what was lost, it's creating something better from the ground up.

This shift echoes what Malcolm Gladwell wrote about in *The Tipping Point*. Significant changes don't happen all at once. They grow slowly, then suddenly accelerate when the right people, message, and moment come together. That's what's happening here.

Policy breakthroughs, new investments, and local leadership are lining up today. And just like Gladwell described, three kinds of people are helping push this moment forward: Mavens, **Connectors**, and Salesman. People who bring communities, businesses, and institutions together.

Gladwell's Three Forces of Change

In *The Tipping Point*, Gladwell asked: What makes change spread?

He gave three answers:

1. **The Law of the Few** – A small number of passionate, skilled people can make a huge difference
2. **The Stickiness Factor** – The message has to matter. It has to stick with people
3. **The Power of Context** – The world has to be ready for it.

Right now, all three are coming together in Appalachia. Whether this becomes an actual turning point for Appalachia remains to be seen, but the energy is real, and the signals are strong

A new identity is taking shape—one that blends **digital power** with **hands-on work**. It's not just about bringing factories back. It's about **networks, sensors, data**, and even buildings that "know" how to adjust themselves in real-time.

Sounds futuristic? In some places, it's already happening.

What's Actually Changing?

One major shift is the rise of **AI powered Digital Spatial Intelligence (DSI)**. It's a big term, but here's the simple version: **DSI with Artificial Intelligence** is the technology that helps buildings, towns, and grids, think. (See chapter 34 for a more in-depth discussion on DSI)

Imagine an old coal plant. Now imagine that same building wired with smart systems—lights and heat that adjust automatically, air that stays clean, machines that fix themselves before breaking. That's DSI and AI. And it's not just suitable for engineers, in fact if you have a smart thermostat, you are using DSI today. Everyone can use DSI, just like we operate our iPhones. It saves money, reduces waste, and creates jobs in both trades and tech, as well as creating a cleaner environment and a more skilled workforce. In the Voltage Valley, these tools are helping turn former coal sites into **innovation centers**. It's the Industrial Revolution—just upgraded. DSI led by AI doesn't just collect data. It helps people make better decisions faster. It turns buildings into partners, not just places.

Why This Matters

When Gladwell talked about the "stickiness factor," he meant ideas that **don't just sound good—they last**. Bringing digital applications and tools powered by Artificial Intelligence is something mentioned in the news every day. A quick Google search details - American reporters published 7.1 million stories on AI between 3/23 – 3/24; the current pace is over 60,000 AI-generated news articles a day.

This transformation solves real problems - sky-high utility bills, outdated buildings, and shrinking job markets.

People: It builds local capabilities by training workers, growing leadership, and creating pathways to lasting careers.

Planet: It modernizes infrastructure for energy efficiency and sustainability, reducing emissions and protecting natural resources.

Profit: It lowers costs, attracts new investment, and strengthens local economies from the ground up.

Appalachia isn't a blank slate; it's a launchpad. The region can have what the future needs:

Land, skilled workers, clean energy, high-speed broadband, and a deep will to grow.

While crowded coasts face rising costs and declining returns, Appalachia is becoming a testbed for smart, resilient communities. Here, people, technology, and the environment don't just coexist; they work together. It looks like this when the places that powered the past start building the future - and the people leading it.

VOLTAGE VALLEY REVOLUTION™

Where Coal Met Code

A quiet revolution is unfolding deep in Central Appalachia.

Where the coal economy once defined towns, new digital infrastructure is rising. This isn't just a cleanup, it's a transformation. The region is building an intelligent grid that senses, learns, and adapts in real time. It's not just concrete and steel—it's a smart revolution in the heart of America.

Case In Point: Appalachia, VA – From Coal School to Tech Training

At Appalachia Elementary School in Wise County, VA—once shuttered in 2017—you'll now find the **Center for Workforce & Innovation** run by Mountain Empire Community College.

- **Reclaimed building, restored purpose**: What was once a school for local kids is now a training center where elements of advanced manufacturing, digital systems, and the high-tech trades intersect.

- **Trades meet tech**: The program teaches welding, HVAC, and electrical wiring alongside data analysis, automation control, and predictive maintenance systems.

- **Safety + Sustainability**: Apprentices learn to install smart sensors and integrate solar modules alongside legacy HVAC equipment, preparing them to manage both physical hardware and digital diagnostics.

- **Community-rooted, globally relevant**: Local students train for jobs maintaining industrial automation systems, not sending their skills offshore—this is coal-country tech, with the jobs staying local.

This smart educational hub is more than a school—it's a testbed for a region in transition. It proves that Appalachia can power the nation again—not with coal, but with code, sensors, and skilled hands. **From coal education to code, from trade school to tech hub—Appalachia is reinventing itself for the 21st-century grid.**

Why Now?

Appalachia was once the engine room of America's economy, but then it became a footnote. Jobs vanished, infrastructure crumbled, and Silicon Valley soared while Appalachian communities were sidelined.

Then COVID changed everything. Supply chains buckled. Global outsourcing failed. America suddenly realized it couldn't manufacture its essentials—from masks to semiconductors. It was a wake-up call.

Example: Kentucky's Mask Pivot. In the early pandemic, a network of small manufacturers in Eastern Kentucky retooled to produce PPE using 3D printing and local labor. They proved that Appalachia had the skills, speed, and networks to intervene when global supply chains faltered.

Now, Appalachia is being re-recognized as a strategic region—not just for recovery but for reinvention.

Context as Catalyst

Transformational change begins with the right context—and today, the policy environment is aligned to support it. Federal legislation has opened unprecedented opportunities for clean energy, advanced manufacturing, and workforce development:

- **Inflation Reduction Act (IRA):** Originally allocated $400 billion to clean energy initiatives.

- **CHIPS and Science Act:** Accelerating domestic semiconductor manufacturing and supply chains.

- **Bipartisan Infrastructure Law:** Over $2 trillion committed to rebuilding roads, expanding broadband, and strengthening workforce systems.

While some federal initiatives—like hydrogen hubs—are being reconsidered or scaled back due to budget constraints, the broader momentum for clean innovation remains. Appalachia is not waiting on Washington. It's moving forward by aligning local strengths with national priorities—training its workforce, modernizing infrastructure, and creating durable business ecosystems.

Clusters of Innovation: Appalachia's New Business Blueprint

Appalachia's revival isn't scattered—it's strategic. Drawing on Michael Porter's cluster theory, the region is nurturing dense networks of companies, talent pipelines, and research institutions working in sync.

1. **Clean Energy**

   From hydrogen and battery tech to smart grids and data centers, the clean energy cluster is growing fast. In **Pike County, Ohio**, a former Department of Energy site is being transformed into an integrated clean manufacturing campus, complete with local hiring and skill development programs.

2. **Semiconductors & Microelectronics**

   Supported by the CHIPS Act, new facilities and talent pipelines are rising. **Central Ohio Technical College**, in partnership with Intel, is training workers in AI-assisted logistics and chip quality control using advanced simulation labs.

3. **Digital Spatial Intelligence (DSI)**

   Infrastructure is getting smarter. In **Athens County**, smart water sensors and GIS mapping cut water loss by 45% and slashed operational costs. Students gained hands-on experience in civic tech—blending education with real-world impact.

4. **Advanced Materials**

   In **Morgantown, WV**, former coal workers are part of cutting-edge R&D efforts in 3D printing, graphene applications, and lightweight alloys. This is not abstract innovation—it's about local people solving real problems with transformative tools.

5. **Data Centers & Cloud Infrastructure**

   Power, land, and fiber make Appalachia ideal for data infrastructure. In one project, a **reclaimed strip mine** is being repurposed into a solar- and natural gas-powered data campus. Waste heat will warm adjacent greenhouses—cloud computing meets regenerative design.

A Revolution Rooted in People

This isn't a spinoff of Silicon Valley—it's *Appalachia 1.0*. Here, people are the platform.

Consider **Youngstown's Mahoning Valley Tech Ladder**: middle schoolers learn to code, local employers co-design the curriculum, and graduates return as mentors. It's a full-circle approach to workforce development—designed by the community, for the community.

This isn't charity. It's strategy. And it's working.

Why This Moment Matters

Economic history rarely offers second chances. Appalachia is seizing this one—not with nostalgia, but with determination. It's not just rebounding; it's leaping forward. This is what it looks like when coal dust gives way to code, and when memory meets machine learning.

This is the **Voltage Valley Revolution**™.

A Different Kind of Revolution

This movement isn't about rebuilding the past—it's about reshaping the future. For decades, Appalachia stood as a cautionary tale of industrial abandonment. Now, it's becoming a model for resilience-driven innovation.

The Voltage Valley Revolution™ is grounded in clean energy, secure supply chains, and homegrown talent. It's powered by strategy, not subsidies; by purpose, not pity.

Meet the People Powering the Change

As Malcolm Gladwell writes in *The Tipping Point*, real change begins with the right people pressing at the right moment. In Appalachia, that moment is now.

VOLTAGE VALLEY REVOLUTION™

You'll meet the **connectors** who bridge policy and practice, the **mavens** who bring technical wisdom to the table, and the **salespeople** who inspire belief in what's possible. These aren't theories—they're people in small towns, rolling up their sleeves, redefining what's next.

This is not just a story of energy and technology. It's a story of hope, grit, and the people who believe that Appalachia's best days aren't behind—it's just getting started.

∞ Connectors

They spark momentum by doing what few others can: bringing the right people together at the right time for the right cause.

Want to see how a movement gets built from the ground up? Meet the Connectors. These are the doers and dot-connectors who turn good ideas into grand coalitions. Their superpower? Making things happen—fast, across silos, and with heart.

David Wilhelm - Helped elect a president and headed the Democratic Party. After leaving Washington politics, he never looked back. David returned to his Ohio roots with a new mission: to use renewable energy to rebuild the towns that built him. His career is a case study in reinvention, and his impact is still unfolding.

Gail Manchin – Her path was not about politics but people. From classroom teacher to Federal Co-Chair of the Appalachian Regional Commission, Gail brings resilience shaped by personal trials and a vision forged in the community. She's turning adversity into action for an entire region.

Arria Hines – Arria's story starts as a single mom returning to school and ends with West Virginia securing billions for a hydrogen future. She built her company from scratch and helped lead the winning ARCH2 hub bid. Arria doesn't just win contracts; she wins trust. And she makes everyone around her believe Appalachia's best days are ahead.

Jennifer Oddo was raised in a coal country and tested by the Great Recession, and she never forgot where she came from. Now, she's building pathways for the next generation with her firm, New Collar Talent. Her work trains and uplifts the Appalachians for tomorrow's economy, blending tech, grit, and heart

Michael Armour – A former apprentice electrician who climbed poles and climbed the ranks. Today, Michael mentors others with that same hands-on experience, directing programs that open doors for those once locked out. Faith and work fuse in his mission to give others the same shot he got.

Chuck Johnson is a developer, community partner, and systems thinker. Chuck sees energy infrastructure not as an endpoint but as a catalyst for trust and transformation. He's a builder who focuses as much on people as on projects.

Tim Petrey – Youngstown native, accountant, and fixer. Tim grew up in the wreckage of the steel collapse and turned pain into purpose. Today, he helps local businesses adapt to new industries and brings backbone to the Voltage Valley economy.

Rick Stockburger – A veteran, a connector, a community rebuilder. Rick's leadership at BRITE turns struggling towns into clean energy innovation hubs. His story—from combat zones to classrooms full of battery tech—proves that redemption and reinvention go hand-in-hand. At time of Publication Rick is now working at the Department of Energy as the CEO – leading energy Security and Innovation foundation.

Tony Montgomery – Pike County's machine-operating commissioner with a passion for clean energy and a deep sense of duty. Tony blends policy savvy with blue-collar know-how, always asking what my county needs next.

Amanda Woodrum – A policy architect with grassroots roots. Amanda co-founded Reimagine Appalachia and helped bring hundreds of millions in federal funds to communities that corporate America had long overlooked. She fights for an economy that includes everyone.

John Holbrook – A union man and workforce trainer who knows that belief can be just as important as skills. John shows people their potential and then helps them build it with their hands. His work is where dignity meets opportunity.

Matt Smith is quiet, deliberate, and deeply wise. A long-time public servant, he spent years at the U.S. State Department, where his work helped shape international partnerships and strengthen national security through diplomacy. His life has centered on service, family, and the slow, steady building of trust and infrastructure—both abroad and at home. That he raised a nuclear physicist says everything you need to know about the values he passed down

Petra Mitchell – A connector between industry and innovation, Petra leads Catalyst Connection, helping small manufacturers across Appalachia adopt advanced technologies. She links factory floors to funding, training, and robotics—bridging the gap between Rust Belt legacy and clean energy opportunity.

⚡Mavens

They're the ones who figure out what's next—and show us how to get there.

Every big leap forward needs a blueprint. The Mavens are the thinkers, the scientists, the obsessive problem-solvers. If someone's asking, "How do we actually do this?"—these are the folks with answers.

Jack Roush – From the back roads of Adams County, OH to the world stage of NASCAR, Jack Roush has always believed in breaking things—so he could rebuild them better. He once said, "We win tomorrow because of our focus today." Jack is more than a racing legend—he's an innovator whose clean energy ventures now help drive the Voltage Valley Revolution™ into the future.

VOLTAGE VALLEY REVOLUTION™

Caroline Cochran – Nuclear engineer and co-founder of Oklo, Caroline is helping Appalachia rethink its energy backbone. Her work with small modular reactors (SMRs) is about unlocking clean, consistent power without legacy grid limitations. She's not just designing the future; she's powering it.

Stephen Dean—Born in the last days of the Great Depression, Stephen's journey spans racial divides, global collaboration, and the dawn of fusion energy. A pioneer in both science and inclusion, he helped bring the international ITER project to life, proving that innovation is at its best when it brings people together.

Benjamin Cross – Raised on a 105-acre farm in the heart of Appalachia, Ben was soloing airplanes at 16. He's helping engineers create clean energy innovation ecosystems to power America's energy transition. Ben blends precision, humility, and an intense local sense of purpose.

Donald Wingate – A Northeast Ohio kid who nearly dropped out of college, Don now helps lead clean microgrid energy projects for Schneider Electric. His work bridges global innovation and local execution. He's not just electrifying regions—he's empowering them.

Zane Rhodes – Zane's gift is taking moonshot ideas—like integrated manufacturing facilities powered by clean energy —and making them real. He's a trench-to-blueprint builder who's just as likely to be elbow-deep in equipment as he is in front of a DOE official. His faith, family, and perseverance anchor big ideas in real soil.

Caitlin Holley – Engineer, mom of four, and clean energy deal-closer. Caitlin lives on a small farm with alpacas, goats, and kids—literal and figurative. She is helping raise $2+ billion to launch the Trillium H2 Power Complex in southern Ohio. For Caitlin, it's not just about carbon—it's about community.

James Valencia—A systems thinker who blends ancestral knowledge with cutting-edge tech, James helps Appalachian farmers use data and drones to build regenerative, resilient food systems. His work proves that the future of farming is both high-tech and deeply rooted.

Bhavin Patel – Bhavin's story started in a tiny family-run motel in Ohio and grew into a regional vision for smart, affordable workforce housing. His builds serve the people, powering Appalachia's clean energy future. From hospitality to housing, he thinks long-term, community-first.

✏ Salesperson

They don't just talk, they move people. And when they show up, people listen.

Every movement needs belief. These voices make the vision real and turn plans into stories and stories into shared momentum.

Wiley Rhodes – The Hydrogen Cowboy. With a background in oil and gas, a journey through grief, and a relentless will to build, Wiley brings soul to the energy transition. His life's pivot to clean hydrogen wasn't a pivot at all—it was a purpose revealed. He's not just pitching projects—he's bringing communities along for the ride.

Samantha Childress – At 14, Sam emailed a climate scientist to ask questions. Now, she's a rising voice in energy justice with real technical chops and a personal drive that hasn't faded. Every project she joins carries her belief that climate solutions should work for people, not just the planet.

Chris Guerri—Chris grew up paving roads with his family and then carved a new path in clean energy. But it's his work building housing for adults with disabilities that proves he doesn't just talk about equity—he builds it. Chris brings practical wisdom and heart to every room he walks into.

Kevin Schwab—Born into a story that embodies civil rights history, Kevin's life is about bridging gaps. From journalism to aviation to economic development, he brings the gift of perspective and knows that access is everything. His leadership in Syracuse shows how belief, roots, and grit can power a region forward.

Chris Montgomery—A trusted voice in Syracuse's integrated circuit chip transition. Chris champions workforce development and veteran training. Whether at job sites or board meetings, he makes clean energy real for communities once left behind.

🏛 *Legacy Figures*

They ground the work in memory, meaning, and long-view purpose.

Every revolution needs roots. These are the ones who remind us why the work matters—and why we don't give up.

Uncle Bill – A WWII veteran whose values—duty, service, humility—echo across generations. He's not just part of the past. He's part of the scaffolding this whole revolution stands on.

Stephen Dean – Also featured as a Maven, Stephen's long arc from fusion labs to international policy is the spine of generational progress. He's a scientist who dared to dream across borders—and time.

The Stickiness Factor

This book aims to strengthen what Gladwell calls the *Stickiness Factor* by telling the stories of real people creating real change. These stories are designed to inspire and inform, making the movement visible and contagious.

You'll meet innovators and builders, veterans and newcomers, workers and leaders, and people who once struggled but now thrive. They share not just skill or vision but something more profound: the will to reclaim their region's future.

VOLTAGE VALLEY REVOLUTION™

A New Industrial Identity

The Voltage Valley Revolution™ is more than just an economic change. It's a cultural shift that redefines Appalachia's identity—not as a region in decline but as a leader in today's economy.

This movement is also changing the story of American industry. It's about more than just bringing back jobs; it focuses on rebuilding the systems that make our country stronger. This includes having dependable supply chains, being energy independent, and keeping our technology at home. The goal is to make sure that future innovations happen here in America, not overseas.

This isn't simply a remake of Silicon Valley. This is the start of the Voltage Valley Revolution™. It's more profound: an ecosystem rooted in community, shaped by place and driven by people.

Why It's Different This Time

Appalachia powered America's postwar boom. It can power this one, too.

But this revolution isn't just about tech. It's about restoring public trust, rebuilding regional pride, and reinvigorating human connection. It blends the digital, physical, and biological. It merges data science with dirt-under-the-nails resilience. It's not just clean—it's just. Not just green—but grounded.

And unlike the last industrial wave, this one isn't trickling down from the coasts. It's rising from the middle.

This Is Where the Story Begins

This book is based on the lived experiences of 25 individuals across Greater Central Appalachia—from Kentucky and West Virginia to Ohio, Pennsylvania, Tennessee, Upstate New York. These aren't abstract trends; these are real lives.

And here's the heart of it: **people make the difference**.

Whether the Voltage Valley Revolution™ becomes an actual tipping point will not be decided solely by the policy. It will depend on how we show up, connect, build, and believe.

We invite you to listen. To learn.

And to decide for yourself: **Is this Appalachia's next tipping point?**

Chapter 6
Coal Miner Son Finds His Place in the World.

Dr. William Paolillo w/Michael Armour

Appalachia's first Industrial Revolution was powered by the People of Appalachia and Coal.

In 1946, to end a 40-day strike, President Harry S. Truman ordered a government seizure of soft coal mines. Under the ensuing settlement with the United Mine Workers Union, the administration agreed to survey the health and safety of the miners' working and living conditions. Under the leadership of the U.S. Navy Medical Corps, 90 mining communities in 22 states, from Wyoming to West Virginia, were surveyed.

Michael Amour's family is highlighted in an exhibit at the National Archives Museum Special Exhibition | O'Brien Gallery titled Power & Light, Russell Lee's Coal Survey. was t Lee asked with visually documenting the study. "Power & Light Exhibit serves as an example of how records can impact the lives of Americans," said Archivist of the United States Dr. Colleen Shogan. "These valuable photographs held by the National Archives helped change the narrative around the coal strikes. Today, they provide us a glimpse into the rich history of coal communities nationwide."

This unprecedented survey and its powerful images were credited for constructing 13 new modern hospitals in the Appalachia, installing washhouses, and improving mine safety and first aid. "Russell Lee's photographs of coal miners are rich sources of historical information about the lives of a group of people unfamiliar to mainstream Americans.

The photographs depict the reality of their plight. Today, the photographs give us a window into Henry Armour, who was one of the top coal loaders in the mines. Henry's last year's income was in excess of $5400. Inland Steel Company, Wheelwright #1 & 2 Mines, Wheelwright, Floyd County, Kentucky.

Michaels Story

We cannot change how people act. We can choose our attitude……. Life is 10% what happens to me and 90% how I react. Charles R. Swindoll

I grew up in Wheelwright, a small coal mining town tucked deep in the heart of Appalachia, Eastern Kentucky. Life was tough. It wasn't all bad—there were a lot of good people there—but it was tough. As an African American in a predominantly white area, it brought additional challenges. It was a way of life. My mother, Hazel, did housework for a wealthy white family in a town 32 miles from where we lived. It was where she grew up but on the other side of the tracks.

Sometimes, mom brought me to her job and then dropped me off to play with my cousins. One occasion I'll never forget—I walked up to the front door instead of the usual backdoor entrance. My mother had a look of shock and fear on her face. She quickly shuttled me off to the back door and let me have it with both barrels. I was stunned. The wealthy white family wasn't home, so what's the problem? "Somebody might see you. That's the problem. There were boundaries that everyone was expected to know and abide by." My father, from Alabama, knew it well. He was respected for his hard work and respectful demeanor. He always taught us kids to do our best but to be smart and know our place and the imposed boundaries. We loved him, but we didn't always listen to him.

We lived in a small five-room house owned by the Inland Steel Coal Company with my father, mother, sister, and brothers. Coal gave the community a livelihood to feed and provide for their families, but it came at a high price and took its toll on most miners. Coal sustained Eastern Kentucky. But, it was a hard way to make a living. It was common to see miners with missing fingers. Some lost their lives in the mines. My father made it out. He started when he was 13 and retired when he was 66. But he died prematurely from black lung and Alzheimer's disease. Just about every man in Wheelwright came down with black lung disease. I knew I did not want to be a coal miner, but I loved the coal miner culture. The coal miner's purpose was to make a better life for their families; my father worked so hard for our family so we could have opportunities denied to him.

My mother and father's example of working hard rubbed off on me without me knowing it. Day after day, seemingly with no respite, although I'm sure there was, they worked. I wondered why my father couldn't seem to stay awake to watch *Gunsmoke* or *My Three Sons* to save his life. He no sooner set down in front of that big old TV encased in a wooden cabinet than his head leaned back against the wall, and he was out. I didn't get it. Years later, I realized that he fell asleep as soon as his back hit the couch. He had been on his feet, working from before sunrise until well after sundown. The poor man was exhausted. It was the same with my mother. She went to bed at 8:30 in the winter and summer. They worked hard to care for us kids and left us an example and a legacy that shaped my approach to employment. My daddy, the top-loading coal miner, year after year, used to tell me, "You make money for the man, and he gonna keep ya."

There were good people in my life who influenced me. There were black people and white people in my life from the time I was a youngster and through high school and beyond that impacted my life. I knew discrimination and prejudice, and there was no mistaking the source. But what goes unnoticed by so many people are those of the other persuasion who loved me, helped me, taught me, and kicked me in the behind when I needed it. I would not be who I am, and I could not have been blessed to go as far as I have been if not for the community of people who did extraordinary things for me under considerable pressure at times. They gave me a hand, not a handout, but a hand to help me and to steer me away from trouble and towards bigger and better things. These relationships taught me about the most important things in life and how to listen, collaborate, and lead.

VOLTAGE VALLEY REVOLUTION™

At sixteen, I felt a call on my life—God. My parents required us to attend Sunday school, and it was in Sunday School that the reality of God drew me to him. I heard the call, but it was not easy to accept. I wanted to go out with my friends on Friday nights and do what they were doing: drinking and hooking up. Instead, I surrendered my life to God. God led me to Akron, Ohio. I served as an associate minister at the Church of God Cole Ave. I attended the University of Akron and worked as an apprentice electrician at First Energy Electric Utility. I was trained to climb poles, splice conductors, and work manholes out in the elements. I did that well for ten years and was recognized as having managerial potential. I was offered a management position at First Energy. I quickly moved up the ranks to director via front-line supervisor, manager, and general manager. First Energy is one of the top 10 publicly traded utilities.

My daddy was a respected man, known for his hard work and respectful nature. He always told us kids to give it our all, but also to be smart about it and know our boundaries. We loved and admired him, even if we didn't always take his advice. I grew up knowing what discrimination and prejudice looked like, and I knew who was behind it. Many people forget those who didn't discriminate. They showed me kindness, taught me important lessons, and pushed me to improve when I needed help.

The lessons of being part of a miner's family shaped me. I am blessed to be able to give back and pay it forward. Times have changed, but the issues that block and hinder folks from reaching their full potential are real and present. I go into the community and serve as a community connector to provide a pathway to those who see no way out of their circumstances. You can go from being an unskilled helper in the electrical field to a journeyman skilled in high-voltage equipment. Then, you can become a director at a Fortune 500 company. Life is 10% what happens to me and 90% how I react.

Michael serves as a community church pastor and most recently served as the director of community outreach for JW Didado Electric, Quanta Services Co. JW Didado Electric will serve as the lead electrical contractor on an advanced manufacturing facility to be located in Piketon, Ohio. The facility is planned to make clean ammonia and support data centers with clean power. The Piketon, Ohio site will be powered by Hydrogen and Natural Gas . In his former role Michael engaged the local community and served as boots on the ground to add value to the community where JW Didado Electric lives and works. Michael helped to support three programs to attract diverse groups to work in the electrical trades:

1. **LIVE CLASSROOM**: Designed to equip students who desire to pursue careers in construction, engineering, or architecture.
2. **TRAIN TO HIRE**: A workforce development program for young adults for 12 consecutive weeks. This program transitions individuals into full-time, part-time, or project-specific employment opportunities.

3. **BRIGHT FUTURE Re-Entry Program**: Provides work opportunities and training to individuals recovering from substance abuse and to individuals who have been incarcerated.

Chapter 7
From Politics to Purpose

Dr. William Paolillo w/David Wilhelm

"It is the hour of the people, not the hour of the politician." – John Steinbeck

David Wilhelm's life took an unexpected turn in the mid-1990s. After achieving great success in politics, David made a surprising choice. He managed Bill Clinton's 1992 presidential campaign and was Chair of the Democratic National Committee (DNC). He decided to leave politics. After the Democratic Party lost the 1994 midterms, he chose to leave Washington on his own terms. "I jumped before I got pushed," he later reflected.

Politics had been the core of David's identity. At 36, he made history as the youngest DNC Chair. He had guided a U.S. president to victory. And, he had navigated the sharp, ego-driven currents of Washington. But as he packed up his office, David realized that the world of political power no longer resonated with him. "Politics was done with me," he admitted. "I fell out of love with it. It wasn't the answer to everything." The bright lights of Washington now seemed hollow, and the weight of it no longer fit him. He needed something real, something deeper.

This was the beginning of his reinvention—a journey back to his roots in Appalachia. David wasn't returning to any place; he was returning to a deeper connection. His ties to Appalachia were personal and strong. David was born in Champaign, Illinois. He spent his formative years in Athens, Ohio, where his father, a German refugee, was a professor at Ohio University. Growing up there shaped him profoundly.

But this return wasn't just about geography. It was about rediscovering a purpose beyond politics. David's ancestors were linked to George Washington. That connection instilled a sense of public service in him. It had long guided him. His Appalachian upbringing fostered a deep sense of responsibility. It was due to the relationships he built there. The people he knew—their grit, their resilience, and their commitment to community—left a lasting impact. He saw the values of hard work and perseverance. They became a legacy he carried with him. They shaped his view of the world and his purpose.

In the hills and valleys of Appalachia, David would find a greater purpose than the fleeting victories of Washington. It was a mission to build a better future for the land and its people that had shaped him.

David's early education at Ohio University in Athens exposed him to the issues and promise of Appalachian communities. He was drawn to grassroots politics. He organized local campaigns and engaged with the region's economic and social issues. These experiences laid the groundwork for his future work in economic development. They instilled in him a lifelong commitment to improving the lives of working-class Americans.

Though David's career took him to the national stage, his heart remained in Ohio. He studied public policy at Harvard. After leaving Washington, he returned to Athens. He reconnected with the community that had shaped him. His roots in Appalachia and his family's public service inspired David. He aimed to develop areas hurt by globalization and the decline of old industries.

When David left the political scene, he knew he wanted to focus on making a tangible impact. Instead of becoming a lobbyist or consultant, he aimed at economic development. He wanted to help areas like Appalachia and the Great Lakes. They suffered from the decline of coal and manufacturing. David recognized that these areas needed new industries to replace the ones that had once provided jobs and stability.

His first big effort in economic development was creating a venture capital fund. It aimed to revitalize distressed regions. The fund's financial success was modest. But, it was a steppingstone for David. It showed the potential to attract investment and spur entrepreneurship in overlooked communities. He continued this work as a founder of the Ohio Appalachian Business Council. It advocated for policies and partnerships to boost the region's economy.

David also played a key role in initiatives like the Ohio Third Frontier. It's a state-funded program that aims to bring technology and innovation to Ohio. David helped lay the groundwork for a sustainable future in Appalachia. He did this by fostering partnerships between government, business, and academia. He aimed to create jobs. He also wanted new industries to provide long-term stability for the region.

In the early 2000s, David became Chief Strategy Officer at Hecate Energy. It is now the fourth-largest private solar developer in the world. This was a pivotal moment in his career. It marked a shift from politics to renewable energy. Much like his earlier journey in the 1990s, David took a leap of faith. Then, he flew to Arkansas to meet Bill Clinton. That meeting led to his role in managing Clinton's successful presidential campaign. This time, he flew to Chicago to meet the Bullinger brothers, a move that would propel him into a new chapter of leadership.

Under David's direction as the Chief Strategy Officer, Hecate Energy played a key role in driving solar energy development across Ohio and beyond. His vision was not to harness renewable energy. It was to use it to revive struggling regions' economies. Factories and coal plants once dominated Appalachia. But, as these industries declined, the region was left behind. Wilhelm saw the potential for renewable energy to breathe new life into these areas. Under his leadership, Hecate's projects grew manufacturing facilities. They created jobs and revived communities that had long been in decline.

Much like his work with Clinton, where he helped reshape the political landscape, David's work with Hecate focused on long-term impact. His leadership aimed to build a sustainable future for Appalachia and other regions. He wanted renewable energy to spur lasting economic growth and resilience for generations.

VOLTAGE VALLEY REVOLUTION™

First Solar expanded its operations in Perrysburg and Lake Township. It created over 700 permanent jobs. It is now the largest solar manufacturing site in the Western Hemisphere. Enel Green Power announced a new solar panel plant in the Mahoning Valley. It will create hundreds of jobs. Also, Illuminate USA celebrated its one-millionth solar panel. It has hired over 1,000 employees at its Ohio facility. These facilities, enabled by Hecate's projects, show the benefits of David's vision for Appalachia.

David's leadership at Hecate extended beyond the United States. As head of Hecate's global operations, David secured agreements. They positioned the company as a major player in the global renewable energy sector. One such agreement was a Memorandum of Understanding (MoU) with Sonatrach, Algeria's state-owned oil company. It aimed to explore renewable energy, including green hydrogen production. This project may serve as a key element in the global transition to sustainable energy.

David's international efforts show that clean energy is vital. It is both an environmental must and a tool for global economic growth. David has used Hecate's solar energy expertise to make it a leader in renewable energy. This has benefited communities at home and abroad.

Solar and wind energy are intermittent. The sun does not shine at night and the wind does not blow all day. Their future depends on storage to fix their intermittency. David views battery storage as essential to maximize clean energy's potential. He has proposed large battery storage projects in the U.S. to stabilize energy supply and modernize the grid. Hecate is behind them. In Ohio, David wants to turn old coal plants into battery hubs. He wants to ensure that communities enjoy the clean energy shift and are not left behind.

For David, the Voltage Valley Revolution™ is more than an economic project—it's a personal mission. His deep connection to Appalachia and his family's history of public service motivates him. He wants the region to benefit from the clean energy revolution. As coal once powered America's industrial rise, David believes that renewable energy can drive the future of Appalachia.

He has helped create an ecosystem that fosters innovation and growth. He did this through partnerships with local governments, businesses, and universities. One partner was Ohio University's Voinovich School. David is Co-Chair of the Voinovich School's Strategic Partners Group at Ohio University. He co-founded its Center for Public and Social Innovation. His work at the Voinovich School let him mentor future leaders. It also promoted economic development and sustainability in the region.

David's vision for Appalachia is not based on idealism but on practical realities. He knows renewable energy jobs must be well-paid and long-lasting. The goal isn't just to build solar farms. It's to create an economic ecosystem that can support the region for generations. David's approach aims to give Appalachians a chance to secure their future. He wants to create jobs and sustainable industries. They will help the region's hardworking communities thrive. He knows the people of Appalachia will take charge of their own success. He believes that, with the right opportunities, the grit of Appalachia's people will drive their long-term success. This will ensure the region flourishes for generations. All the people of Appalachia need is the opportunity, and they will do the rest.

Chapter 8
Make It, Break It, Make It Better

Dr. Benjamin Cross

"We win tomorrow because of our focus today." — Jack Roush

In 2002, on Jack Roush's 60th birthday, he was left unconscious and submerged in eight feet of water. A plane Jack was flying struck a power line in Troy, AL, and crashed into a small lake. As terrible as the incident was, Roush had two things in his favor: the plane landed in the water, and a retired member of the U.S. Marine Corps, Larry Hicks, witnessed the crash. Had the plane not plummeted into the lake, the impact with the ground likely would have killed Roush. Hicks, using underwater rescue training he learned during his tenure with the Marines, rushed to the crash site where, after several attempts, he removed Jack from the cockpit. Once on the surface, he administered CPR to Roush, who was unconscious and not breathing. Emergency personnel soon arrived, and Roush, who suffered a broken leg, collapsed lung, broken ribs, and a head injury, spent the next several months recovering from his injuries.

The 2002 crash wasn't the only aircraft mishap for Roush. In 2010, he crash-landed his jet at the Experimental Aircraft Association's annual Air Venture in Oshkosh, WI. The incident left Jack with a broken back and jaw and resulted in the loss of his left eye. Jack continued to fly his own planes — which include two P-51 Mustangs — at every opportunity. Jack enjoys saying, "I tell people I don't fly anymore, but I don't fly any less either."

Jack Roush was born in Covington, KY, in 1942. When his father returned from World War II, he returned to Manchester, Ohio's farming community, where he was raised. Manchester, which is designated as the Boyhood Home of Jack Roush, is a small farming community along the Ohio River in Adams County, OH. Jack rebuilt his first lawn mower at nine and built his first go-cart out of lawn mower and wagon parts when he was 11. Jack operated on whatever he could get out of the junkyard, generally Ford vehicles. By age 16, Jack had built four cars out of junkyard parts. Jack was racing on the back roads of Adams County at the age of 16. On his way to pick up his date on a Friday evening, he ran across Bobby Jenkins in his modified 1940 Chevrolet. Jack pulled out to pass Bobby, going around 60 miles per hour. Bobby was having none of that; he sped up to keep Jack on the left side, and Jack slowed down to get behind Bobby, and he put on the brake to keep me out there. It was dusk, and there was a creek on the left side of the road, a tributary for the Ohio River that's probably 9 to 10 feet deep, and no guardrails. Bobby lost the front end of his car—it started to slide—and he bumped Jack in the quarter-panel. Jack recalls, as my car was sliding, God was on my shoulder, he had plans for me, and he said, "Boy, you better brace yourself because it's gonna roll." Sure enough, it took the roof on the passenger side; nobody was with me, but it took it down to the top of the seat. The right-hand door came off immediately as I rolled up the creek bed—all the glass was broken. Any place you could touch that car with your hand was bent, broken, or missing." Jack lost his penny loafers and his new suede jacket on the seat beside him was covered in battery acid and coolant. Besides a little bit of battery acid on his face, he didn't have a scratch, bruise, or a mark on him.

In 1960, there were 30 Ohio applicants for Berea College scholarships, which accepted two, and Jack was one of those two. Berea allowed him to get an education without taking on unacceptable debt - this was the Appalachian way. Berea College was a great experience. Being a liberal arts college, it did not have the engineering program that Jack wanted. So, Jack majored in mathematics and minored in physics. Jack took as many elective courses as possible in the Industrial Arts Department. The instructors allowed him to have a toolbox in the shop, where he would repair bicycles and cars belonging to Berea staff and the few students permitted to have cars. In the shop, he also built a 1954 Dodge for himself.

In May 1964, Jack's daughter Susan was born in the Berea hospital ten days before graduation. She was his graduation present, but he also ordered a new Mustang without seeing anything but pictures, and he was hired by Ford. When the Mustang was built in early June, Jack was already working on quality control issues at the Ford plant in Dearborn, Michigan, and he likely saw his car go through the assembly line. At Ford, Jack soon became acquainted with the "Fastbacks," a group of employees involved in drag racing cars. Jack was immediately hooked on racing and, in 1970, formed his own team with partner Wayne Gapp. Roush and Gapp combined to win multiple championships in NHRA, IHRA, and AHRA Pro Stock drag racing between 1970-75. Jack established Jack Roush Performance Engineering in 1976, supplying racing engines and components for drag, oval-track, hill-climb cars, and offshore powerboat contenders. Jack later partnered with Bob Corn and Ron Woodard to create ECS/Roush, a precursor to today's Roush Industries.

In 1984, Ford commissioned Roush to develop cars and engines for the SCCA Trans-Am and IMSA Camel GT racing series. Roush's cars dominated the Trans-Am manufacturer's championship for Lincoln-Mercury in 1985, won 119 national events, and secured 24 national championships between the two series. Jack expanded his racing operations in 1988 when he established his immensely successful NASCAR team. Roush Fenway Keselowski Racing has claimed two NASCAR Cup Championships, four NASCAR Xfinity championships, and one NASCAR Truck Series title. Jack has also made significant safety contributions to stock car racing, including developing roof flaps to prevent rollovers. Jack has won over 400 national events and more than 30 championships across numerous different motorsports.

Once, an interviewer asked, "Jack, what makes you so great? What makes you a world-class engine builder?"

"It's really quite simple," Jack said. "Here's what we do: we get an engine and put it on the engine block in the shop. We start the engine, let it warm until we can get it to full throttle — like putting a brick on the gas pedal — and my team and I get a cup of coffee. We don't come back until that engine has blown up. Then we tear it apart and see what broke. Let's say it's a piston ring. I will build a better, stronger, and faster piston ring." Jack and his team then put the engine back together and repeat the process. "While all my competitors are afraid of breaking, here at Roush Industries, we embrace breakage. We encourage it because I'll build a better, faster, stronger machine." Additionally, Jack stated, "Early in his racing career, someone told me they assumed we'd take Monday off to celebrate our victory on Sunday. I told him we focus on the future; we win tomorrow because of our focus today."

Culture is critical to Jack. Roush Enterprises defines its culture as "Fueled by a culture of enthusiasm, innovation, and collective purpose. It's a world-leading set of minds combined with a Midwest roll-up-our-sleeves and get-it-done attitude. Working with our clients to push beyond the expected — never satisfied until we reach extraordinary." This ethos, born out of the challenges faced in motorsports, aligns perfectly with the spirit of Appalachia and the Voltage Valley Revolution™. Just as the region has risen from economic decline, transforming its industrial base, Roush Enterprises has channeled its innovative strengths into addressing the future of clean energy and sustainable manufacturing. These same principles are driving Appalachia's resurgence as a hub for advanced technology and renewable energy.

Jack's story, rooted in the Appalachian values of hard work, resilience, and innovation, mirrors the journey of the region itself. While his legacy in motorsports is legendary, Jack Roush's most profound impact may well be the inspiration he provides for the people of Appalachia—those striving to reinvent their future and build a cleaner, stronger, and more sustainable tomorrow. Jack, a son of Appalachia, exemplifies the spirit of the region, proving that with determination and vision, even the toughest challenges can be overcome.

Appendix

On July 15, 2010, Roush CleanTech was legally formed as a cornerstone of this vision. **ROUSH CleanTech**, the clean technology division of Roush Enterprises, has taken the lead in providing sustainable energy solutions, initially focusing on vehicles powered by propane autogas—a cleaner alternative that reduces greenhouse gases and harmful emissions. Now, Roush CleanTech is expanding its efforts to assist in the transition of fleets to electric vehicles (EVs), positioning itself as a crucial player in the green energy transformation taking hold in Appalachia and the Voltage Valley Revolution™.

Jack Roush's legacy is one of relentless commitment to clean energy solutions and advanced manufacturing, perfectly in line with the vision for Appalachia's future. As Roush Enterprises states: "We're obsessed with sustainable progress. Going further, faster, and doing more — all with less impact, less waste, and more long-term vision." These efforts are driving the Voltage Valley Revolution™, which is centered on sustainable growth and innovation, with a focus on:

- **Lightweighting**: Leading the way in advanced composites that reduce weight while increasing strength, durability, and performance—key for both motorsports and the new industries emerging in Appalachia.

- **Sustainable Energy**: Developing the infrastructure needed to scale renewable energy, much like the transformation of the Voltage Valley into a clean energy powerhouse.

- **Life Cycle Management**: Continuously improving processes to maximize efficiency and minimize environmental impact, a philosophy central to the revival of Appalachia's industries.

- **Innovative Spirit**: Encouraging teams to think beyond traditional methods, driving the creative solutions necessary for Appalachia's continued growth in advanced manufacturing and green technology.

- **Why Not Culture**: Asking tough questions and examining processes to make collective improvements, a mindset that has empowered the people of Appalachia and propelled the Voltage Valley forward.

VOLTAGE VALLEY REVOLUTION™

Chapter 9
Love, Resilience, and Community

Dr. William Paolillo w/Gayle Manchin

"Our progress as a nation depends not on individual achievement alone but on our shared commitment to each other, the strength of our communities, and the resilience we show together."
– President John F. Kennedy

The call came before dawn, shattering the quiet with an urgent ring that jolted Gayle awake. She sat up, her heart racing. At twenty, she had just married Joe. Now, she was ready to start the fall semester at West Virginia University. They had planned every detail, excited for the life they were building. But at that moment, none of it mattered. Her father had suffered a heart attack and a stroke—both in one brutal blow.

Within the hour, she and Joe were on a plane, racing toward Beckley, West Virginia, where her parents lived. Gayle stared out the window. The early light caught the clouds below. Dread and determination swirled inside her. Her father had always been strong, a steady presence with hands that had worked tirelessly for their family. Yet the voice on the line had left her suspended in a place where certainty vanished. She walked into a sterile hospital room. Her father lay motionless against the crisp sheets, surrounded by the relentless hum of machines. Doctors spoke clinically, predicting he'd never walk, likely never speak, and be dead in a year. But when she looked into her dad's eyes, she saw he was not done.

Over the following weeks, Gayle stayed by his side, putting her classes on hold. She coaxed him through tiny, painful movements. She ignored the doctors' impossibilities. She matched his quiet defiance with her own. Bit by bit, he proved them wrong. He walked. He spoke slowly but surely again, and Gayle's strength grew alongside his. She would carry a lesson forward. Adversity must be met head-on, no matter what the odds.

A year later, Gayle faced another trial. She was pregnant with their first child. Joe's business had burned to the ground. They stood together in the ashes, unsure of the future. Yet Gayle's father's defiance had left a mark; surrender was not an option. Together, they faced each new challenge. This built a resilience that would carry Gayle through every role. It would see her through her journey as a teacher, an advocate, and a leader in Appalachia's rebirth. Gayle now leads an effort to make Appalachia a hub for advanced manufacturing, all-in energy, technology and innovation.

A Vision Rooted in Education, Family, and Community

Gayle Manchin's path to the Appalachian Regional Commission (ARC) was shaped more by a deep commitment to education and Appalachian roots than by political ambition. From her early days as a teacher to now, Gayle's life has been about uplifting others. She is ARC's first Federal Co-Chair from West Virginia. The region is known for its resilience and strong sense of community.

It all began in the classroom. After graduating from West Virginia University, Gayle began her education career in Marion County. She quickly learned that teaching was more than sharing knowledge. It meant opening her heart and meeting students where they were. A powerful memory from her early teaching days shaped her view of being truly present for others. She had watched a young boy, frustrated with his grade, tear his paper in half and felt her throat tighten. After class, he returned to apologize and ask for help. This exchange moved her deeply. "You have to be there for them," she would later say. "That's what they're really looking for." It cemented her philosophy: teaching was not just a job but a chance to demonstrate her commitment to supporting her community's youth.

Her dedication to students went beyond the classroom. Gayle believed that authentic learning came from engaging with the community. She helped create Fairmont State University's first Community Service-Learning Program. It connected students' studies to local service projects. It was a hands-on initiative. As the AmeriCorps Promise Fellows director in West Virginia, she expanded this vision to the whole state. She instilled in students the values of compassion, collaboration, and self-reliance.

Family has always been central to Gayle's life and work, grounding her values and giving her purpose. As an only child, she watched her parents face life's challenges with quiet strength. Her father taught her a lasting lesson in resilience. After the severe heart attack and stroke, with determination and family support, he defied the odds. Through tough physical therapy, he regained his ability to walk and speak and lived for eighteen years. Those hours spent helping him taught Gayle the power of persistence and faith in each other.

As a mother, Gayle taught her children these values. She and Joe built a family centered on love and support. Thanksgiving became a cherished time. She told her kids, " The greatest gift children can give to their parents is to love each other." Her ten grandchildren, more like siblings than cousins, are a testament to nurturing family bonds.

Gayle's passion for family and community has guided her in every role. Her work with Reconnecting McDowell, an initiative to revitalize one of West Virginia's most troubled counties, shows her commitment to meeting people where they are. This project proved that authentic leadership is hands-on. It means knowing the community's needs from the inside out.

In a state with a complex history, Gayle has fought for fairness in education and economic growth. She knows Appalachia's struggles well. She has seen the effects of the opioid crisis and an economic downturn in many of the region's communities. Through Reconnecting McDowell, she reminded them, "Be there for them. Help."

Appendix

In 2021, Gayle's commitment to her community reached new heights when she became Federal Co-Chair of the ARC. Her role represents the culmination of a lifetime devotion to service and growth in Appalachia. She works with thirteen state governors. They aim to build economic resilience across Appalachia. They address issues like broadband access, infrastructure, and opioid recovery-to-work programs.

The Appalachian Regional Commission is an economic development entity of the federal government and 13 state governments focusing on 423 counties across the Appalachian Region. ARC's mission is to innovate, partner, and invest to build community capacity and strengthen economic growth in Appalachia to help the region achieve socioeconomic parity with the nation.

VOLTAGE VALLEY REVOLUTION™

Chapter 10
A Mother's Love

Dr. William Paolillo with Arria Hines

"The stone age didn't end for lack of stone, and the oil age will end long before the world runs out of oil." – Sheikh Ahmed Zaki Yamani, former Saudi Arabian oil minister

As Arria stared out the window of her childhood home, she stood at a crossroads. After a tough divorce, she returned to West Virginia with her two young kids and an unfinished college degree. She knew what she had to do: provide for her family, but the path wasn't clear. In a state where jobs were scarce and the economy had seen better days, her future seemed uncertain. Still, she wasn't the type to run from a challenge.

There were no shortcuts for Arria. She had to finish her education. Then, she had to support her children. But she had to do it in a place with few opportunities. It wasn't easy, but leaving West Virginia wasn't an option. This was her home. She walked into West Virginia Wesleyan College with a bold request: help. With one child in school and another needing daycare, she couldn't manage alone. Asking for help wasn't in her nature. Appalachians are proud, self-reliant people. But if she was going to move forward, she had to make sacrifices, including setting aside her pride.

It worked. She secured daycare and went back to school, determined to finish what she had started. Her accounting degree became the foundation for her next steps. More than that, she learned a lesson that would change her life: relationships mattered. The support from her professors and the community gave her the strength to push forward. This network would be vital as she advanced her career. It proved that no one can succeed alone.

After earning her degree, Arria's career began in an unexpected place—managing a local golf course development. It wasn't glamorous, but it was valuable. The project taught her to handle budgets, lead teams, and manage large operations. It taught her the essential value of building trust in the community. In Appalachia, success isn't just about skill; it's about trust. People need to know that you're in it for the long haul, that you're not going to abandon them when times get tough.

This skill, building relationships, opened doors for Arria. One led her to National Aeronautics and Space Administration, NASA. A small business contractor secured her a project management job. There, she learned to manage complex government contracts and large projects. It was a turning point for her. Working for NASA boosted her confidence and expertise. It deepened her understanding of large systems and managing high-stakes projects. Still, even with her success, she felt the pull of home. Appalachia needed people like her. She often asked herself, "If everyone leaves, what happens to this place?" So, she stayed.

VOLTAGE VALLEY REVOLUTION™

In 2009, Arria took a leap and founded her own consulting firm Allegheny Science and Technology, AST. At first, her company focused on providing financial and project management services to small oil and gas companies. Fossil fuels had long been the backbone of West Virginia's economy, but even then, she knew change was coming. The energy landscape was shifting toward sustainability. Arria was determined to help Appalachia keep up. Her company started small. She grew it by connecting with people. She earned their trust and built relationships along the way.

Her reliability and trustworthiness let her expand to bigger projects. Her big break came when she got a contract with the Idaho National Laboratory (INL) to work on nuclear energy. It was her first real exposure to clean energy. It opened her eyes to the potential of these technologies for Appalachia. The more she learned, the more she believed that West Virginia's future lay not in coal or gas, but in something new, clean energy. It had to create jobs, revitalize communities, and ensure a sustainable future for the region.

As her work in clean energy expanded, so did her role in reshaping the future of Appalachia. This became especially true when she entered the U.S. Hydrogen Hub competition. It aimed to fund 6-10 regional Hydrogen Hubs with $8 billion. Arria knew hydrogen could transform energy. She wanted West Virginia to lead in this new era.

Hydrogen, especially blue hydrogen, offered a unique opportunity for West Virginia. The state is the second-largest natural gas producer, after Texas. West Virginia has vast natural gas reserves. So, it is ideal for blue hydrogen production. This process makes hydrogen from natural gas. It captures and stores carbon emissions. The abundance of natural gas could fuel a clean, hydrogen-based energy future. Arria saw a chance for West Virginia. It could use its natural resources and reduce carbon emissions.

Her leadership in the hydrogen sector was not just about her skills. It was about her ability to unite people. Due to West Virginia's key role in the ARCH2 initiative, Arria was asked to lead the Request for Information (RFI) development. This was a crucial step to secure federal support for a multi-state project that involved Ohio, Pennsylvania, and Kentucky. The effort required a diverse group of stakeholders. They were energy companies, government officials, and local communities. The aim was to make the region's bid competitive. Arria worked hard with the team to organize industry days and form partnerships. Their first event brought over 300 participants into the conversation.

West Virginia's natural gas industry positioned the state as an ideal candidate for Appalachian Region Clean Hydrogen Hub (ARCH2), particularly for blue hydrogen. The hub would use the state's existing infrastructure. It would use pipelines and gas production to make hydrogen. This could power industries, cut emissions, and boost the local economy. The ARCH2 project spanned multiple states. It aimed to create a self-sustaining hydrogen ecosystem. It would produce, distribute, and store hydrogen, all in the region. This would boost the economy of West Virginia and the broader Appalachian area.

"The ripple effect of this project is incredible," she said. "This isn't just about hydrogen. It's about creating jobs and industries. It's about building infrastructure. These will transform the region for generations."" Her vision was broad. She saw that the hydrogen hub could do more than create energy. It could create opportunities, build careers, and provide long-term economic stability in Appalachia. The ARCH2 hub would create thousands of direct jobs in construction, operations, and maintenance. Supporting industries, like manufacturing and logistics, would create even more jobs.

The Inflation Reduction Act (IRA) funded critical support. In the end, West Virginia and its neighbors in the ARCH2 hub secured billions in federal investment. The ARCH2 project won a multi-billion-dollar investment. It would produce clean energy and create high-paying, long-term jobs in the region. Arria's work positioned Appalachia to lead the global energy transition, with West Virginia at the forefront.

For Arria, the hydrogen hub wasn't just a project, it was a lifeline for her community. "The ripple effect of what we're doing is about more than energy," she said. "It's about creating jobs and building a future for the people of this region." The project would bring sustainable industry to Appalachia. The region has long struggled with economic instability. The hub would create new industries and businesses. It would reshape the region for years to come.

Arria's ability to connect with people made her a key figure in Appalachia's transformation. She built trust and led projects from start to finish. But she wasn't done yet. The hydrogen hub was just the beginning. The ripple effect she had spoken of would continue to shape the region. It would create opportunities across industries, not just in energy.

Looking ahead, Arria remains optimistic. "The best is yet to come," she says, confident in the work she's done and the future she's helping to build. Appalachia is evolving. With leaders like Arria, its best days are ahead. The Voltage Valley Revolution™ is more than an economic shift. It's a cultural one. Arria is ensuring that West Virginians will lead the charge into this new energy era.

Appendix – Technical Facts

ARCH2, the Appalachian Regional Clean Hydrogen Hub, was initially awarded up to $925 million by the U.S. Department of Energy. It brings together 12 Project Development Partners (PDPs) to advance clean hydrogen initiatives in Appalachia. The hub was selected from over 70 applicants, showcasing the potential of its projects to meet the DOE's goals of accelerating the hydrogen economy. The partners have been chosen for their expertise and commitment to the region, with projects targeting rapid deployment of hydrogen technologies to support diverse applications, from transportation to industrial use.

VOLTAGE VALLEY REVOLUTION™

Key partners and their projects include:

- **Air Liquide**, a global leader in gases and technology, will contribute to hydrogen production and infrastructure development, leveraging its expertise in industrial gases and clean energy solutions.

- **CNX Resources** will utilize Appalachian natural gas to produce low-carbon hydrogen, focusing on integrating carbon capture technologies to minimize emissions during production.

- **Enbridge**, known for its energy infrastructure, is working on advancing hydrogen production, integrating renewable energy sources such as wind and solar power, and enhancing hydrogen delivery systems.

- **EQT Corporation**, the largest natural gas producer in the U.S., is developing projects to use hydrogen to decarbonize energy production and support industrial applications in the region.

- **Fidelis New Energy** is focused on producing decarbonized fuels and offering solutions that address climate change challenges through clean hydrogen and energy services.

- **Empire Diversified Energy** brings its experience in recycling, logistics, and energy production to support sustainable hydrogen projects in Appalachia.

- **Hope Gas**, a local distribution company, aims to incorporate hydrogen into its existing natural gas network, promoting the use of blended hydrogen for residential, industrial, and commercial customers across West Virginia.

- **Hog Lick Aggregates** is collaborating with other companies in West Virginia to bring economic, environmental, and community benefits through clean hydrogen projects.

- **Independence Hydrogen** focuses on delivering hydrogen fuel solutions for mobility and transportation, promoting the use of clean hydrogen in heavy-duty vehicles.

- **KeyState Natural Gas Synthesis** is developing a project to produce hydrogen and other products from a stranded gas asset in Northern Pennsylvania, integrating geological storage for carbon management.

- **Plug Power** is constructing an end-to-end green hydrogen ecosystem, covering all stages from production and storage to distribution and utilization to support industrial decarbonization and transportation.

Program management and support come from **AST**, which leads project coordination and community outreach, **and Battelle**, which brings research expertise in public-private partnerships and technical insights from **GTI**, **NETL**, and **TRC** to cover all phases of the hydrogen lifecycle. Together, these partners are positioning Appalachia as a hub for clean hydrogen innovation, driving sustainable energy development and economic growth in the region.

Chapter 11
Smart Enough to Try

Dr. William Paolillo w/ Dr. Benjamin Cross

You need to be smart enough to know what to do and dumb enough not to let anybody tell you any different. My Daddy –Marion Donald Cross

Benjamin Cross was raised on a 105-acre farm near Cherry Fork, Adams County, Ohio. Adams County was the second poorest county in Ohio when Ben was born in 1954. Today, over 19% of the country's population lives below the poverty line. At age 4, Ben crashed the big Oliver tractor through a closed barn door and into a chicken house – no one was hurt. You would think Ben might lose his driving privileges with such a significant accident. At 5, Ben drove tractors to pick up hay. At 7, he spread manure on the farm's fields using a 1947 Ford Ferguson tractor. If Ben's older brother Alan could do it, so could he.

Once, Ben missed the school bus. His dad had no time to take him to school. So, Ben drove the 1947 Ford Ferguson tractor to school. Ben remembers pulling up to school just behind his classroom, getting off the tractor, and going to class. Some students commented, but that was about it, and everyone went on with their day. Growing up in Appalachia, Ben's dad often said, "You need to be smart enough to know what to do and dumb enough not to let anybody tell you any different."

Ben's parents foresaw the changing economy in Appalachia. So, they decided to move to Florida. Ben's father saw that the small farm was unsustainable. The trend was shifting to larger, more industrialized farms. After graduating high school, Ben's oldest brother moved to Florida in 1961. In December 1962, at 8, his parents sold everything they had except the land. The five family members then loaded into a new 1963 Ford Fairlane and drove to Florida. Florida was cheap back then, but they didn't have much money. Ben, "We were never hungry, but I only had two pairs of jeans and a suit to wear to church on Sundays. What we typically got for Christmas was an apple and underwear." What Ben lacked in material things was made up for by an encouraging and intelligent family. Ben's sister Brenda taught him to read, and his cousins Ken Roush and Wayne Malone became engineers. They inspired Ben to follow his dream of becoming an engineer and participating in the space program.

Growing up in Central Florida in the 1960s was about NASA and Disney. Ben's dream of space travel compelled him to learn to fly small aircraft at 15. Ben's parents were supportive; if he could pay for it, he could learn to fly. When you start driving tractors at 5, flying lessons at 15 and soloing at 16 are no big deal. Once in 12th grade, Ben and a fellow student flew a Cessna 150 to New Smyrna Beach during lunch. When they got back to English class, they were fifteen minutes late. The teacher asked where they'd been, and he said, we flew to New Smyrna. They were honest with her, and she didn't believe them, but all the kids laughed as they knew it was true.

Ben worked at Amtrak to pay for college and graduated from the University of Maryland. While he worked handling baggage and going to college, he was promoted to Manager of Special Projects - Energy. Ben traveled the country finding ways to save Amtrak money on energy costs – he saved over $440,000 the 1st year. Ben was a rising star at Amtrak. But, after he graduated from the University of Maryland, he wanted to travel. So, he took a job with the US government at the Norfolk Naval shipyard as a mechanical engineer in the propulsion piping section.

Ben would always work late and took Self-Study Naval Engineering courses. While working late, Ben would answer the phone and try to help whoever called. Larry Dutton, the Shipyard's Chief Engineer, would call looking for Ben's boss. Larry Dutton previously worked for Admiral Rickover, the godfather of the nuclear navy. Admiral Rickover directed the original development of the naval nuclear program. Larry promoted Ben to a Field Engineer, acting as the design liaison for a nuclear-guided cruiser. Ben's role involved daily meetings with the ship's captain, chief engineer, and electrical officer. They covered the ship's power plant and all its systems, including the weapons. Ben would routinely visit the navy ship. He would identify the work, approve design changes, oversee job planning, and sign off on acceptance tests. Once Ben started working to advance nuclear technology, he never looked back.

Ben's career in the commercial nuclear industry began at the Fort St. Vrain Nuclear Generating Station. He later worked at the Savannah River Site and the Savannah River National Laboratory (SRNL). He was promoted to Manager of Nuclear Energy Programs. He led various initiatives, showcasing his leadership and deep knowledge of nuclear energy. Ben applied his Appalachian farm boy work ethic and smarts. His father taught him to be smart enough to know what to do and dumb enough not to let anyone tell you different.

In 1992, Ben got his dream job. He became program manager of Fusion/ITER, the International Thermonuclear Experimental Reactor. It is a large experiment to test fusion energy. The "magic" and global reach of the Fusion/ITER project lie in its potential to revolutionize energy generation. It offers a renewable, eco-friendly, and abundant energy source.

ITER is one of the world's most ambitious energy projects. It involves collaboration from the EU, India, Japan, China, Russia, South Korea, and the US. In 1998, the US canceled its participation in the program. Global travel, working with brilliant minds, and a chance to save the world from global warming with nuclear fusion were put on hold. Something else in Ben's life was also happening; his son was reaching his teenage years, and Ben was needed at home.

Taking a step to the side, Ben continued at the Savannah River Site and SRNL. He worked in various roles, honing his skills in sustainable energy and manufacturing. As his son grew older, Ben reflected more on the future – not just his own, but that of the planet and the next generation. While there was a setback, the cancellation of the US participation in the ITER project catalyzed a new direction in Ben's career.

With his son now 17, Ben had a new focus. He wanted to combine integrated energy systems with closed-loop manufacturing. It was a groundbreaking idea. This concept promised a revolution in industries' operations, with sustainability at its core. This idea wasn't just about changing one facility and setting a new energy usage and manufacturing standard worldwide.

A closed-loop, clean energy-powered, integrated energy system is a big step. It will improve energy production and use efficiency. It's about creating a system where everything is connected, and nothing is unnecessarily wasted. This system uses output of one system as the input of another. It can greatly improve efficiency and sustainability. It's a way of producing what we need without the waste and environmental damage that traditional manufacturing brings.

Ben's vision took form in a proposal. It was to develop an Integrated Energy System – Closed Loop Manufacturing Complex in Piketon, Ohio, near his hometown. This wasn't just a return to his roots but a step towards the future he wanted to create. In Piketon, he saw a chance to build a model for the world. It would be a manufacturing hub that's productive, sustainable, and eco-friendly. The Piketon facility will create 300 high-paying jobs. It will employ 2,000 constructors to build it. The manufacturing complex will be powered by clean energy.

This project would be more than a professional achievement; it is a personal mission for Ben. It was about creating a legacy for future generations. It was built on Daddy's belief: be smart enough to know what to do and dumb enough not to let anyone tell you otherwise.

Chapter 12
Forging a Path forward

Dr. William Paolillo with Don Wingate

"Success is not final; failure is not fatal: It is the courage to continue that counts." – Winston Churchill

A transformation was quietly taking root in the heart of the industrial Midwest, where the steel mills had fallen silent, and the coal mines were closing. This change was called the Voltage Valley Revolution™. It represented a shift from old industries to clean energy, innovative technology solutions and advanced manufacturing. It was about rebuilding what was broken and finding a path forward. For Don Wingate, it was not just about technological progress; it was about rebuilding a future for his community and preserving the values he had grown up with.

Don grew up in northeast Ohio, in a working-class family whose rhythms were tied to the hum of the local factory. His mother kept the house spotless, the faint smell of lemon polish always in the air. Don was their only child, and life was steady, predictable. Summers smelled of fresh-cut grass and the charcoal smoke of neighborhood barbecues, with days filled with baseball games, Boy Scouts, and family dinners where the rich aroma of his mother's pot roast signaled everything was as it should be. The kind of life you didn't know you'd miss until it was gone. Then, in his first year of college, at Kent State, everything changed. His father died in a car crash. A van crossed the center line and slammed into his father's Chevy Impala. It was sudden and brutal. When Don arrived home his mother was alone, waiting at the kitchen table with his father's lunch still on the counter.

Don had a choice: stay in school or drop out to help his mother make ends meet. She decided to work as a secretary at Republic Steel, which was her first time working outside the home since marriage. She told him to stay in school, to finish what he started. So, he did. He stuck it out, one class at a time, driven by a sense of duty and the need to prove that the loss wouldn't break them.

He graduated with a business degree in 1973. Still trying to figure out what to do next, he applied for an MBA at Kent State. They turned him down. Don took a job with Burroughs Corporation, selling computer systems. It was the career in technology he had imagined but different from the time frame he imagined. A few months later, another letter came from Kent State. They'd made a mistake and sent the wrong letter. He had been accepted all along. By then, it didn't matter. He was already on his way. He didn't look back.

From Burroughs, Don went to General Electric and then ran his own business for a while, selling minicomputers. He learned the hard truths of running a small company in a market dominated by giants. It wasn't easy. He shut down the business after four years and shifted to selling database systems for companies like Cullinet Software and Oracle. It was decent work, but it wasn't enough for Don to provide the underlying technology. He wanted to use technology to solve real problems and create business solutions.

Then, one day, he found himself at Telvent, leading sales and marketing—selling technology solutions to the utility industry. That's when everything changed again. Schneider Electric bought the company. He had never heard of them before. He thought they were just hardware manufacturers. Then, he discovered what they were about—sustainability, resilience, and a vision for the future. It wasn't just another company. Schnieder Electric's mission made sense to Don.

At Schneider Electric, Don learned about microgrids, small, self-sufficient systems that produce sustainable, resilient, and cost-effective energy. When the primary grid fails, systems that power commercial and industrial customers can also power entire communities. He saw the potential, not just in technology, but in its impact on places like Appalachia. The coal mines had closed, the factories were boarded up, and families were struggling. The promise of a new kind of energy—clean, reliable, and local—could change everything. This would help Ohio move from being called the rust belt, to a hub of innovation and industry.

Don's role at Schneider Electric soon evolved from software sales to a deeper engagement with sustainability and digitization that drove the energy sector's transition. He became involved in developing microgrids—localized energy systems that could operate independently or in conjunction with the larger grid. The significance of microgrids extended beyond technology; they offered a solution for regions like Appalachia, where economic decline and aging infrastructure had left communities struggling. The Voltage Valley Revolution™ aimed to turn such regions into clean energy and advanced manufacturing hubs, and microgrids were key to this transformation.

As Don immersed himself in the intricacies of energy resilience and renewable integration, he realized that this work was about more than technology. It was about people and communities—about making energy accessible and reliable in places left behind by the collapse of traditional industries like coal. The transition wasn't just about replacing one form of energy with another; it was about rethinking how energy was produced, distributed, and consumed in a way that benefited everyone.

The work became a natural extension of Don's career, combining his experience with utilities and his newfound focus on sustainable energy solutions. One of the most significant projects that defined this shift was the Trillium H2 initiative, a hydrogen production facility that aimed to harness clean hydrogen - as a key component of the future energy mix. The project presented significant challenges, including integrating hydrogen production of electricity to power potential data centers, manufacturing facilities and the existing grid. It required a level of innovation and coordination that had never been done before.

To tackle these challenges, Don recognized the potential of digital twins—virtual replicas of physical systems. By using digital twins, the facility could simulate different scenarios, optimize processes, and predict potential issues before they occur. This cutting-edge technology was essential for ensuring the plant's efficiency and sustainability. However, not everyone was convinced. Some stakeholders expressed skepticism regarding the practical benefits of such a new technology.

Don's solution was to bring all the key players together. He organized a series of meetings that brought engineers, contractors, developers, and local leaders into the same room. The first meeting occurred at his trout fishing club, an informal and neutral setting where everyone could discuss their concerns openly. Don's calm and methodical approach helped build trust and facilitated honest conversations about the challenges ahead. He emphasized the importance of collaboration and showed how a coordinated effort could bring the project to fruition.

The meetings at unconventional locations like the trout fishing club reflected Don's belief that relationships were central to success. His experience taught him that no person or company could solve every problem in the complex energy landscape. Projects like the Trillium H2 and the broader efforts in Voltage Valley required a network of partners with complementary expertise. By fostering genuine and enduring partnerships, he helped align various stakeholders toward a shared goal of building a sustainable and resilient energy future.

The work was hard. It took more than a good idea. It took partnerships, trust, and a willingness to try something new. Don knew that technology alone wouldn't solve the problem. It took people working together, putting aside doubts, and finding a way forward. That's how the Trillium H2 project came about—a planned hydrogen production plant that would power the production of data centers and clean ammonia.

But nothing came easy. The idea of digital twins—virtual replicas of physical systems—seemed like science fiction to some. People were skeptical. They didn't see how a simulation could help build a plant or run an energy grid. Don brought them all together. They met at his trout fishing club, a place where they could sit down, have a meal, and talk plainly. Engineers, contractors, and local leaders all came. He laid out the plan and showed them what was possible. Technology wasn't the hard part. It was getting everyone to believe in the use of technology.

Slowly, things began to move. The meetings turned into agreements, and the ideas turned into plans. They worked on the microgrids, figuring out how to tie solar, wind, and hydrogen into a network that could power plants and, eventually, entire communities. The digital twin helped them catch problems before they started, keeping costs down and progressing steadily. What seemed impossible a year ago was beginning to take shape.

Don continues to work closely with local utilities, government agencies, and private companies to ensure that the new energy systems being built were environmentally friendly, economically viable, and resilient enough to withstand future challenges. The broader implications of his work extended beyond Appalachia. The principles of integrating renewable energy, enhancing grid resilience, and fostering community partnerships are applied to energy projects across the country. As Don continued to champion these efforts at Schneider Electric, he saw firsthand how technology, combined with the right people and vision, could change the course of entire communities.

For Don, the journey wasn't just about advancing his career or achieving professional milestones. It was a personal mission to contribute to a cause bigger than himself. He often thinks back to his early days, the loss of his father, and the resilience that his mother showed, and he continues to count on the support and love his wife and children provide today. Those experiences shaped his resolve to push forward, even when the path was uncertain. The Voltage Valley Revolution™ became a way to give back—to help rebuild regions and lives in a way that honored the spirit of resilience he had known all his life.

As he continues his work, Don remains focused on the future. The road ahead is still full of challenges, but with the right technology, partnerships, and dedication, the Voltage Valley Revolution™ is more than just a hopeful idea; it is becoming a reality, one project and one community at a time.

In Voltage Valley, Don saw more than an energy project. He saw a way to give back, to bring life back to a place that had been left behind. He worked with utilities, government agencies, and private companies to ensure that the new systems weren't just good for the environment and the people who lived there. It was about making energy affordable, reliable, and available for the next generation.

The revolution wasn't just about technology. It was about redemption. For Don, it was a way to honor his father's memory and ensure that his mother's hard work and sacrifice hadn't been in vain. The lessons he learned grew about resilience, sticking it out, and supporting his family when things got hard—were the heart of what will make the Voltage Valley Revolution™.

As the projects grow and the momentum builds, Don looks out over the trout fishing club where it all began. There's still work to be done, and it won't be easy. But the path is clear. It's not just about changing the grid. It's about changing lives. And that's a job worth doing. He's looking for the next set of meetings to hold while he enjoys fly fishing for trout.

Appendix Digital Twin Technology – Technical Talk

Integrating Schneider Electric's Digital Twin into the Trillium H2 Power's project will bring significant expected efficiency and cost management improvements. This digital twin technology allowed for virtual modeling and testing across the facility's systems, including hydrogen production, metallurgical silicon manufacturing, and ammonia synthesis. As a result, the project was projected to achieve a 60% reduction in commissioning time, streamlining the path from design to operation.

Additionally, virtual testing and optimization anticipated a 20% reduction in quality-related costs by identifying and addressing potential issues early in the process. Operationally, the digital twin was projected to boost manufacturing efficiency by 30%, ensuring a seamless integration of hydrogen-powered processes. This reassures stakeholders about the project's sustainability and resilience, contributing to a more resilient and sustainable production system.

VOLTAGE VALLEY REVOLUTION™

These expected gains in time, cost, and operational efficiency demonstrated the transformative potential of digital twin technology in complex projects like Trillium H2 Power, the integration of clean energy into the grid, and Advanced Manufacturing. The Digital Twin is paving the way for a clean energy future in Voltage Valley. Learning and mastering Digital Twin technology is one way to join the Voltage Valley Revolution™.

VOLTAGE VALLEY REVOLUTION™

Chapter 13
Powering Possibilities

Dr. William Paolillo w/ Samantha Childress

"It always seems impossible until it's done." – Nelson Mandela

Samantha, or Sam as her friends called her, was only 14 when her life took a sharp and unexpected turn. Her parents' divorce changed the steady rhythm she had always known. Suddenly, she had to balance life between two homes while stepping up to care for her younger brother. The burden of responsibility could have been heavy for someone so young, but Sam became more independent and focused instead of being overwhelmed. She realized early on that she would have to take control as her family adjusted during these formative years. This moment sparked a new, strong determination in her. It would, unexpectedly, shape her future.

Around the same time, Sam's interest in the environment blossomed. A significant turning point came during a biology class project. Each student was allowed to choose a topic, and Sam was instantly captivated by the issue of climate change. While many classmates chose easier subjects, Sam was drawn to the complexity of global warming and its potential solutions. She was not just intrigued by science. She wanted to make a real, tangible difference.

To fuel her curiosity, Sam watched a documentary called *Too Hot to Handle*, which explored how people fought climate change. The film showed new technologies, from biofuels to small renewables. It sparked something in her. She began to see energy not just as a technical issue but as a human one, something that had the potential to change lives. Eager to dive deeper, Sam decided to reach out to an expert. She took a bold step. She emailed the Dean of Duke University's Nicholas School of the Environment, Norm Christensen. She asked thoughtful questions about global warming and renewable energy.

At just 14, Sam wasn't sure what to expect, but to her surprise, the dean responded with thoughtful, detailed answers. This exchange opened her eyes to the fact that even as a young teenager, she could impact the world. From that moment on, Sam wanted a career in the energy sector. She wanted to tackle one of the planet's biggest challenges: climate change.

Her growing passion for renewable energy didn't detract from another essential part of her life: soccer. The discipline and focus she learned in the field fueled her determination in other areas. Soccer had been a constant in her childhood. It taught her the value of teamwork, perseverance, and pushing her limits. "I wanted to be a professional soccer player," Sam recalls. "That was my dream for the longest time." While her path ultimately led her away from professional sports, the lessons she learned on field - resilience, competitiveness, and determination, would serve her well as she navigated the energy industry's complexities in the years to come.

As Sam started looking at colleges, she was torn between her love for soccer and her growing interest in renewable energy. Many schools recruiting her for soccer didn't have the programs she wanted. But then Appalachian State University, nestled in the Appalachian Mountains, caught her eye. At first, she was hesitant. "I thought, no way, it's too cold and windy up there," she laughs. "I didn't want to be playing soccer in the cold." But when she toured the campus, everything changed. She saw the university's commitment to renewable energy. It had a large wind turbine and a solar decathlon home that students had built. The university's hands-on approach to sustainability won her over.

Appalachian State's *Appropriate Technology* program was exactly what Sam had been searching for. It was one of the few programs in the country that focused on small-scale renewable energy systems. The university's location in the Appalachian Mountains made it ideal for studying sustainability. She knew immediately that this was where she wanted to be. The decision was made more accessible when she realized she could pursue both her passions—soccer and renewable energy—at the same time. "It was a perfect fit," Sam says. "I could keep playing the sport I loved while diving into the world of renewable energy."

During college, Sam had the opportunity to travel to Nicaragua, where she and her classmates installed solar panels in remote schools and community centers. The experience was transformative. In these rural areas, electricity was scarce, and the impact of providing solar energy was immediate. Children could study at night, and community centers could host events that unite people. "That trip changed everything for me," Sam recalls. "Seeing firsthand what access to energy could do for these communities made me realize that energy is about more than just technology. It's about empowering people."

After that trip, Sam knew she wanted to dedicate her life to bringing renewable energy to underserved communities. She began volunteering with United Solar Initiative, a nonprofit that focused on providing solar power to remote regions. Over the years, she became more involved, eventually rising to the role of president of the board. Under her leadership, the organization expanded its reach. It provided solar systems and battery storage to schools, clinics, and community hubs in Kenya and Guatemala. "It's about so much more than just lights," Sam says. "It's about giving people the tools to improve their lives, in education, healthcare, and economic development."

Sam loved small renewable energy projects. She knew the world needed larger solutions to meet its energy needs. After her undergraduate degree, she pursued a master's at Duke University. She focused on power markets and the economics of renewable energy. It gave her a broader view of the challenges of scaling renewable energy. She learned that the energy transition is complex. Political and financial barriers often slow progress.

During this time, Sam became acutely aware of the challenges facing regions like Appalachia. As coal mines shut down and communities struggled to adapt, she saw firsthand the human cost of the energy transition. "It's not just about closing coal mines and building wind farms," she explains. "It's about people—families whose livelihoods have been tied to these industries for generations. You can't just tell them to move on. You have to bring them along and provide them opportunity out of the transition."

This realization guided Sam's next steps. She joined Schneider Electric, a global leader in energy management. Its mission is to provide access to clean, reliable energy. That aligns with her values. Schneider Electric was named one of the world's most sustainable companies. Sam was excited to join a firm that pursued, not just talked about, sustainability. "I joined Schneider Electric for their commitment to sustainability. They believe access to energy is a basic human right," Sam says. "That's something I could get behind."

At Schneider Electric, Sam worked on commercializing Distributed Energy Resources (DERs) and microgrids. These systems use solar power, battery storage, and other local, appropriate, energy sources. They let communities and businesses generate and manage their energy. It reduces their reliance exclusively on the power grid. It boosts resilience to climate-related disruptions. "We're building technology, but we're also building partnerships," Sam explains. "We need to figure out how to monetize and finance these solutions so that they're accessible to everyone, not just the big players."

A thrilling part of her work was driving the adoption of microgrids. They let communities produce and control their electricity. Sam's work was centered on making these technologies scalable and cost-effective. "The cost of battery storage has come down significantly, but there's still a long way to go," she says. "At Schneider Electric, we're creating business models to access this tech without high upfront costs."

Sam and her team aimed to make microgrids more accessible. They also wanted to use digital tools to optimize energy use. Schneider Electric's digital work lets businesses and communities monitor energy use in real time. They made changes that saved money and cut emissions. "We're not just talking about hardware; we're talking about data," Sam explains. "Our data from these systems helps us use energy better. It shows where it's needed most.""

Sam's work at Schneider Electric embodies the spirit of the Voltage Valley Revolution™, merging advanced technology with a strong commitment to people and communities. She is dedicated to making the energy transition inclusive, ensuring clean energy benefits everyone, not just a privileged few. "Many U.S. and global communities lack reliable energy," Sam emphasizes. "My goal is to change that." Her mission aligns seamlessly with the Revolution's vision to reshape the energy landscape and empower people to control their future.

For Sam, working at Schneider Electric is more than just a career; it's about aligning her values with her work and making a real impact. "Every day, I get to help build the future of energy," she says. "It's gratifying to know that my work contributes to a more sustainable and equitable world." Like the Voltage Valley Revolution™, Sam's efforts focus on not only producing clean energy but also ensuring that underserved communities benefit from the transition.

Her optimism mirrors the movement's momentum. "The best is yet to come," she says. "We're at the forefront of an energy revolution, and I'm proud to be part of the organizations who are leading the way." Her focus on using digital tools to improve microgrid access and optimize energy use is creating smarter, more sustainable systems. "We're not just talking about a single hardware technology; we're talking about an ecosystem of cohesive, data-driven solutions," she explains. Her team's data-driven approach helps communities make informed energy decisions, reducing costs and emissions that are driving an equitable and resilient future.

Through Sam's leadership, the Voltage Valley Revolution™ is not just an idea—it's already making a tangible difference, proving the shift to clean energy is happening now, one step at a time.

Chapter 14
A Child Breaks Through the Cycle of Poverty

Dr. William Paolillo w/ Amanda Woodrum

"In this era where 'Otherism' reigns and divides grow deep. Zeros and ones, a silent guide. From hearts that refuse to be mere pawns. Born from a troubled past in impoverished lands, her mother's past is a guiding hand" – inspired by Amanda Woodrum.

Amanda sat in the stalled subway car, deep under the streets of New York City, the train stuck in the dark tunnels like the city itself was holding its breath. It was November 2001, sixty-five days since the Twin Towers had fallen on 9/11, leaving the city scarred and its people haunted. The hum of the train's engine had gone quiet, replaced by an eerie stillness that made the distant echoes of an uncertain world above even louder. There was talk of another threat—anthrax.

Armed National Guard soldiers patrolled the subways, rifles across their chests. Their presence reminded her of all the terror that had ripped through the city. Fear hung thick in the air, etched into every nervous glance, every white-knuckled grip on the subway poles. Amanda had grown up a military brat, moving around the world. She graduated from high school in Guam. But nothing prepared her for this city under attack. She felt fear deep in the pit of her stomach, a fear that came from the unknown within the city and within herself.

Amanda had come to New York City to attend St. John's University Law School, the only place she had applied because they offered her a full scholarship. She didn't know any better and had no one to tell or guide her through the complex web of higher education. Amanda's mother, Starre, had escaped from an abusive home, an alcoholic mother and poverty in the hills of upstate New York. Starre's second marriage was to a military man, in part to find stability for herself, Amanda and Amanda's brother. Starre did her best to raise and support her kids. But there was only so much wisdom she had to offer Amanda aside from staying in school, stay in school, stay in school, stay in school (which is why Amanda later became a schoolaholic).

Amanda spent her own childhood moving from base to base—always with a roof over their heads, a safe place to live and food on the table, far more than her mother had growing up, but never staying longer than a few years in one place. She attended three different elementary schools, two junior highs and three high schools. While this life and her lack of roots wasn't always easy, it did provide her with a unique perspective that made her who she is today. She believes that while every place may have unique attributes, cultures and circumstances, people at their core, everywhere, are 99% the same.

After attending college in Ohio, the City of New York had represented something different to Amanda. A place that better reflective of her own worldview. It was a city where the diversity of people was respected, where the possibility of an "us" without a "them" seemed within reach. It was a place where all backgrounds blended into the city's identity. Here, your worth was based more on your character, less on your skin color, gender, or past. The city, with its bustling streets and excellent public transportation, promised a life of opportunity, connection, and purpose. Or so she thought.

But now, deep in the city's bowels, the train was unmoving. Fear of another attack hung in the air. Amanda felt the weight of her choices pressing down on her. The city that had once seemed so full of promise now felt cold and indifferent, where dreams could be crushed as quickly as they were born. The fear and uncertainty gripping New York mirrored the turmoil in her heart. She wondered if this was the life she had fought for. Or was she just a lost soul, buried deep beneath a city struggling to find its footing after unimaginable loss?

The scholarship to law school, once a lifeline, now felt like a chain. It bound her to a path she wasn't sure she wanted to follow. She had come to New York with a sense of purpose, believing that a law degree was the key to making a difference in the world. But now, caught in a city reeling from tragedy and its economic aftermath, putting her on the verge of homelessness, she began to rethink her priorities. The law, which Amanda had once seen as a tool for change, now seemed remote and irrelevant in the face of such overwhelming loss. As the train sat motionless, Amanda's mind drifted back to the journey that had brought her to this moment.

As she sat there, Amanda realized something. This wasn't the first time she had felt lost, and it wouldn't be the last. Life had always been about survival, about finding a way forward even when the path was unclear. Her mother had done it and so had she. The fear and uncertainty that gripped the city were the same forces that shaped her life. But instead of being defeated by them, she could use them to fuel her resolve.

When the train finally jolted back to life and began to move, Amanda felt a shift within herself. The city was still wounded, struggling to heal, but it was also moving forward, refusing to be paralyzed by fear. And so would she. She would finish her law degree, not because it was easy, but because it was the right thing to do. She would find a way to make a difference, not just for herself, but for the people and communities who needed it most. She had grown up with a deep-seated need for community, for a place to call her own. But in the wake of 9/11, New York felt like the last place where that was possible.

With her mother having relocated back to Ohio, Amanda felt lucky to have a safe home to return to, a more stable environment in which to recover and regroup- back with her family. Her mother may have come from poverty and an abusive upbringing, but they were breaking the cycle. She decided to transfer to the University of Akron to finish her law degree. She wanted to build a meaningful life in Ohio. She also wanted to contribute to the community in a way that matched her values. She wanted to help make Ohio and the region the kind of place she wanted to live.

After returning to Ohio and earning her law degree at the University of Akron, Amanda wanted to challenge the "otherism" she had seen. Growing up in a military family that moved frequently, she had witnessed firsthand the impact of being seen as an outsider. Her alienation in New York also fueled her desire to change Ohio.

As Amanda got more involved, she pursued a master's in economics. She wanted to better analyze and address the structural inequalities she saw. This expertise let her view problems from both a legal and an economic angle. It gave her the tools to craft better solutions.

Amanda quickly joined groups that shared her goal of creating inclusive communities. She joined local groups like Policy Matters Ohio, the Apollo Alliance, and Cleveland Emerald Cities. They focus on social justice, environmental sustainability, and economic equity. Amanda worked tirelessly to bridge gaps between groups and breakdown silos. She used her legal training and knowledge of systemic issues. This made her a powerful advocate for change.

Amanda's work led her to launch Reimagine Appalachia, for which she now serves as the co-director. This coalition of diverse stakeholder groups aims to create a sustainable, inclusive economy in the Ohio River Valley of Appalachia, better known as coal country. The group help earn Appalachia's place at the nation climate infrastructure table and was pivotal in helping secure passage of a package of legislation—including the Inflation Reduction Act, the Bipartisan Infrastructure Law, CHIPS+ and others—that prioritize climate infrastructure investments into coal communities, creation of good union jobs and pathways out of poverty for low-income and disadvantaged communities. These federal resources are now bringing hope back to a region that has long been exploited by absentee corporations in the extractive industries, funding projects to revitalize the region and hopefully transform Appalachia into leaders of the new clean economy.

Through her work with Reimagine Appalachia, she united labor, environmental, and racial justice movements. She ensured marginalized communities were heard in the push for a sustainable, equitable future. She came to understand how good the military was at building pathways out of poverty—from their recruitment efforts in poor neighborhoods to the provision of paid training opportunities, family-sustaining wages and benefits, housing accommodations, and transportation solutions, among other things—and began to apply that understanding instead towards creating pathways out of poverty towards good union jobs building out the infrastructure needed for the future clean economy in which she wants to live.

Reimagine Appalachia is a broad coalition formed with a shared vision. It includes unions, environmentalists, and social justice advocates. Her work was key in shifting the conversation in Appalachia. It moved from economic decline to one of opportunity and resilience. Amanda helps the region by promoting unity and challenging otherism. Her vision aids the push for a more inclusive, sustainable future.

Chapter 15
The New –Collar Revolution

Dr. William Paolillo w/ Jennifer Oddo

"The measure of who we are is what we do with what we have." – Vince Lombardi

Jennifer Oddo's story begins in the heart of Appalachia, a place of rolling hills and small towns that were the backdrop of her youth. In the summer, the air carried the earthy scent of the coal mines and cornflowers. On winter mornings, you would smell wood-burning stoves mixed with the faint smell of diesel fumes from passing trains. Born and raised in Bridgeport, Ohio, along the Ohio River, Jennifer grew up in a tight-knit community where neighbors were like family and simple joys were the foundation of life. Her childhood days were filled with walks along railroad tracks, visits to the candy store, and evenings at local baseball fields by old coal mines. They lived a humble, picturesque life, but the harsh realities of the coal economy would soon test it.

In her junior year of high school, the coal mine where her father worked shut down, a story repeated by countless families across Appalachia. "It was a turning point," she recalled. "One moment, I thought the world was full of possibilities. The next, my parents told me we couldn't afford college."

The mine's closure forced the family to leave Bridgeport and move to Powell, Ohio, a busy Columbus suburb. For Jennifer, the move was a shock to her system. Bridgeport was a town of under 1,000 people with no traffic lights, while Powell was a rapidly growing town on the cusp of suburban expansion. Her father became a butcher, returning to his old trade, and her mother joined Sears and rose to a managerial position.

Jennifer refused to let the loss of the coal mine define her future. Determined to pursue higher education, she enrolled at the University of Akron, where she worked tirelessly, balancing her studies with multiple jobs to pay her tuition. "I was lucky," she said. "Not everyone from my high school had the chance to go to college. I had to fight for it but knew it was the path forward."

Jennifer faced a new world at the University of Akron, with its sprawling campus and over 20,000 students – starkly contrasting her graduating class 94 in Bridgeport. To find her footing, she joined a sorority, which gave her a sense of community and helped her build connections. "The sorority was a strategy for me,' she admitted. "It was about surrounding myself with like-minded people who could elevate me."

Jennifer's college years were marked by resilience and determination. She worked multiple part-time jobs to pay for her education, cultivating a deep sense of curiosity and drive – qualities that defined her career. "One of my professors once told me I asked too many questions," she said. "But curiosity became my greatest asset."

The Great Recession: Losing It All—Again

Jennifer's career began with tech and quickly rose through the ranks. By her late twenties, she worked for Whitman Hart, a consulting firm that grew from $40 million to over $1 billion in revenue during her time there. International travel and managing high-level projects opened Jennifer's eyes to a world beyond the Appalachian hills of her youth.

But life has a way of circling back. In 2008, the Great Recession dealt another blow. Her husband's tech company, Four Tech Work, had been on the verge of a lucrative acquisition, but the deal collapsed as markets crashed. Their largest client, National City Bank, was acquired, wiping out 25% of the company's business. To make matters worse, banks called in loans, forcing the couple into survival mode.

Jennifer returned to work full-time to provide stability for her family. She juggled motherhood and a demanding career with two young sons, Holden and Christopher, born 10 months apart, and a six-month-old daughter. "Those years were tough," she admitted. "But growing up in a coal-mining town teaches you resilience. You keep going because you have no choice."

Reinvention at IBM: Creating Pathways for the Underserved

At IBM, Jennifer became a crucial voice in the movement to democratize access to high-demand tech jobs, a defining moment in her career. Central to her work was the "New Collar" job concept—a term popularized by IBM's former CEO, Ginni Rometty. New-collar jobs differ from white-collar and blue-collar roles, valuing skills over degrees and focusing on short training, certifications, and stackable credentials that prepare people for cybersecurity, advanced manufacturing, and cloud computing careers.

Jennifer's initiatives embodied the New-Collar ethos, creating innovative apprenticeships and digital credentials to give equal access to tech careers. One of her most notable achievements was launching a cybersecurity apprenticeship program in Rocket Center, West Virginia, among whose participants were a former Air Force veteran and a professional poker player, showing that talent and potential are not limited to any background. "It was about giving people a chance," Jennifer said. "We proved that skills—not degrees—should be the entry ticket to opportunity."

Ivanka Trump, a senior advisor to the Trump administration, noticed her work and championed workforce development, focusing on alternative education that matched Jennifer's mission to connect traditional industries with emerging tech sectors. As Jennifer noted, "Ivanka made people more aware of micro-credentials and apprenticeships."

In 2018, a turning point happened at the Consumer Electronics Show (CES) in Las Vegas. This is the world's largest tech conference. Here, the focus shifted to the future of work. Jennifer sat in the front row. She's a workforce strategist. She was there to explore how technology could transform careers for everyday Americans. The keynote event included Ivanka Trump, who is the

President's Advisor, and Gary Shapiro, the CEO of the Consumer Technology Association (CTA). The CTA organizes CES.

Shapiro, who advocates for modernizing the workforce, highlighted IBM's apprenticeship programs. These programs offer alternative routes to high-tech jobs, and you don't need a college degree. He pivoted sharply. He challenged Ivanka and the federal government on a long-standing issue: degree requirements in federal hiring and contracting policies. He claimed these old rules left out millions of skilled workers. Many of these workers have training from apprenticeships, technical schools, or hands-on jobs. Because of this, they miss out on good-paying jobs in growing industries.

Ivanka didn't deflect. She responded quickly and decisively, promising to address the issue. The moment was brief, but powerful. In just a few months, the public exchange led to a Presidential Executive Order. Signed by President Trump in June 2020, it told federal agencies to focus on skills-based hiring. It also aimed to remove unnecessary college degree requirements for government jobs.

This policy shift was a **watershed moment** for workforce development. It opened doors for millions of Americans who once faced barriers. This is especially true in fields like clean energy, cybersecurity, and advanced manufacturing. In these areas, skills are more important than background. In Appalachia, four-year degrees are less common, but the work ethic is strong. This change created a chance to link federal opportunities with local talent.

"That moment validated years of effort," Jennifer said. "It wasn't just about IBM – it was about redefining what makes someone qualified and capable."

IBM's work with the federal government led to partnerships with industry leaders like Google, Microsoft, and Ford, setting standards for apprenticeships and digital credentials to ensure quality and consistency across sectors. Jennifer said, "We wanted to create frameworks for industries to adopt, making New Collar jobs a sustainable part of the workforce." She added, "This wasn't just a moment – it was the beginning of a movement." She appreciated Ivanka's focus on the greater good. "Her platform helped drive real change," she said. "And that made a tangible difference in places like Rocket Center, where lives were transformed."

Reflecting on her journey, Jennifer tied it back to her own roots. "At the end of the day, this wasn't about politics," she said. "It was about creating opportunities for people like the ones I grew up with in Bridgeport. That's what New Collar is all about – giving people the tools they need to succeed."

The Voltage Valley Revolution™: Returning to Appalachia

In 2019, Jennifer's work returned her to her roots in Appalachia. General Motors had announced the closure of its Lordstown plant, displacing thousands of workers. Jennifer partnered with Youngstown State University, creating a strategy to retrain these individuals for advanced manufacturing and tech roles.

VOLTAGE VALLEY REVOLUTION™

This partnership introduced her to Jim Tressel, then-president of Youngstown State University and a beloved figure in Ohio. He was celebrated nationwide for leading Ohio State's football team to a national championship. His legendary 9-1 record against Michigan cemented his status as a Buckeye icon. Tressel had seamlessly transitioned his leadership skills to academia. "Within minutes of our first meeting, I knew he understood the importance of workforce development," Jennifer said.

Together, they launched an IT Workforce Accelerator, funded partly by a $5 million investment from GM. The accelerator aims to equip workers for the new economy, including roles in automation, robotics, and electric vehicle production. "It wasn't just about jobs," Jennifer emphasized. "It was about giving people hope and keeping communities together."

Jennifer's work in the Voltage Valley was more comprehensive than workforce training; she also helped bridge cultural divides. Companies like LG Chem and Foxconn built advanced regional factories, and "the workforce needed more than technical skills," she explained. "They needed to navigate cultural differences, embrace teamwork, and adapt to automation."

At Ultium Cells, a GM and LG Chem joint venture, Jennifer's team trained leaders to manage a mix of Midwestern and Korean cultures. Foxconn's arrival in Lordstown brought new challenges and opportunities, and the region had to adapt to its new role as a hub for electric vehicle production.

Jennifer saw these developments as a continuation of Appalachia's legacy of industrial innovation. "Appalachia powered the first industrial revolution with coal and steel. We're leading the next one with clean energy and advanced manufacturing."

Throughout her journey, Jennifer's family remained her anchor. Her children, Holden, Christopher, and their younger sister saw their mother's resilience and drive to make a difference. "I want them to know that no matter how hard things get, you can always find a way forward," she said.

Her work has also been a way to honor the community values she learned in Bridgeport. "Growing up in Appalachia, I saw how neighbors cared for each other," she reflected. "That spirit of community has guided everything I've done."

Today, Jennifer leads New Collar Talent, a consulting firm dedicated to bridging the gap between academia and industry. Her mission is clear: to ensure workforce development keeps pace with the industry's speed. "We're in a new era," she said. "This isn't just about creating jobs. It's about creating opportunities and a sense of purpose."

For Jennifer, the Voltage Valley Revolution™ is more than an economic movement; it's a testament to the power of love, resilience, and community – a chance to give back to the region that shaped her. "Appalachia has always been about grit and determination," she said. "Now, it's about innovation and hope. And I'm honored to be part of that journey."

Jennifer Oddo's story shows the power of resilience and the spirit of Appalachia. From her childhood growing up supported by the coal mines to Voltage Valley Revolutions™ factories, she has devoted her life to improving the region and its people. Through her work, Appalachia is lighting the way for America's next industrial revolution.

Appendix

New Collar Talent is a workforce development organization dedicated to bridging the skills gap in today's rapidly evolving industries. Inspired by the "new collar" concept popularized by former IBM CEO Ginni Rometty, the organization emphasizes skills-based training and hiring over traditional degree requirements.

Recognizing the shift towards technology-driven roles in sectors like application development, cybersecurity, data science, and cloud computing, New Collar Talent offers innovative solutions tailored to various stakeholders:

- **Adult Learners**: Providing career assessments and online training programs to facilitate workplace advancement.
- **Employers**: Delivering workforce and training solutions aimed at optimizing talent development and addressing specific organizational needs.
- **Academic Institutions**: Developing integrated training strategies to equip students with in-demand industry skills.

The organization's mission focuses on three core pillars:

1. **Accessible Training**: Innovating pathways to ensure equitable participation in quality new collar training and employment opportunities.
2. **Employability Outcomes**: Co-creating talent solutions that enhance job readiness and access to quality positions for both early-career and experienced individuals.
3. **Social Impact**: Implementing sustainable workforce and education strategies that prioritize diversity, accessibility, and inclusion.

Through these initiatives, New Collar Talent aims to empower individuals and organizations to thrive in the Voltage Valley Revolution™ by fostering a skilled and adaptable workforce.

Chapter 16
Courage Forged in Steel

Dr. William Paolillo w/ Rick Stockburger

"Success is not final, failure is not fatal: It is the courage to continue that counts." – Winston Churchill

Every day, the steel mill's sharp, metallic scent followed Rick Stockburger's father Bill home. It became as much a part of their household as the region's rolling hills and railways. The Mahoning Valley was once an industrial powerhouse. It was a community built around the mills and factories that fueled the nation's economy. For Rick, the smell was more than a reminder of his father's job. It represented strength, stability, and pride.

"My dad operated a blast furnace," Rick recalls. "He made couplings that connected train cars. As a kid, I thought that was the coolest job in the world. He was connecting trains—linking billions of dollars' worth of goods nationwide. It made me proud to know my dad was part of something big and important."

The steel mill was more than a job. It was a foundation for families in the Mahoning Valley. It provided their livelihoods, a sense of self, and a purpose. But, as globalization changed the economy, steel's security and pride began to unravel. When Rick was in high school, his father returned home with devastating news: the plant would be shutting down.

For Rick, his father, older brother Mike and his mother Joann, the closure marked the end of an era. The industry had defined their lives and their community. It was now disappearing, leaving uncertainty and a need to find a new path.

A Family's Struggle

Rick's father had put in nearly 30 years at American Steel Foundry, but globalization proved too strong. The plant didn't close due to bad management or a lack of customers - it was a business decision that hit Rick's family hard. The company offered Rick's father a job at their Indiana plant, but his mother, a practical and strong-willed woman, didn't want to move the family. As it turned out, she made the right decision - the Indiana plant shut down just a year later. Losing his father's job, however, had a deep and lasting effect.

"For my dad, it wasn't about losing a paycheck—it was about losing his identity," Rick says. "When you see the man you respect as a pillar of strength questioning his place in the world, your view of everything changes."

The closure didn't just affect Rick's father—it changed the trajectory of Rick's own life. "I always thought I'd follow in my dad's footsteps," he says. "But when his job disappeared, that path disappeared. The work that defined him no longer existed."

As the family struggled to regain stability, Rick's mother JoAnn was fighting for her life. When Rick was a teenager, doctors diagnosed her with cancer and told her she had only six months to live. Yet, with unrelenting determination, she battled the disease for ten years.

"She was tough as nails," Rick says. "She refused to give up, even when the odds were stacked against her." "She was our family's anchor during those years. She kept us going when everything felt uncertain."

Her fight against cancer left a lasting impression on Rick. "She taught me what it means to be resilient, to fight for what matters even when it feels impossible," he says. "Her strength shaped how I approach everything in life."

His father's job loss and his mother's illness left Rick untethered. He struggled to make sense of the upheaval. So, he turned to alcohol in high school. That habit lingered for years. "I was angry, confused, and didn't know how to deal with everything happening," he recalls. "Drinking felt like an escape, but it didn't solve anything. If anything, it just made things worse."

After high school, Rick made what he describes as a "paradoxical" decision - a choice that seemed self-contradictory or illogical at first glance—he joined the Army. In his mind, it was a rebellion against the chaos of his life. Yet, it was one of the most disciplined paths he could have chosen. "It felt rebellious at the time," he says with a laugh. "But in hindsight, it gave me the focus and purpose I desperately needed.

Learning to Lead in the Army

Rick's time in the Army became a crucible for growth. His first deployment to Kosovo forced him to face his personal struggles. But it was his second deployment to Afghanistan that genuinely shaped him.

Rick was in a 23-person unit of the Ohio Army National Guard. They were stationed in northern Afghanistan. He worked with a larger group of Hungarian Special Forces and Afghan soldiers. Rick's role was as a combat advisor. This placed him at the center of the action, coordinating efforts between the groups. "Some days, we'd be under fire. I'd have to use two interpreters, one Hungarian and one Afghan, to get instructions across," he recalls. "It was chaos, but it taught me the importance of clear communication and building trust."

The imbalance in numbers also heightened the risks. The threat of betrayal was a constant reality. A 150 Afghan soldiers were placed at the same base as Rick's unit. A simple $50 bribe could turn an ally into an enemy overnight. "Living with that kind of uncertainty changes you," Rick says. "There were nights when I went to sleep knowing that the guy I had trained could walk into my room and betray me. It was a lesson in vigilance and the fragility of trust."

Despite the tension and danger, the deployment offered Rick profound lessons. "I learned how to fight from my mom," he says. "And in Afghanistan, I proved to myself that I could."

Finding Purpose Back Home

Returning to Ohio after his time in the Army, Rick faced new challenges. PTSD and his struggles with alcohol made the transition difficult. But meeting Carly, the woman who would become his wife, marked a turning point. "She was the best thing that ever happened to me," Rick says. "Her love and support gave me the foundation I needed to start rebuilding my life."

Becoming a father to Reagan and Jake gave Rick an even greater sense of purpose. "Having kids changes everything," he says. "It made me realize I had something bigger than myself to be responsible for. They gave me the motivation to get my life together."

In 2011, Rick's frustrations grew when Forbes magazine named Cleveland the most miserable city in the US. "I was living in northeast Ohio at the time, and I thought, 'That's not true,'" Rick says. "So, I sent an email to the author, asking if he'd ever visited Cleveland. His answer was no."

Rick and a friend wanted to challenge the narrative. So, they decided to throw a party. They invited young people from all over Cleveland to discuss the city's future. "We thought 20 or 30 people would show up," he says. "Instead, 400 people came, along with eight local politicians running for county executive. The Harvard Business Review and the Atlantic even showed up."

That night, Rick and his friend started a media company, **Saving Cities**. It focused on revitalizing Rust Belt cities. They made feature-length documentaries, such as *Red, White & Blueprints*. It showed grassroots efforts to rebuild cities like Cleveland, Detroit, and Pittsburgh. "We didn't earn much, but we shared stories that counted," Rick says. "It reminded us of the strength that comes from community and working together."

The Power of Connection

Rick Stockburger's gift to connect with people has been a driving force behind the success of BRITE Energy Innovators and the Voltage Valley Revolution™. Rick credits his father for this skill. It mirrors ideas in Malcolm Gladwell's The Tipping Point. It explores how "connectors" can shape communities and drive change. "My dad had this way of making everyone feel important," Rick says. "He could meet someone for the first time and, within minutes, make them smile or feel like they belonged. Watching him taught me to value people and build trust. It helped me form meaningful relationships. That's at the heart of my success."

Gladwell describes connectors as rare individuals. They love making introductions and finding synergies between people. They build networks that lead to tipping points. A tipping point is when small changes lead to a big change. Rick embodies this role. It was vital when he became president and CEO of the Tech Belt Energy Innovation Center. The organization was struggling. It had a $400,000 budget and no clear direction.

Rick saw the need for a new identity. So, he transformed the center into BRITE Energy Innovators. The new name better reflected its mission to foster clean energy innovation. But the rebranding wasn't just about a name, it was about rallying people around a shared vision. Rick's "connector" instincts kicked in. He built ties with investors, industry leaders, and the community to transform the organization.

Rick's father had a gift for connection. He could make a friend anywhere and was always open to talking to anyone about anything. "My dad didn't need to say profound things to make an impact," Rick reflects. "He showed me, through his actions, that relationships are built by being open, approachable, and willing to engage with people from all walks of life. I really appreciate that about him."

Rick deeply connects with Gladwell's idea of connectors—not just knowing many people but bringing them together to create something more significant. Under his leadership, BRITE has grown from a struggling startup to a cornerstone of the Voltage Valley Revolution™. With a $5 million budget, BRITE supports over 150 Ohio startups, helping to make Appalachia a hub for clean energy and advanced manufacturing.

Rick's leadership style is deeply personal, shaped by his father's example and the principles in *The Tipping Point*. "One of the best compliments I've ever received was from a stranger at a networking event who said, 'I just met you, and I feel like I've known you for 10 years. You put yourself out there and set the tone, and that made space for me to do the same.' That's my dad's influence, Rick says. "He showed me that success isn't just about what you can do alone, it's about the opportunities you create when you bring the right people together."

For Rick, connecting with people isn't just a skill, it's a responsibility.

"When I meet someone, I think about what they're good at and what they need," he says. "That's the information that sticks in my head. It's not just about solving problems—it's about creating opportunities." Rick Stockburger's work at BRITE and Voltage Valley proves Gladwell's theory. The right connections can tip the scales and transform people, organizations, and communities.

A Best Day at Work

One of Rick's most memorable days at BRITE began with a visit from a youth group at Second Baptist Church. The children were learning about battery technology in BRITE's lab. At the same time, upstairs, 100 new hires were being trained for jobs at Ultium Cells. It is a cutting-edge electric vehicle battery plant run by General Motors. The plant and the surrounding jobs created thousands of new jobs in the Mahoning Valley.

BRITE's facility buzzed with activity. The lab had state-of-the-art equipment. It let the kids do hands-on experiments to explore how batteries worked. In the mezzanine classroom, Ultium employees were being trained on battery manufacturing. It overlooked the lab. It was to prepare them for their roles in a growing industry.

As Rick walked through the lab, he noticed a boy waving excitedly to a person in the Ultium training. "That's my dad," the boy said proudly when Rick asked who he was waving to.

Rick learned that the father had struggled with unemployment for years. Then, he found a job at Ultium. Now, his son was dreaming of following in his footsteps. "It was a full-circle moment," Rick says. "It reminded me of my dad and my pride in what he did. Seeing that connection between generations, that's what this work is all about."

The Heart of the Voltage Valley Revolution™

Rick's story is part of a larger tale. It is the Voltage Valley Revolution™. It aims to make Appalachia a hub for clean energy and advanced manufacturing. Once known for its steel mills and coal mines, the region is now a leader in renewable energy. Organizations like BRITE are at the forefront.

"What's happening here is nothing remarkable," Rick says. "We're taking the lessons of the past and using them to build a better future. This isn't just about creating jobs—it's about restoring hope and pride in our communities."

Rick is grateful for his journey. It shaped him, even the hard, painful parts. His father's struggles and his mother's resilience shaped him. So did his Army service and his work at BRITE. They taught him to fight for a greater cause.

"My story isn't unique," Rick says. "It's part of a larger tapestry of people. They refuse to give up. They see challenges as opportunities. They believe in the region's potential."

For Rick, the Voltage Valley Revolution™ is more than a movement, it's a promise. It promises that Appalachia's past can fuel its future. It says resilience can lead to renewal. The best days for the region and its families are still to come.

Appendix

BRITE Energy Innovators, a 501(c)(3) advanced energy accelerator, is at the forefront of powering the Voltage Valley Revolution™. Headquartered in Warren, Ohio—the heart of the Voltage Valley—BRITE drives innovation by equipping founders with the capital, customers, and talent they need to bring transformative energy technologies to market. Each year, BRITE-supported companies generate nearly $250 million in economic impact for Ohio, creating thousands of jobs in the advanced and clean energy sectors. With a dedicated team spanning the state, BRITE is igniting a new era of energy leadership, innovation, and economic growth in Ohio and beyond. At the time of publication Rick has accepted a position with the Department of Energy as the CEO to lead Energy Security and Innovation Foundation.

Chapter 17
The Heart of Voltage Valley™

Dr. William Paolillo w Tim Petrey

"In the middle of every difficulty lies opportunity." – Albert Einstein

Youngstown was once the beating heart of America's steel industry. The skyline had smokestacks, and the streets buzzed with factory workers ending their long shifts. This city fueled the nation's growth. It made steel for bridges, cars, and skyscrapers. My grandfather worked in a steel mill. His labor shaped metal and built our community. His work ethic and resilience are now part of our family legacy. They show the strength that defines Youngstown. But that prosperity didn't last. The steel industry's collapse in the late 1970s, known as "Black Monday," shocked the community. Thousands of jobs disappeared overnight. Many people lost the security their families had relied on for generations. Buildings lay empty, neighborhoods felt deserted, and many lost hopes in the American Dream. Youngstown became a symbol of industrial decline. The community's resilience tested by economic hardship, crime, and population loss. But even in its darkest days, the spirit of Youngstown never broke. It waited for a new spark.

I was born and raised on the west side of Youngstown, Ohio. My story begins with loss—my mother passed away from colon cancer when I was four years old. Soon after, my father, struggling with dependency issues, left us. I have not seen my father since he left, and now, at 37 years old, that absence still lingers as a silent chapter in my story. My mother's family took in my older brother, who was 13 then, and me. They became the foundation of my life, a patchwork of relatives who stepped up when we needed them most.

My Grandma Honey was the heart of our family. She lived in a small, 1,200-square-foot house. It always smelled like butter and onions, the signature scents of her Polish cooking. The rich, savory scent greets you as you open the door. It's a warm hug of comfort and tradition. She never got a driver's license. Instead, she used public transportation to travel around Youngstown. She raised five children, including my mother, and embodied resilience and kindness. "Grandma Honey" was a fitting nickname for her. She truly was the sweetest woman you'd ever know.

Her home was the epitome of community connection. In the Polish neighborhood of Youngstown, everything was within walking distance. We walked to McDonald's, to playgrounds, and to local shops. Kids played in the streets. Neighbors chatted. It was a place where everyone knew each other's names. The bonds formed here felt like family, not just friendship. Community connection means more than geography. It's about the unspoken understanding that we are all part of something bigger.

During the week, I lived with my Aunt Marsha and Uncle Jim Nadasky in Ellsworth, Ohio. They owned Youngstown Cycle Supply, a small shop for British motorcycle parts. They specialized in brands like Nortons, BSAs, and Triumphs. Megan and Nikki, their daughters, were older than me. My brother and I changed the flow of their family life. But they made room for us, integrating us into their lives with patience and love.

I grew up in two worlds. One was Ellsworth's quiet, rural life. The other was the busy, close-knit community with Grandma Honey in Youngstown. This shaped me, giving me an appreciation for hard work and community connection.

High school brought new challenges and responsibilities. I played baseball, basketball, and football. I soon saw that sports wouldn't shape my future. So, I started working. At 15, I was washing semi-trucks at Blue Beacon Truck Wash. The grime was relentless. It seeped into my skin, under my nails, and every crevice of my clothes. Cold water mixed with industrial soap splashed back, covering me in dirt, grease, and sweat. My hands were often chapped. My muscles felt sore. But this taught me the value of hard work in a real way.

I remember cleaning up in the truck stop bathroom before school. I scrubbed the grime from my face and arms, trying to look presentable.

By my junior year, I was juggling full-time work with school. I wanted to get ahead, so I joined a Pre-college program. This let me leave high school early. I could attend college and earn credits for both at the same time.

College marked a turning point. I lived on my own. I paid my bills, moved between family homes, and worked full-time. By my junior year, I had climbed the ranks at the truck wash, traveling across the country to train others. But I wanted more. I left the truck wash to focus on my education, taking odd jobs to make ends meet and sleeping in study halls. I graduated in 2009, right into the heart of the financial crisis. Jobs were scarce, especially in Youngstown.

After countless interviews with no offers, I planned to move to Washington, D.C., for a job. God had other plans. Before leaving, I met Harold Davis, who owned a small accounting firm in Liberty. He hired me as a receptionist, paying $9 an hour. It wasn't glamorous, but it was an opportunity.

Six months later, when it was time to move to D.C., I realized I didn't want to leave. Youngstown was home. I loved the community, the people, the spirit. Harold thought about selling his business. I wasn't ready to buy it, but I wanted to learn as much as I could. I stayed, earning less than I would have in D.C. but gaining invaluable experience.

By 24, I took over the firm, which had $400,000 in revenue and three employees. Today, we've grown to $8 million in revenue with 70 employees and operate in 42 states. We've helped businesses grow and supported startups. In recent years, we've received a variety of recognitions nationally for what we've built, including being named as the top CPA firm for Women by Accounting Today in 2021 and being named to the top 200 CPA List by Forbes in 2024.

What drove me wasn't just ambition—it was survival. I worked hard because I had to. I washed trucks, studied in parking lots, and solved tough business problems. I did whatever was needed.

Harold saw something in me: a relentless problem solver. I didn't have all the answers, but I was determined to discover them.

One early success story stands out. A client, drowning in debt and tax issues, was miserable running a business he hated. When I visited his office, it was buried under unpaid bills and tax notices. I asked him a simple question: "What do you love doing?" His eyes lit up when he showed me a back room where he crafted custom motorcycle parts. It was like crossing a threshold into his true passion. I encouraged him to pivot. We fixed his finances, revamped his business, and helped him create a multimillion-dollar company doing what he loved. That simple question changed the course of his life—and mine.

This experience taught me an important lesson: success is not only about profit; it's about having a purpose. That belief shapes my work in business and community development today.

Youngstown and Voltage Valley Revolution™ show resilience and the power of reinvention. The Voltage Valley Revolution™ isn't just about electric vehicles. We want to make our region a center for advanced manufacturing, clean energy, innovation, and technology. We're leveraging our industrial roots to build a sustainable future.

I saw the potential in Youngstown, the Voltage Valley™ early on. In fact, we were the original Voltage Valley™. We established the brand before COVID-19 disrupted the world. I trademarked the name I made social media accounts and got community leaders to adopt the brand. Voltage Valley™ stands for more than just electrification. It symbolizes renewal, growth, and a bright future beyond the Rust Belt.

I've partnered with the Youngstown/Warren Regional Chamber, the Ohio Commodores, and various business incubators. These efforts help create connections that energize this revolution. We've helped companies like Youngstown Clothing Company. Now, they make over $1 million in annual sales. They've also donated $400,000 to local charities. Our community has teamed up with big names like Foxconn. They are transforming the old GM Lordstown plant for advanced manufacturing. This includes making autonomous electric tractors.

These tractors aren't just machines; they're symbols of innovation. They built the Monarch Tractor where they used to build regular cars. It shows us what farming will look like in the future. Their tractors are autonomous and electric. They reduce the need for harmful chemicals and cut emissions. Monarch Tractor uses advanced AI technology to improve farming. This makes agriculture more efficient and sustainable. They're not just changing farming—they're redefining what's possible in manufacturing and technology.

LG Energy Solution and Honda are building battery plants. Also, downtown Youngstown has additive manufacturing hubs. These hubs are driving new ideas in 3D printing technologies.

My personal journey mirrors the story of Voltage Valley™. Both come from hardship. They are driven by resilience and a desire to create something meaningful. Youngstown isn't just where

I'm from—it's who I am. I believe in our future because I've seen firsthand what's possible when you refuse to give up.

This is more than economic development—it's the Voltage Valley Revolution™. It's about transforming challenges into opportunities, just like I did in my own life. It's about creating a legacy. It honors the past and builds a brighter more sustainable future.

I see myself as a connector. A connector brings people and ideas together. This helps create meaningful change. I aim to connect the right people with the right opportunities. This can happen through business relationships, community development, or new ventures. And through those connections, we're building something remarkable here in Voltage Valley™.

HD Growth Partners is an accounting and advisory firm that is built for the future. We leverage technology and artificial intelligence to empower business owners. We guide them through the lifecycle of business ownership, from formation, growth and eventual success planning and sale consulting. We strive to provide value to every conversation with our clients and work tirelessly to make a positive impact on everyone we interact with.

Chapter 18
A Fathers Dream

Dr. William Paolillo w/ John Holbrook

"Hardships often prepare ordinary people for an extraordinary destiny." – C.S. Lewis

John Holbrook remembers a time when jobs were abundant in northeastern Kentucky. In the 1990s, John was a young pipefitter. He worked at the steel mill, the coal-fired power plant, and the petroleum refinery. Each was an industrial giant that powered the local economy. They provided steady, well-paying jobs for the region's skilled tradespeople. Ashland, the town where he grew up, called itself "Where Coal Meets Iron" with pride. Fossil fuels and heavy industry were its lifeblood.

But over the years, that world began to fade. In 2022, they demolished the steel mill that once dominated Ashland. The coal-fired power plant switched to natural gas. Thousands of coal jobs vanished as mining became more mechanized. New, strict environmental rules also took hold. Families moved away, leaving homes and memories behind. Those who stayed had to travel far for work. Appalachia, once a thriving industrial heartland, found itself fighting to survive. But survival is in their blood.

"I used to be able to find work right here," John said. "Now, a lot of our guys are driving hours to get to job sites." He speaks of it in a straightforward manner, but there's no denying the undercurrent of grit in his words. The people of Appalachia know hardship. They've faced life's storms with a resolve passed down from generations of coal miners, steelworkers, and tradespeople.

For John, who now leads the Tri-State Building and Construction Trades Council, the region's change is personal. It represents union workers across Kentucky, Ohio, and West Virginia. Like many of his peers, he grew up in a trade's family. His father was a 69-year-old member of UA Local 248, the same union where John began his career as a pipefitter. But his father had a different vision for him.

"My dad regretted not getting an education. So, he pushed me to go to college before joining the trades," John recalls. Many of John's friends were starting in the trades right out of high school. But his father was insistent. He told me, "Get that degree, then we'll see about a job." John honored that promise. He earned a degree from Morehead State University. Then, he followed his father's footsteps into the union. He learned that hard work wasn't just about swinging hammers. It was about fighting for a future worth building.

VOLTAGE VALLEY REVOLUTION™

In the early 2000s, local union leadership saw potential in John and asked him to run for office. He accepted, without asking about to pay or hours. He knew he was meant to serve the workers and the community where he grew up.

John won five consecutive, often unopposed, terms. This showed his fellow members' trust in his leadership. But as the economy in the region declined, John's role became less about managing work and more about finding it. The shift away from coal wasn't just an economic challenge, it was an existential one. For generations, coal had sustained the people of Appalachia. Now, they needed to find new ways to survive.

Then came the COVID-19 pandemic. It pushed a struggling region to the brink. "COVID was tough," John recalls. Jobs dried up, projects were put on hold, and workers fought to keep their benefits. "A lot of people had to find other ways to get by," he says. Through it all, John fought for his members. He advised them to take any work they could find to keep their insurance and pay the bills. It was survival mode, pure and simple—something Appalachians know all too well.

Despite the hardships, John hoped the region could find a new path. He believed clean energy could solve the downturn. This included hydrogen and cleaner uses of old coal technologies. For Appalachians, it wasn't just about survival. It was about making something new from what they had. They weren't waiting for a handout; they were ready to build.

In 2023, officials announced the Trillion H2 Project in Piketon, Ohio, just over the state line. A major opportunity emerged. The project aims to use clean energy for power manufacturing. It could be one of the largest of its kind in the country. It could turn the Ohio River Valley into a hydrogen hub. It would bring back high-quality jobs the region hasn't seen in decades.

For John, the hydrogen project represents hope. They did this for the region's tradespeople. There is a need for skilled labor to build hydrogen infrastructure—piping, safety systems, and plant operations. "Hydrogen can be a game-changer for this region," John said. "We have the infrastructure, the skills, and the workforce. This is a project that could really help put us back on the map." That drive is the cornerstone of Appalachia's spirit. It is a quiet strength that pushes on despite the tough road.

Besides hydrogen, Century Aluminum's "green" smelter could be a lifeline. If the project goes ahead in northeastern Kentucky, it would be the first new U.S. aluminum smelter in 45 years. It would create over 5,500 construction jobs and 1,000 full-time union positions. John and his team are ready to provide the workforce. But he's cautious. Past disappointments, like the failed Braidy Industries plant, have made him wary of celebrating too soon.

"We just need a crumb or two, just a little giant smelter," John said with a grin. He knows the people of Appalachia are tough. They don't need much. But, when opportunity knocks, they'll seize it with both hands.

John grounds his optimism in his deep connection to his community. He and his fellow labor leaders are working with Governor Andy Beshear's administration, local officials, environmentalists, and clean energy advocates. They aim to prepare the workforce for a new chapter—whether it's hydrogen, green aluminum, or clean coal technologies. Appalachia's future is not like the past. It's about evolving and thriving in tough times.

John's focus on education has been constant. An alumnus of Morehead State University, he was appointed to the Board of Regents in 2024. He is deeply honored to hold this role. "I'm proud to give back to the university that gave me so much," John says. His wife, Sandy, a high school principal, is also a Morehead State graduate. They believe in education's power to change lives in their community. It's the same grit that made his father push him to get a degree before entering the trades. His father believed that hard work and knowledge together can build a future stronger than alone.

As clean energy projects like the Trillium H2 Project and the Century Aluminum smelter continue to take shape, John remains steadfast in his belief that Appalachia is poised for a resurgence. "It would be region-changing," John says. "And life changing."

The people of Appalachia persist in the face of challenges. They've endured, adapted, and fought for every inch of progress. As the region nears a new era, John Holbrook and his workers are ready to lead the way. They will build cleaner, smarter industries to carry Appalachia forward for generations.

Chapter 19
Celebrating Loving Day

Bill Paolillo w/ Kevin Schwab

In 1959, interracial marriage was illegal in Virginia. Police raided a Virginia home and found Richard Loving, a white man, and Mildred Loving, a black woman of Native American descent, sleeping in bed. They were arrested. They were each sentenced to a year in jail. They were forced to move away from Virginia.

Supreme Court Decision: Loving vs Commonwealth of Virginia, 388 U.S. 1 (1967) A unanimous Court struck down state laws banning marriage between individuals of different races.

Kevin Schwab is proud to be the child of an interracial couple. They met in Chicago at the height of the Civil Rights movement. When Kevin asked his devout mother why they weren't married in a church, she replied, "In 1961, who would've married us?" My church in Tennessee, where I grew up; how about the small town in western Illinois where your father grew up? On a snowy February day, Kevin's parents went to a Chicago courthouse with some friends. They fought together against many pressures that weighed on their marriage for a long time. They went to L.A.; they liked southern California but felt disconnected from family. So, ultimately, they moved to Washington, DC. That's when Kevin came around - 1966.

Kevin remembers as a child when his mother, a librarian, and his father, an attorney, bootstrapped their educations. They were both educated, learned people. Both were the first in their family to go to college and were enjoying some financial success. Kevin remembers they were ready to buy a house when he was four. A joyous milestone towards the American Dream proved uniquely stressful for the Schwab family. "Perhaps the first time I remember my parents arguing was about this house. My father liked Northern Virginia, particularly Alexandria. It was beautiful, stately, historic – *George Washington had lived there*. However, even as a small child, I remember my mom saying that I was never moving to Virginia. So, they found a house in a nearby Maryland suburb."

This was just three years after the Supreme Court's *Loving v. Virginia* decision. "The thing I remember even more than the fights was that my father went house hunting himself. This was a decision both of my parents had made. My father is white. I didn't go, my mother didn't go. My father went with the realtor. He would then come home and tell us about what he had seen. We would later drive through the neighborhoods. We would see the houses he had looked at to find a place to buy their first home. And, of course, the reason for that was if a black woman were there, we would have been shown an entirely different set of houses."

Kevin and his family made Takoma Park, Maryland, their home, a three-bedroom cape cod house. They presented a united front against the world for years, then fractured. Conflicts grew. Kevin's parents separated when he was in fifth grade. Kevin's father moved to Alexandria. Kevin and his mother moved to Tennessee, where she had grown up. She later moved to Florida because Tennessee wasn't it. Kevin was that kid flying back and forth from Tennessee to D.C. and Florida to D.C. every other weekend.

Court insisted that Kevin decide between residing with mother or father. "It was the most difficult question anyone could ever ask a child. I love my parents, and I could not walk into the courtroom, sit on a witness stand, and say I loved one more than the other." The court had appointed a separate lawyer to represent Kevin, and the attorney delivered that message. Ultimately, the judge decided that Kevin would live in Alexandria with his father. Kevin's mother moved back to the northeast to be closer to her son and see him more often.

Kevin chose Syracuse University for its strong academics and its welcome of all backgrounds.

In Central New York, Harriet Tubman chose to live near Syracuse University. Frederick Douglass lived up the road in Rochester. The Women's Rights Movement began in Seneca Falls. Early in the Holocaust, Oswego, NY, 30 minutes from Syracuse and located on Lake Ontario, took in a thousand Jewish refugees. In Syracuse, there are monuments to the abolitionist movement. Everybody knows the story of Jim Brown, or whether you're talking about Floyd Little, the 44 is here, the first black football player ever to win the Heisman.

In the City of Syracuse, the population from 1970 to 2000 declined from 197,000 to 147,000, over a 25% decrease. Kevin's time at Syracuse University was precisely what he had hoped for – a welcoming environment where he would be challenged, learn, and grow. When Kevin graduated with a Broadcast Journalism and Spanish degree, he accepted a job at an ABC affiliate in New York. At that time, Syracuse graduates didn't stay in Syracuse. But he had just met a woman – who would later become his wife - he followed his heart. "I declined the new job, returned to WSYR, where I had worked while a student, begged to get my job back, and even got the security deposit back from my new apartment – that never happens! Three amazing kids, three dogs, and a house later, Kevin and his wife, Deborah, are still in Syracuse."

"There's a reason we're supposed to be here in Syracuse. "We had job offers that would've paid us much more in D.C. several years ago. Deborah, who's a successful labor and delivery nurse, receives frequent calls from recruiters all over the country. We sat down and did the math, and we were like, wow, we'll double our salary! Then we realized that money would pay the mortgage every month and not much more. Damn. It was one of those things where we said, what are we getting? And so, it's why we've stayed. And then we've said, if we're going to stay here and believe in this place, let's put our proverbial money where our mouth is. And I left journalism.

Kevin was the chief of staff to the majority leader in the New York State Assembly. He left after just a couple of years because my wife said it was changing you and not in a good way. She noted that I had reached a point where nearly every sentence had an F-bomb. Kevin became an associate publisher for a paper focused on the communities across upstate New York. Kevin then became a consultant on aviation issues. Syracuse's regional business group hired him. That was how he worked his way into economic development because Syracuse lost air service in the post-9/11 period. "Without air links, your city dies." Syracuse saved their air service by working with the community and others. Then Kevin was brought on staff at what became CenterState CEO. He worked with partners across the region to create a vision for a prosperous Syracuse region in the near future.

Kevin has two titles at Center State: CEO and VP of public policy. He is also a senior aviation industry advisor. CenterState CEO's name speaks to its business leadership and economic development organization role. Centerstate envisioned taking on a broader role than a typical chamber or economic development group. So, the name CenterState CEO appeals to its business membership. Our full name is the CenterState Corporation for Economic Opportunity. They envisioned a mission: to build a region of growing opportunity, where business thrives and all people prosper. The economic development role and people like Kevin is key to making the Voltage Valley Revolution™ a reality. Deborah and Kevin stayed in Syracuse and saw the area build on its history and start to fulfill this mission. And, yes, Kevin and Deborah celebrate *Loving Day* – June 12 – every year."

VOLTAGE VALLEY REVOLUTION™

Chapter 20
Figuring it Out

Dr. William Paolillo w/ Chris Montgomery

"In sports, as in life, it's not always about having a clear playbook. It's about 'just figuring it out,' adapting to each play and learning from every move. "Victory is about navigating uncertainties and turning challenges into opportunities." – Inspired by Chris Montgomery

And then it was over. I would no longer work for U.S. Representative Dan Maffei as the Immigration & Agriculture representative; he lost the election. This was a dream job. It helped refugees, citizens, and immigrants. It also helped farmers and migrant workers. I had a beautiful son. His mother and I had recently agreed to co-parent in separate homes. I remember sitting on a curb in my old neighborhood and thinking it was time to double down. I worked two jobs, 80 to 120 hours a week. I helped kids with dual disabilities and worked for human resources agencies. I assisted the homeless with rehousing and relocation. I worked these jobs while finishing my degree, and it was time to try to figure it out while figuring it out.

Chris grew up in a working-class neighborhood on the east side of Syracuse. His family-owned Coker and Sun Pavement. Chris started working there at 13, doing odd jobs, and in six months, he was driving the 2-ton dump truck. What stood out about our business wasn't just the task. It was the sheer number of family members involved. They ranged from my grandfather, the revered patriarch, to me and my four cousins, the youngest in the lineage. We were a diverse, multi-generational crew. It included my grandfather, Lee, and uncles Dwight, Angelo, and Anthony. Then there were us younger ones: Chubb, Darien, Xavier, and Antoine. We even had the 'babies' of the family there, including 3-year-old Dante, a constant bundle of energy.

One job I remember was straightforward: connecting the rural road to the steps of the house – about a half mile. That sunny summer morning is unforgettable for the job and an unexpected encounter. As we cleared the area for paving, my grandfather instructed me to move a log to the other side of the house. Simple enough, until I rounded the corner and came face-to-face with a Great Dane. The owner had left the cage door open. Initially unimposing as it lay there, the dog transformed into a towering figure as it stood. I was just a kid, barely four feet tall, and the sight of the Great Dane sent me sprinting back to the safety of our truck and family. Chris's eventual 4.3 forty speed was put to good use that day.

Chris had a God-given ability to run and jump – at 5 foot 7, he could dunk a basketball and was lightning fast on the field. Growing up, he played all sorts of sports, from football to soccer, and was pretty good at them. Chris joined a program called Shooting for A's. The highlight for him was an impromptu invite to join a shootaround with the Syracuse basketball team, including Alan Griffin, Ryan Blackwell, and Eton Thomas. Then, as they were balling, Jim Boeheim, the renowned head coach of the Syracuse men's basketball team, appeared unexpectedly. Seeing Coach Boeheim, a figure Chris had only watched on TV, made him think, maybe I can play Division One ball one day.

Chris started college at SUNY Morrisville. He excelled on the football team. He majored in English and secondary education. Chris's coach at Morrisville eventually came to him and said, it is time to move on and play division one ball. Then came the move to Temple University, where Chris walked on at Temple to play slot receiver. There was another ball game besides football to play in inner-city Philadelphia – busy streets, lots of noise, and people everywhere. When Chris initially went to Philadelphia, he worked out financing for Temple. Then, with the financial crisis of 2008, his finances for college dried up, and he did not have the 40k to continue his studies at Temple. Chris returned to Syracuse, trying to figure it out while figuring it out. He was blessed with his first son as he returned to Syracuse and finished his degree at SUNY Morrisville in 2015. As Chris continued to figure it out, he also graduated from Syracuse University and its professional studies program. During this time, Chris also worked at two nonprofits in the Syracuse area, Catholic Charities and Liberty Resources.

While Chris was doubling down, something else was happening. His network was watching, especially Tim Penix, VP at SUNY Syracuse's Educational Opportunity Center. Lifted by his network and the community, Chris is currently figuring it out in his new role as the Director of Syracuse Builds. In today's world, no one succeeds by themselves.

Chris will focus on developing talent for the I-80 corridor and Micron's chip plants in his new role. These projects will create the need for 6000 construction jobs. A key part of the workforce program will be the Syracuse Builds Pathways to Apprenticeship program. This program is key to the Syracuse Builds initiative. It aims to prepare community members for construction jobs.

Key Features of the Pathways to Apprenticeship Program:

Targeted Training: The program offers comprehensive training designed to prepare participants for apprenticeships in the building trades. It aims to equip them with the necessary skills and certifications required in the construction industry.

Focus on Underrepresented Groups: A significant aspect of the program is its emphasis on inclusivity. It targets women, minorities, and veterans, groups that have historically been underrepresented in the construction sector.

The training includes an 11-week course. It uses the nationally recognized Multi-Craft Core Curriculum (MC3). This curriculum ensures that participants receive a standardized and high-quality education in construction basics.

Practical and Safety Training: Participants undergo practical training. This includes CPR, first aid, and OSHA (Occupational Safety and Health Administration) training. This enhances their skills and prepares them for real-world construction environments.

Industry Exposure: The program gives enrollees direct exposure to various construction trades through field trips, union visits, and shadowing. It helps them understand the construction industry and guides their careers.

Pathway to Employment: Graduates are ready for union apprenticeships or other construction jobs. Some participants have been invited to join unions or have applied for union apprenticeship opportunities.

Community and Economic Impact: The program aims to help the community by preparing residents for construction jobs. It will provide jobs and boost the local economy.

Chapter 21
Catalyst for Change

Dr. William Paolillo w/ Petra Mitchell

"My parents sacrificed everything for me. They came to America with nothing, but they made sure we had opportunities they could only dream of." – Petra Mitchell.

The year was 2008, and the world was unraveling. Financial markets crashed. Banks collapsed. People lost homes, jobs, and savings. Lehman Brothers fell, and the ripple effects spread like wildfire. Panic swept across industries, and companies struggled to keep their doors open. Pennsylvania wasn't spared. It cut economic development funding by 40%. Businesses and organizations are struggling. For Catalyst Connection, that meant a $2 million cut, almost half its budget—gone overnight.

Petra had become the CEO. Catalyst Connection was a non-profit consulting firm. It helped small and medium-sized manufacturers survive in a tough world. With the global economy in freefall, its future was in jeopardy. On top of the state cuts, the federal government was considering cutting MEP funding. The Manufacturing Extension Partnership (MEP) National Network is a public-private partnership that delivers comprehensive, proven solutions by helping small and medium-sized manufacturers grow, make operational improvements, and reduce risk. MEP was a vital source of support for Catalyst Connection. The walls were closing in. It was a Friday afternoon. The sky outside was a dull gray, reflecting the mood inside Petra's office. She sat across from Jean, her CFO, a woman who had been with Catalyst Connection for over two decades. They had faced challenges before, but nothing like this.

"We're going to have to shut this down," Petra said, staring out the window. Her voice was steady, but the words hung heavy in the room. Jean, her trusted confidante, nodded slowly. There was no sugarcoating the situation. The numbers didn't lie. They discussed the grim details: layoffs, which projects to abandon, and what they might save.

It felt like the world was crumbling. "It was one of those moments where you feel the weight of everything," Petra recalled later. "The future of the organization and its workers felt like it was slipping through my fingers." But, this was not Petra's first encounter with adversity. She developed her resilience much earlier. Her family emigrated from Slovenia when she was five.

In the late 1970s, Petra's parents made the decision that would change everything. Slovenia, then part of Yugoslavia, was under a communist regime. It was not the life her mother wanted for her daughter. Petra's mother gave her father an ultimatum—leave now or never. They packed their things and flew to Pittsburgh, Pennsylvania. Petra's father's sister had settled there years ago. They moved in with her and her husband until they could get on their feet.

"For me, the transition was smooth," Petra said. "I was young, and I adapted quickly. For my parents, it was much harder. "They didn't speak the language. They worked long hours in factories. And, they bore the burden of starting over in a new country."

Petra's family wasn't alone, though. They were part of a close-knit Slovenian community in Pittsburgh. Every holiday and birthday was celebrated together. "It was always on the actual day," Petra remembered with a smile. There was no waiting until the weekend. "Cake, ice cream, and family marked our milestones." The parents were hardworking and driven. They had blue-collar jobs. But, they were set on their kids going to college. For them, education was non-negotiable. "It wasn't a question of if we would go to college, but where," Petra explained. That determination laid the foundation for Petra's future. She excelled in school, especially in math and science. This led her to pursue engineering.

Petra attended the University of Dayton on a scholarship. She juggled college life with her tough studies. But, she aimed to make her parents proud. "They had sacrificed so much for me," she said. "I couldn't let them down."

After graduating, Petra got a job at General Electric (GE) in their Aircraft Engines division. The work was intense, but the company offered Petra a chance to continue her education. Through GE, she earned a master's degree while working full-time. Yet, despite her success, something was missing. The corporate environment wasn't fulfilling her. After seven years at GE, Petra left and returned to Pittsburgh, drawn by the desire to be closer to her family.

She found Catalyst Connection. There, she managed projects, working directly with manufacturers. It was work that made sense to her—practical, hands-on, and impactful. But, as she rose through the ranks, Petra was pushed into a role she resisted: business development.

"I hated it," she said bluntly. "I didn't want to sell. I wanted to be in the field, working directly with manufacturers." Business development felt too abstract. It was too far from the results of the manufacturing projects she loved. But, over time, Petra saw that funding and partnerships were key. They were essential for Catalyst Connection to survive and grow.

When Petra became CEO in 2007, she had to step into the role of a leader, not just a doer. The transition wasn't easy. "At first, I tried to do everything," she admitted. "I micromanaged because I didn't trust anyone else could do it how I would." But the crisis of 2008 forced her to rethink everything.

As the financial downturn deepened, Petra's role changed. She had to guide others through uncertainty, not fix problems. She learned to trust her team more, delegate, and focus on the bigger picture. She once dreaded business development. Now, it was her main focus. "Now, I love it," Petra said. "I see it as the lifeblood of the organization. "Without new funding and partnerships, our work with manufacturers is impossible. A major project funded by the Heinz Endowments shows this transformation." It was a $1 million initiative to help local manufacturers innovate and grow.

In the past, Petra would have been deeply involved in every aspect of the project. As CEO, she had to step back. She had to trust her team to manage daily operations. She would focus on securing funding and partnerships.

This shift let Catalyst Connection expand its impact. It helped manufacturers survive and thrive in the post-recession economy.

Under Petra's leadership, Catalyst Connection is now a key player in the Voltage Valley Revolution™. This movement aims to revitalize Appalachia. It will invest in clean energy, advanced manufacturing, and innovation. Catalyst Connection and its partners helps small and medium-sized manufacturers in five states. It aids their transition into new industries, providing tools and resources for success.

One of Petra's biggest successes has been securing federal funding for these efforts. Catalyst Connection manages over $11 million in grants. This includes a $10 million ARISE grant from the Appalachian Regional Commission. "We've grown tremendously," Petra said, reflecting on how far the organization has come. "We're helping manufacturers expand into solar, broadband, and clean sectors." Petra sees a clear evolution in her leadership, looking back on her journey. "In the beginning, I wanted to be involved in everything—hands-on, maybe too much," she laughs. "Now, I focus on the big picture. I need to secure resources to keep growing and serving our community.""

Under Petra's leadership, Catalyst Connection has faced tough times. It is now a vital resource for manufacturers across Appalachia. Her immigrant upbringing and early career struggles shaped her. They built her resilience. It has driven her success. "My parents sacrificed everything to come to America with nothing. But, they ensured I had opportunities they could only dream of. The Voltage Valley provides new hope for Appalachia as well. It forges the path for the next industrial revolution. With the same drive, we aim to bring those opportunities to a region once defined by hardship. We want to make it a hub of innovation and sustainable growth.

Appendix: Catalyst Connection

Catalyst Connection is a nonprofit consulting firm that provides technical assistance, strategic planning, and business growth consulting to small and medium-sized manufacturers in the Appalachian region. Founded in 1988, the organization aims to help manufacturers innovate, improve processes, and remain competitive globally.

Catalyst Connection is part of the Manufacturing Extension Partnership (MEP), a nationwide network that supports manufacturers through technical assistance and training. In recent years, Catalyst Connection has played a vital role in the Voltage Valley Revolution™, helping manufacturers transition into clean energy and advanced manufacturing sectors.

Through its work, Catalyst Connection has secured over $30 million in federal funding, including significant grants from the Appalachian Regional Commission and the Economic

Development Administration. The organization's impact has been felt across five states, providing manufacturers with the resources they need to succeed in the modern economy.

Chapter 22
Building More Than Walls

Dr. William Paolillo w/ Bhavin "B." Patel

"True success isn't just about working hard; it's about working smart and leaving a legacy that uplifts the community." *Inspired by Bhavin "B." Patel*

During the 2008 financial crisis, as the global economy crumbled, Bhavin "B." Patel found himself in Ohio watching his once-thriving business fall apart. He had staked everything on the region's future in energy and real estate, but as the world unraveled, so did his meticulously crafted plans. Banks came knocking, loans vanished, and B was left scrambling to salvage whatever he could. Long, lonely nights saw him walking through his properties, shutting off lights and heaters to cut costs. What had once felt like a promising future now seemed like a fleeting dream slipping through his fingers, a painful reflection of the broader economic collapse around him.

B's properties weren't just businesses – they were vital hubs. They housed the workers who built and maintained the infrastructure of a new energy era. Around this same time, **horizontal fracking began in Ohio (2011–2012),** marking the start of a dramatic shift in the region's energy profile. Over the next decade, **Appalachia's energy production steadily transitioned from coal to natural gas.** That change not only reshaped the region's economy but also helped revive American manufacturing, because the pipelines, roads, and energy infrastructure were already in place.

The 2008 recession didn't just threaten B's finances; it challenged everything he knew about business and success. "I never thought, in a million years, Wall Street could hurt me," he would later reflect. The lesson was harsh but invaluable, forcing him to step back and reconsider his entire approach. B wanted to build something that would survive, thrive, and build community. He needed to think about the long game, not short-term wins.

However, B's story doesn't begin with fracking, shale, or the financial crisis. It has its roots in a modest Ohio town, where the values of family, hard work, and perseverance were deeply ingrained in him by his immigrant parents. His father, a former teacher with a degree in education from India, worked tirelessly at a factory in Ohio and owned/managed a small 11-room motel on the side. His mother, who held a degree in accounting, ran the household, quietly shaping B's view of business and life. These family values played a significant role in shaping his character and his approach to business.

The motel sat on a three-acre plot. B's entrepreneurial spirit was nurtured there. After dinner, most kids his age were playing, but B sat beside his mother in the dim glow of a lamp, watching her work through numbers in a notebook. She wasn't just writing down hymns; she often taught him the basics of financial literacy without realizing it.

One evening, when B was around 13 years old, he sat beside his mother with his own notebook. His head was full of dreams, and as he scribbled, he turned to her and said, "Mom, I think I want to buy a business." His mother paused, her pen hovering over the page. "So, you want to buy a business?" she asked softly, her accent still heavy with the echoes of their homeland. "Yes, I think I can do it," B replied, his voice brimming with the naïve certainty of a teenager.

His mother thoughtfully nodded. "All right, let's see if you can really do it. What's the income?" B thought for a moment. "Well, the motel has ten rooms. If we rent them all for thirty dollars a night, that's three hundred dollars daily." She raised an eyebrow. "That's if every room is full every night. What if only half the rooms are rented?" B recalculated. "Then it's a hundred and fifty dollars a day." His mother smiled, seeing the wheels turning in his young mind. "And what about your expenses? You'll have to pay for electricity, water, and taxes. What about maintenance?" For the next hour, B's mother guided him, teaching him to think critically about income, expenses, and risk.

It wasn't just his mother who shaped B's approach to business. Though quieter and less involved in the day-to-day finances, his father had a way of imparting just as impactful wisdom. One hot summer day, B, then 14, had spent hours mowing their property. He trimmed the hedges, weed-whacked the gravel lot, and left the yard pristine. As he sat on the porch, waiting for his father to come home, he couldn't wait for the praise he was sure to receive. When his father finally arrived, B grinned and puffed out his chest, ready for the approval he craved. But his father barely glanced at the yard. He walked inside, showered, and returned to the porch with a cup of tea.

B's pride couldn't contain itself any longer. "So, what do you think, old man? Looks pretty good, right?" B asked, his voice full of confidence. His father took a slow sip of tea and then looked at him calmly. "Even a donkey works hard." The words hit B like a bucket of cold water. He had expected admiration, not a rebuke. "What do you mean?" he asked, wounded and confused. His father leaned back in his chair and crossed his arms. "You worked hard, yes. But what did it get you? You did all this labor, but it won't get you anywhere in the long run. I don't need you to mow the grass, Bhavin – I labor so you can do more. I need you to think. I need you to figure out how to buy more property, not just maintain what we already have."

That moment was a turning point for B. His father valued hard work, but he wanted him to see the bigger picture. There is a difference between working hard and working smart. That lesson, plus his mother's financial wisdom, gave B a foundation. He would later use it to build a business.

As B grew older, those lessons became even more critical. By age 20, he had bought his first motel, using the critical thinking his mother taught him and his father's strategic mindset. He didn't just dive into the work blindly; he calculated every risk, negotiated terms, and always kept the long game in mind. By 2005, his businesses generated over $300,000 a year, a far cry from those humble beginnings in Ohio.

Then, the 2008 financial crisis hit, and B was forced to rely again on those early lessons. The crisis was a turning point for him and reshaped his understanding of weathering economic storms. He began thinking even more long-term, developing a vision that would carry him through future challenges.

These family values carried forward into B's own adult life and marriage. His wife, **Shivani**, shared that same ethic of hard work, resilience, and care for others. Just as his parents worked together to provide for their family, Shivani became both a partner in his ambitions and a guardian of their home life. She was his anchor during his graduate school years. From 2010 to 2012, she ran the motel B was managing while he attended evening classes and spent 10–12 hours in class on weekends. Whether ensuring the kids were on track with school, keeping their household running smoothly, or encouraging him to stay healthy and grounded, she embodied the same steady commitment to family and community that B grew up with. In 2014, he founded GHC, and in 2015, their first child was born.

Now, as B looks to the future of Appalachia, he sees a region on the brink of a new industrial revolution. This revolution will be fueled by energy, infrastructure, and advanced manufacturing. Voltage Valley, as it's now known, is more than just a profit opportunity for B. It's a personal mission, a chance to give back to the region that shaped him. His plan is ambitious: to build affordable, modern housing and hotels to support the influx of workers arriving for new energy projects. But for B, it's more than just business. He believes that creating sustainable communities in Appalachia will revitalize the region and offer families like a way forward.

B has even convinced **major hotel franchisors** to invest in new lodging concepts specifically designed for Appalachia. These partnerships will help create innovative housing solutions for the transient workforce, blending short-term and extended-stay options. Thanks to B's leadership, **major hotel flags** are now testing a new concept in Appalachia—one that combines modular construction with eco-friendly designs.

His use of modern construction methods, like modular and prefab housing, demonstrates his practical yet forward-thinking mindset. These techniques allow for faster, more cost-effective construction while maintaining high standards of quality. B's developments are energy-efficient, designed to minimize residents' costs, and seamlessly integrate with the larger infrastructure projects taking place in Voltage Valley. Cleaner energy, high-speed internet, and easy access to transportation hubs are all integral components of his vision for these communities.

For B, the future of Appalachia is not just about building housing, it's about building a better future for the entire region. His projects, rooted in the values of hard work, strategic thinking, and family, are laying the groundwork for Appalachia's next chapter.

Appendix

This success didn't happen overnight. **The first unconventional horizontal shale wells in Ohio were drilled between 2010 and 2011,** prompting the state to expand regulations and staffing. In 2011, Ohio passed a law allowing fracking in state parks. By 2015, more than 1,200 wells had been drilled across the Marcellus and Utica/Point Pleasant shale formations. Over that same decade, Appalachia's energy base shifted decisively from coal to natural gas. And when COVID struck in 2020, the federal government's massive stimulus programs accelerated real estate appreciation sooner than expected. That, in turn, fueled both housing and manufacturing growth across the region.

Green Harvest Capital (GHC)

Founded in 2014 by Bhavin "B." Patel, Green Harvest Capital is a mission-driven real estate investment and development firm based in Northeast Ohio. GHC specializes in sustainable housing and hospitality projects that support the region's workforce and communities. Using innovative methods like modular and prefabricated construction, the company delivers affordable, energy-efficient developments. Guided by values of resilience and long-term strategy, GHC aligns business success with revitalizing Appalachia and helping shape the future of Voltage Valley Revolution™.

Hydrogen Posse Section

Chapter 23
Hydrogen Scientist

Dr. William Paolillo w/Zane Rhodes

My children and my wife have taught me all things are possible - Zane Rhodes

When my son, Quenten, Zane, Rhodes III, QZR III, a bouncing baby boy, did not meet his milestones at six months, we thought he was a "late bloomer", no big deal. As more and more milestones were missed and more and more tests were done, doctors began to say things like, "well, he has some issues." Some said he may never walk. He may never talk. He might live to the age of eight. Just enjoy the time you have. But parents can see more than tests can ever show. Zane and Tracie never believed the limitations and dire news the doctors shared. First they got to praying, and then they got to work.

When the therapist said that he might never walk and they needed to be OK with that, Tracie said "he will walk before he is two." People often say they taught their children to walk you, but for most, the reality is that they were around while their kid learned to walk. Most do not spend hours each day teaching their child how to place their feet or position their body. QZR III did not start crawling until he was 18 months old. Then, through lots of work on everybody's part, he walked at 22 months.

Zane was the fifth of six children. Growing up, we moved around and followed the oil and gas boom in Texas. Then, in the first grade, we moved to Giddings, Texas, where I learned to read in the third grade – I was a late bloomer. When we moved to Giddings, there was a lot of land. We would play in the pond, where I learned to swim. We would go fishing, build forts, and cut down trees. It was very much a feral childhood. Family gatherings were cool when everybody came together. Thanksgiving is my favorite holiday because we all get together, and our family tells stories.

In the fifth grade, I started to find my way in school – I would read a novel a week. I stayed up too late and went to the library early to get the next book. About this time, I started to enter academic competitions. Whenever there was an option to give a book report, play, or anything, I volunteered. I was horrible at it; I stuttered and stammered. But, I kept at it and put one foot in front of the other. Then, I was the MC for the sports banquet in the eighth grade. I told a few off-the-cuff jokes, everybody laughed, and I thought, well, maybe this public speaking thing will be okay after all.

In high School, my eighth-grade science teacher was a major influence, and he said you should look at this academic world. But in my brain, that was not even an option. It is just not something you could do. Then, I was on the high school speech debate and science teams. I was a drum major. In NASA state science competition, our team, sponsored by the librarian from

Giddings, Texas, won state and won a trip to Huntsville, Alabama. The following year, the competition was national, and we won and earned a visit to Washington D.C. to meet President George H.W. Bush. The national contest was to design a manned mission to Mars That was when I realized I could go to college. Being a nice guy, my dad wanted me to understand that he still loved me if it did not work out. He kept saying, "You are in a small town. You're going to a very big school. You'll be a small fish in a big lake. You are always welcome home." My high school graduating class had less than 100 people; at Texas A&M, my first engineering class had 300 people.

I met my future wife, Tracie, in honors history. This class was different. The professor would call on students. If they didn't know the answer, they'd try to make something up. The professor would then make fun of them and move on to the next student. When he gets to Tracie, she says I do not know. The professor asked again, and Tracie said I did not know because I did not do the reading. Tracie is straight forward and honest she does not lie about even the small stuff. My wife is an open and honest person who takes life head-on, and I love her for it. At A&M, I excelled, became a lecturer, and received a University-Wide teaching award. Tracie and I had the deal that she would be a stay-at-home mom when we started having kids. When that day came, I left A&M with a Ph.D., all but a dissertation. I got a better-paying job designing marine cranes and launch recovery systems for remote-operated vehicles – a Department of Defense project. Nine months later, we had QZR III.

So QZR was walking ahead of schedule, 22 months versus two years. The doctors also said he would never talk. So, Tracie teaches our son sign language, and then he learns two or three phrases. Then, amazingly, we put QZR III on a special diet- in a week, he was speaking in sentences. Now he is 6'3", and 230 pounds and talks 1000 miles an hour. QZR III can read and write. My wife held his hand to write for 12 years before he learned to write on his own. Life is different than we planned, but life his good, and he is a fantastic young man. Success is about paying attention to the details.

We wanted to have other kids, but that didn't work out the way we had planned. Then, one day, we got a call about a beautiful, brown-eyed girl with brown hair. She was born very prematurely at 27 weeks - one pound, seven ounces, three months in the hospital on a ventilator. We were her third home in two years. Elizabeth had stopped talking.

No big problem: we know sign language. So, one day, Tracie's trying to get her to say red. So, she shows her. And then she finally took Elizabeth's hand and did red, and then she said, okay, say red. And that girl sat on her hands like, "I'm not doing it." This would be of many challenging moments. Then, one day, Tracie broke down when Elizabeth was particularly defiant. They were both crying when Tracie said, "Okay, here's the deal. You are our family. We are a family. We love you. We are never giving you up. No matter how mad you are, no matter how stubborn you are, no matter what you do, we're family. We love you. As long as it's in our power, you're here forever." And that little 2-year-old girl who did not want to talk took a deep breath and was an angel for the rest of the day. There were still issues – we went on the highway, and she would scream because she thought she was being taken elsewhere.

She needed to learn that family doesn't walk away, and they never give up on each other. Today, Elizabeth has grown into a lovely young woman with a big heart and a deep love for family and connections who plays the piano beautifully. The engineer and the musical artist do not always speak the same language, but their bond is strong and unbreakable.

Zane's journey to design a clean, hydrogen-powered plant in Piketon, Ohio began with a nudge from his brother Wiley. In 2002, Wiley invited him to join Newpoint Gas. At Newpoint, Zane's innovative spirit thrived. He developed helium purification systems. He also helped expand the company globally by pioneering modular amine plants. Zane's dedication to innovation shone as he tackled methane emissions with novel thermal oxidation technology. His work led to a more sustainable industrial future and challenged skeptics with his effective solutions.

Zane's approach to helping save the Planet is the same as his approach to family. Zane's, Tracie's, Quenten's, and Elizabeth's legacies show love's power. They proved that, when it seemed impossible, family could find a way. Or, As Tracie told Elizabeth, "Okay, here's the deal. You are our family. We are a family. We love you. We are never giving you up. No matter how mad you are, no matter how mean you are, no matter what you do, we are family. We love you. You are here forever. **Substitute the word Planet for family, and you begin to understand it is people like Zane, Tracie, QZRIII, and Elizabeth who will power the Voltage Valley Revolution™.**

Appendix: Reimagining the A-Plant in Piketon, Ohio

The planned hydrogen-powered facility in Piketon, Ohio, is a groundbreaking project led by two brothers - Wiley and Zane Rhodes. Located at the historic A-Plant site. The A-Plant produced enriched uranium during the cold war. At its peak the top-secret A-plant employed 10,000 people (cold war warriors) and used five percent of the United States electricity production. The new plans for the A-plant site mark a significant step forward in sustainable manufacturing and clean energy.

The technological innovation at the heart of the planned Piketon project begins with hydrogen, the universe's simplest and most abundant element. This hydrogen, produced at a capacity of 500 metric tons per day, is the lifeblood of the facility. It powers the various manufacturing processes, reducing the overall carbon footprint efficiently and clearly. This is not a complex dance of gears and circuits but a clean, efficient cut. The planned Piketon facility leverages cutting-edge technology to produce hydrogen, clean ammonia, and power datacenters. The process starts by removing carbon before combustion. This results in a cleaner, more efficient energy production method. This innovative approach minimizes emissions and maximizes sustainability. The sequestered carbon will be stored in geological formations, over a mile under the earth's cap, specific to Appalachia, ensuring it is safely and effectively contained.

Water, a precious resource, is captured and reused in the process. This isn't a grand gesture but a necessary step to ensure sustainability and minimal impact on local resources. It's about making the most of what you have, a lesson learned from years of experience and hard living by the people of Appalachia.

This facility is more than just a technological marvel. It's a beacon of hope, a testament to what can be achieved when innovation meets determination. It's not just about the machines and processes but the people who make it happen, the community that supports it, and the future it promises. Ultimately, it's a simple, powerful story of progress written in the language of a sustainable mindset, hard work, and clear vision.

Chapter 24
The Rhodes Brothers' Journey – Vision to Reality

Dr. William Paolillo w/Zane & Wiley Rhodes

In the story of the Voltage Valley Revolution™, Zane and Wiley Rhodes are pivotal. Each brother brings unique skills and views. This section links the visionary designs of Zane Rhodes with the practical, hands-on work of his brother Wiley Rhodes. Their complementary strengths are the backbone of this transformative project, driving it from concept to completion.

Zane Rhodes, the visionary architect, conceptualized the revolutionary hydrogen-powered facility. His designs laid the groundwork for a cleaner, more sustainable future. Zane's approach was deeply rooted in formal education, technological innovation and engineering excellence. He wanted a facility that would produce hydrogen, power datacenters and clean ammonia. It would also set new standards for efficiency and sustainability. His detailed plans and methods were the first key step in making the Voltage Valley Revolution™ a reality.

However, vision alone is not enough to bring a project of this magnitude to fruition. This is where Wiley Rhodes steps in. Wiley, the pragmatic developer, can make grand plans a reality. He must navigate the complexities of implementation. He must ensure Zane's designs lead to success. Wiley's expertise in project management, coupled with his deep understanding of the energy sector, makes him the ideal person to lead the construction and operation phases of the Piketon facility.

Wiley's journey into environmental advocacy was profoundly influenced by personal experiences, particularly the holistic cancer treatments his wife, Debbie, chose to pursue. This path introduced him to a broader, more progressive world that contrasted sharply with his background in oil and gas. These experiences made Wiley committed to sustainable energy. He is a key player in the Voltage Valley Revolution™.

The collaboration between the brothers is a blend of vision and execution. Zane's designs aim to remove carbon before combustion. This results in cleaner energy and lower emissions. Wiley's task is to ensure these designs are implemented effectively, managing the construction of the facility and overseeing the operations that will produce hydrogen, clean silicon, and ammonia. The project includes advanced water capture and reuse systems. They are a testament to Zane's sustainability goals, brought to life by Wiley.

The Inflation Reduction Act (IRA) and Department of Energy (DOE) grants play a significant role in supporting this endeavor. These federal initiatives provide the necessary funding and regulatory framework to advance the project. Wiley's ability to secure these resources and manage their application is critical to the project's success. His leadership ensures that the facility not only meets but exceeds environmental standards, contributing to the broader goals of the Voltage Valley Revolution™.

Malcolm Gladwell's change model, as outlined in "The Tipping Point," offers a useful lens to understand the brothers' impact. Zane can be seen as the Maven; a subject matter expert whose innovative designs provide the foundation of knowledge for the project. Wiley, on the other hand, embodies the Connector and Salesman roles. He bridges the gap between various stakeholders, from government agencies to local communities, and persuades them of the project's viability and benefits.

Together, the Rhodes brothers represent the dynamic interplay between vision and execution. Zane's forward-thinking designs and Wiley's Unique blend of leadership skills are the dual engines driving the Voltage Valley Revolution™. It shows that, with effective leadership, visionary ideas can transform industries and communities.

Rudyard Kipling's poem "If': published in 1910, encapsulates ideals of stoicism, resilience, and integrity. It provides a framework for personal conduct and character, qualities that are essential for the challenges faced by pioneers like Zane and Wiley Rhodes in the Voltage Valley Revolution™.

If—

If you can keep your head when all about you Are losing theirs and blaming it on you, If you can trust yourself when all men doubt you, But make allowance for their doubting too; If you can wait and not be tired by waiting, Or being lied about, don't deal in lies, Or being hated, don't give way to hating, And yet don't look too good, nor talk too wise:

If you can dream—and not make dreams your master; If you can think—and not make thoughts your aim; If you can meet with Triumph and Disaster And treat those two impostors just the same; If you can bear to hear the truth you've spoken Twisted by knaves to make a trap for fools, Or watch the things you gave your life to, broken, And stoop and build 'em up with worn-out tools:

If you can make one heap of all your winnings And risk it on one turn of pitch-and-toss, And lose, and start again at your beginnings And never breathe a word about your loss; If you can force your heart and nerve and sinew To serve your turn long after they are gone, And so hold on when there is nothing in you Except the Will which says to them: 'Hold on!'

If you can talk with crowds and keep your virtue, Or walk with Kings—nor lose the common touch, If neither foes nor loving friends can hurt you, If all men count with you, but none too much; If you can fill the unforgiving minute With sixty seconds' worth of distance run, Yours is the Earth and everything that's in it, And—which is more—you'll be a Man, my son!

Chapter 25
Hydrogen Cowboy

Dr. William Paolillo w/ Wiley Rhodes

If you can make one heap of all your winnings; And risk it on one turn of pitch-and-toss, and lose, and start again at your beginnings; And never breathe a word about your loss.

Rudyard Kipling

In 2013, life threw a curveball. Debbie, Wiley's beloved wife, was diagnosed with cancer. She chose holistic treatments, a far cry from their day-to-day life in Texas and Oklahoma's oil and gas industry. They found themselves in Reno, Nevada, immersed in a progressive crowd. Mention organic juice, and folks smiled. Mention oil and gas, and they called you a villain. It was a clash of worlds.

"My career in oil and gas began in Texas and Oklahoma. I climbed the ranks, eventually found Newpoint Gas. Newpoint Gas became a global player with offices across the globe in the United States, Africa, Europe, and the Arab world. We specialize in natural gas processing, earning a reputation for innovation and reliability. Our focus was always on efficiency and cutting-edge technology. But Debbie's illness shifted my perspective."

Debbie's cancer and holistic treatments were my wake-up call. I realized people enter conversations to understand, not change their minds. Despite the villain label, we tackled methane emissions, a significant concern in 2013 and 2014. I told my team, "Let's figure this out. We know where methane comes from and how to stop it." This journey introduced me to new people and places.

Debbie's treatments in Reno involved long hours in a room with other patients. We shared stories, bridging our differences. Chuck, a commercial fisherman from Oregon, questioned my balance between holistic treatments and the oil industry. Our talks highlighted a shared goal: reducing environmental harm. Chuck focused on ocean plastic, while I emphasized consumer choices. Individual actions drive change.

We spent a lot of time in Reno and Lake Tahoe. The beauty and serenity of Tahoe were spiritual for Debbie. Our drives down the mountain for treatments fostered a bond among patients and caregivers. Fighting cancer together transcends our differences. George, a brain cancer survivor from California, embodied resilience. His spirit shone through physical and speech challenges. Debbie and I spent countless hours in treatment rooms, connecting deeply with others facing similar battles.

Debbie's treatments involved a low-dose IPT protocol, starving cancer cells before chemotherapy. This rigorous regimen initially worked, but Debbie struggled to maintain it, leading to recurrences. Her determination to fight naturally, despite the odds, taught me about persistence and hope. In 2018, we went to Tijuana, Mexico, to receive Debbie's final treatments.

This was our last resort. Tijuana's alternative treatments weren't covered by insurance, straining families financially. We spent $2.6 million out of pocket, but those five years were our best together. We cherished every moment, shedding petty conflicts. In Tijuana, we met Tom and Cheryl from Columbus, Ohio. Tom's humor lightened the heavy mood. His skepticism about treatments, especially the coffee enemas, brought much-needed laughter. An Amish couple who had left their community shared their lives openly, fostering intimate conversations.

Despite these connections, cancer's toll was evident. Many patients, including Cheryl, our new Amish friend, didn't survive. These experiences underscored our shared human struggle and the importance of compassion.

After Debbie passed in December 2018, I retreated to Aspen, Colorado, for reflection. Listening to Pink Floyd, journaling, and reciting Kipling's "If" became my solace. This introspection helped me plan for the future. Without Debbie, I needed to rely on family more than ever. My brother, Zane, and I had always been partners, but after Debbie's death, I needed his support. We consolidated efforts, shared ownership equally. Together, we focused on environmental work, especially methane emissions. Despite clear solutions, the world needed more time to be ready for change.

In 2016, I attended the Climate Change Conference in Morocco, seeking global solutions. This opened my mind. It showed the need for balance. We must consider both environmental and social impacts. Meeting Andrew Rice and Alice Madden deepened my ecological advocacy.

Andrew Rice is a former Democratic state senator from Oklahoma. He is a strong advocate for many progressive causes. He has worked on many political and social issues. They include environmental advocacy, healthcare, and education. Rice's work often aims to unite diverse groups to tackle tough social issues.

Alice Madden was the principal deputy assistant secretary at the U.S. Department of Energy. She worked in the Office of Energy Efficiency and Renewable Energy during the Obama administration. She has strongly supported renewable energy and sustainability. She works to advance policies that promote clean energy and reduce carbon emissions.

Our work on methane emissions led to the "well site of the future," a zero-emissions facility. Collaborating with the Rocky Mountain Institute, we demonstrated the feasibility of these solutions. Yet, monetizing our work proved challenging. Our focus shifted to hydrogen, a cleaner fuel. Zane's method to remove carbon pre-combustion to produce hydrogen and water was groundbreaking. It positioned us ahead in the hydrogen space. My work with the American Renewable Energy Institute in Aspen showed me the need to balance environmental goals with social impacts. It is crucial to ensure that transitions don't leave people behind.

Lessons from Debbie's cancer battle remained central. Hope, resilience, and compassion guided my approach to personal and professional challenges. Understanding our interconnectedness and the impact of individual actions became my philosophy. Our environmental and social journey, rooted in personal loss and professional transformation, highlighted the connection between people and the Planet. Wiley Rhodes' journey is one of resilience and innovation. It is a story of a rodeo cowboy who became a leader in sustainable energy. He is committed to family and community. His leadership in the Trillium H2 Power Project in Piketon, Ohio, exemplifies the transformative power of combining technological advancements with a deep understanding of social and environmental impacts.

Or, as Tracie, Zanes wife told her daughter Jennifer, "Okay, here's the deal. You are our family. We are a family. We love you. We are never giving you up. No matter how mad you are, no matter how mean you are, no matter what you do, we are family. We love you. You are here forever." Or as Wiley says each day as he imagines the possibilities of helping to save the planet. "Ok, here's the deal. You are our **planet**. We love you. We are never giving you up. No matter how mad you are, no matter how mean you are, no matter what you do, we are family – in this together. You are here forever. We love you."

VOLTAGE VALLEY REVOLUTION™

Chapter 26
Little Red Heifer

Dr. William Paolillo w/ Carrie and Tony Montgomery

"Appalachia teaches us that adapting is more than survival. It's about thriving in new ways while staying true to our roots." - Skid Montgomery

When Tony was eight, he overheard his dad, Skid Montgomery, tell his brother-in-law, "Boys, if something doesn't change, we will lose this farm. In the mid-1970s, interest rates went from 8% to 17%. Tony did not know about interest rates, but he remembers being scared. This was not the first time Skid Montgomery had to adapt. By age 12, Skid was entirely in charge of his needs, from clothing and shoes to school supplies.

In the mid-40s, in Magoffin County, Kentucky, Skid Montgomery would arrive early to the one-room schoolhouse to start the fire. He made 10 cents a day/ 50 cents a week. That paying job wasn't available from spring through the fall, however. Little Skid had to regroup. So, he obtained a little red heifer. He walked that heifer to school with him daily, tying it up outside to graze on the grass while he was in class. He fattened and grew her older, had her bred, raised the calf, then sold the calf.

Skid Montgomery moved to Ohio for good in 1956 to follow land and work. Skid married and raised his family. He started in construction, like almost everyone, then onto owning a few small grocery stores along the way and landing on farming. For much of his life, Tony Montgomery's son grew up on a farm in Pike County, Ohio, in the heart of Appalachia. He relates that the farm was a great place to grow up, even though it was hard work for him and his brother, and he felt included in everything. Tony absorbed every word as adults discussed finance, politics, and family aspirations. So, how did Skid Montgomery adapt and save the farm?

A man named Stan came looking for Skid. He introduced himself and said, "Hey, I want to buy five acres of ground from you." Dad's like, what will you do with five acres? Put in a hog pen? There's not much you can do with five acres. The man replied, "I'll give you $10,000 for those five acres." Well, that was unheard of for somebody to pay $2000 an acre for a piece of land. Dad's like, what do you want to do with five acres? The man stated, "Well, I will put a trailer on it. I need somewhere to live. I want to buy five acres." And so, it clicked in Dad's head. I have a very valuable farm, and milking cows is not why it's valuable. The basic existence of real estate makes it valuable; the earth will always have value. Tony learned that day that if something is not working, you need to change and move forward or "lose your farm." In Appalachia, you adapt

Tony relates that from there, his dad cut up a section of land connected to his farm, which got them into the real estate business. And they're still doing some of the same business 40-50 years later. Now, they build affordable housing for local families. They provide 70 rentals and 234 land contracts. In some countries, you can't own your land. In the U.S., you can. Montgomery's help makes that happen. They make down payments reasonable and ownership attainable. Then land purchasers keep up their monthly payments, and now you're living the American dream. Tony says he's seen people come in to make a payment and see his dad. They are as proud of that $ $200-month piece of ground as any farmer in Texas because they own a piece of land.

Tony remembers a farm auction he and his dad had attended. It was a farm and a little house with the Muncy family living in it, who were now renting off current owners. It was an old house. Mr. Muncy came to my dad and said, "We only pay $150 a month rent on this house. If you buy it and need a bit more, I'm not sure how much more I can pay. But, if you just give me some time, we'll move." The thing is, my wife is blind, and she knows every inch of this house. She doesn't need a cane. She can walk around this house because she went blind while we've been living here." Skid went and found Tony and said, "We are buying this farm even if we pay too much money for it." Tony asked his dad why that was, and Skid replied, "Ms. Muncy knows how many steps it is to her clothesline out back." They bought the farm and paid too much for it. Following the auction, they told Mr. Muncy that if you and your wife lived there, it would be $150 a month. Mr. Muncy just cried. Then he went in and told his wife, "The next thing you know, he's leading her out into the yard. And she's saying, "Where are they at? And so, he led her to them, and she hugged them and thanked them repeatedly. Mr. & Mrs. Muncy lived in that house, continuing to pay $150 a month till they passed. You will not find a house in the country to rent for $150 a month. Their kids then rented for a while but now are buying their land from us on the same farm they lived on for years.

When land contracts get paid off, the Montgomery's aren't finished with the buyers. They then help them use that land for bank loans, i.e., buying more land, remodeling, or buying their kids a car. They will contact the bank and explain what people are looking to do. This way, the bankers and landowners are on the same page. The Montgomery's, while running a sound business model, respected people. They valued what was essential to their lives and helped them attain it. Skid eventually retired. Tony took over the business. He continued his dad's work and started new ventures.

Tony Montgomery Pike County Commissioner

Tony Montgomery was elected the Pike County commissioner in 2016. His wife of 38 years tells the story of their first date in high school. While driving to town, Tony waved at someone. She asked him if he knew them. Tony responded, "No, future voter." As the county commissioner, Tony sits on the SODI board. SODI stands for the Southern Ohio Diversification Initiative. SODI is responsible for deciding how to use the Piketon Gaseous Diffusion plant. The plant was turned on in 1952, consuming 5% of all the electricity used in the United States. The Piketon facility was a cornerstone in the U.S. deterrence strategy during the Cold War. In 2011, the Piketon facility was closed and decommissioned by the Department of Energy after 10 years of standby. Under SODI's stewardship, a significant portion of the plant is set to be revitalized by Trillium H2 Power.

This venture will create thousands of jobs. It will also build a sustainable, Integrated Manufacturing Facility. It will produce clean blue hydrogen. This process uniquely works in Appalachia's unique geological capacity for carbon capture.

The planned Phase 1 of the estimated $2.0 billion plant will create 2,000 construction jobs and 300 at the IMF. The IMF has up to 300 megawatts of power. It provides 500 metric tons daily of clean blue hydrogen. This hydrogen is for advanced production of clean power for a data center and ammonia. Blue Hydrogen is clean energy. CO_2 from the hydrogen and other manufacturing processes is stored in a level 6 well under the earth's cap. Appalachia's unique geology allows the mine to capture the CO_2. The ground required for the Blue Hydrogen facility is 10 acres. A Green Hydrogen facility to make the same amount of Hydrogen would take 40 square miles of solar panels and wind turbines.

Tony and the team at SODI apply the same wisdom his father used to save their family farm. The most impactful solutions don't require vast resources but a vision to use what's available effectively. The team sees the choice between 10 acres for a hydrogen facility or 40 square miles for solar panels and wind turbines as a testament to the Appalachian spirit. It is about using your resources to maximize opportunity. Tony and SODI have a vision. It values the land and the community. It aims for jobs, good stewardship, and a clean energy ecosystem in Pike County.

Chapter 27
Community, Family, and Clean Energy

Dr. William Paolillo w/Caitlin Holley

"You need to know where you came from, to get to where you're going." Inspired by Maya Angelou

For Caitlin Holley, this guiding principle has shaped every step of her career and personal life. Her early days in academia, fueled by a passion for STEM, began her journey. An unexpected turn introduced her to the clean energy revolution in southern Ohio. It is a journey marked by a deep sense of community, family, and purpose.

"You never forget when cancer touches your life," Caitlin thought, sitting across from the man who had just poured his heart out to her in a restaurant near Ohio State. It was an odd place for such an intimate conversation, but life caught you off guard and drew connections where you least expected them. Wiley Rhodes, a man she'd never met before that afternoon, had opened the floodgates of his life's story in a lunch meeting - and somehow, it made sense to her.

In the summer of 2022, Caitlin was at ENGIE. She managed a five hundred-million-dollar portfolio of utility projects for Ohio State University. Then, she got a LinkedIn message from a man she had never met: Wiley Rhodes. The message was simple—Wiley wanted to meet and talk about carbon sequestration. He was working on a clean energy project, H2 Trillium Complex. It aimed to transform southern Ohio's economy and environment. While Caitlin had moved on from her direct work in carbon sequestration, she was intrigued. "I've been out of it for a few years, but sure, let's have lunch," she replied.

The lunch meeting, held at a restaurant near Ohio State's campus, would change the course of her career. Wiley Rhodes wasn't just pitching a clean energy project—he was telling Caitlin his life story. Wiley's path was anything but conventional. He struggled to get a high school diploma. Then, he rose rapidly in the West Texas midstream gas industry. Caitlin was most impressed by his commitment to family. His wife's battle with cancer shaped his outlook on life and business. Wiley's story struck a chord with Caitlin. Her mother was undergoing cancer treatment. A close friend had faced the disease, choosing to forgo chemotherapy for a better quality of life. The parallels between these experiences forged an instant connection between them.

As Wiley outlined his vision for the Trillium H2 Complex. A clean energy hub integrating natural gas, renewable energy, and carbon sequestration. Caitlin found herself both fascinated and slightly disoriented. This was no ordinary business meeting. "It was the strangest and most important lunch meeting of my life," Caitlin later recalled. "Wiley shared everything—his family, his work, his dreams. It wasn't just a pitch; it was a story, and I realized that I wanted to be part of it."

Wiley's project was ambitious, to say the least. The Trillium Complex aimed to leverage old infrastructure in Appalachia. It would repurpose it for clean energy technologies that could revitalize the region's economy. Appalachia, once the heart of America's coal-driven Industrial Revolution, was now facing economic challenges. The coal industry was vital to America's past. But, it had left environmental and social scars that could no longer be ignored. Wiley and Caitlin saw potential in this: they could take the lessons of the past and use them to shape a cleaner, more sustainable future.

For Caitlin, this project wasn't just about carbon sequestration or energy; it was about people. She had deep ties to the area, having grown up in central Ohio and now living on a 50-acre farm with her husband, James, and their four children. The farm, a slice of paradise nestled near Circleville, Ohio was a refuge for their growing family and their many animals, including alpacas, goats, and cows. What had started with a single goat had quickly expanded into a small menagerie, much to the delight of their daughter, Maisy. The farm showed Caitlin and James' shared vision. They wanted to raise their kids in a place connected to the land. There, they could learn hard work, responsibility, and the value of community.

Their home life was a beautiful chaos—three dogs, a pony, seven goats, six alpacas, and a barn cat made sure of that. Maisy, their energetic four-year-old, had recently taken to feeding the animals every morning. Her younger brother, Mason, was just beginning to explore the world from his stroller. Caitlin's stepsons, James' boys from his first marriage, were now young men. They were finding their own paths but always returned to the farm for family gatherings. The farm was more than just a place to live—it was a multi-generational haven where lessons were passed down, stories were told, and a strong sense of belonging was cultivated.

Caitlin saw the Trillium Complex as an extension of that vision. This wasn't just about building a clean energy facility; it was about revitalizing an entire community. The people of Appalachia, who had been the backbone of America's first Industrial Revolution, could now be at the forefront of this new, cleaner revolution. The coal that had once powered the nation had also taken a toll on the environment and the people who mined it. This new revolution, fueled by renewable energy and carbon capture technology, had to do better. It had to prioritize the health of the planet and the well-being of the people who lived there.

But the vision was clear: Appalachia could be transformed once again, this time into a hub for clean energy and innovation. The Trillium H2 Power Complex was not just about building a new facility; it was about creating jobs, improving lives, and giving the region a sustainable future.

Caitlin's role in the project quickly became more than just technical expertise. As the Vice President of Trillium H2 Power, she was responsible for securing the $1.4 billion in financing needed to bring the project to life. This meant working closely with the Department of Energy. It meant navigating complex regulations. It meant making sure the project's environmental impact and community engagement aligned with the broader vision. It also meant bridging the various stakeholders. These were Wiley's dream & vision, Zane's practical engineering skills, and the community's needs. Her ability to communicate across these different worlds, much like she had done earlier in her career, became one of her most valuable assets.

For Caitlin, this project was deeply personal. It wasn't just about her career—it was about her community. Southern Ohio, and the broader Appalachian region, had faced decades of economic decline. The people there were hardworking, resilient, and proud, but they needed new opportunities. Caitlin knew that the Trillium Complex could be that opportunity. It could bring billions of dollars in investment, create hundreds of jobs, and provide a model for how clean energy projects could benefit local communities. And Caitlin wanted to ensure that those benefits were shared equitably.

The community aspect of the project was crucial. The local workforce needed to be engaged, trained, and empowered to take part in this new industrial revolution. The goal wasn't just to bring in outside talent but to lift up the people who already lived in the area. Caitlin worked closely with local leaders, union halls, and schools. She aimed to make the jobs from the Trillium Complex accessible to Appalachia's people.

As the planned project moves forward, Caitlin couldn't help but reflect on the journey that had brought her here. From her early days learning STEM, to her work in carbon sequestration at Battelle, to her leadership role at ENGIE, every step had prepared her for this moment. And yet, it was her family, her roots, and her community that gave her the strength and motivation to keep pushing forward.

For Caitlin, the Voltage Valley Revolution™ was more than just a clean energy initiative. It was a chance to give back to the land and the people who had shaped her, to build something lasting for future generations. And just as her children were growing up surrounded by animals, stories, and the hard work of farm life. The people of southern Ohio will grow with the Trillium H2 Power Complex. They will find new ways to thrive in a fast-changing world.

In the end, Caitlin's story is one of connections. It is a connection to family, to the community, and to a vision for a better, cleaner future. It's a story of building bridges between worlds, whether those are the worlds of academia and industry, or the past and the future. And it all started with a simple LinkedIn message and a lunch meeting that would change everything.

Chapter 28
Finding Purpose in the Pandemic

Dr. William Paolillo w/Chris Guerri

"Faith is taking the first step even when you don't see the whole staircase." – Martin Luther King Jr.

Chris jumped into the van leaving Dongguan, China in route to Hong Kong where he entered the airport terminal., The air thick with the tension of a world on the brink. It was early 2020, and the streets outside, once bustling with life, were now eerily quiet. The virus had started as a murmur in the news, a distant threat, but now it was real, sweeping through the city like a silent storm. The government's response was swift and brutal. The talk of nailing people into their homes was no longer just talk. Armed guards patrolled the streets, and Chris could feel the walls closing in.

He had come to China for business. He was to oversee the production of Victory Innovations' latest product—a line of electrostatic sprayers for sanitizing large spaces. But now, with the virus spreading and the country locking down. The world was changing faster than he could grasp, and the only thing on his mind was getting out. He barely made it onto one of the last flights out of the country before the borders slammed shut, leaving behind a land that had suddenly become a cage.

Back in the United States, the virus followed him like a shadow, turning everything it touched into chaos. However, where others saw only fear, Chris saw an opportunity to make a difference. Victory Innovations' sprayers, once a niche product, were suddenly in demand. The sprayers became a symbol of hope, a tool to fight back against the invisible enemy.

A video of one of their sprayers disinfecting people exiting a plane in Indonesia went viral, racking up over 11 million views on TikTok in just a week. The phone rang constantly, news outlets wanted interviews, hospitals needed supplies, and everyone looked to Chris for answers.

Victory Innovations' success soared as the world grappled with the pandemic. The sprayers were everywhere—on TV, in stadiums, and in airports. They were used to sanitize planes, locker rooms, and sports arenas. The company grew at an unprecedented rate, and soon, private equity firms took notice. Private equity firms eventually bought Victory Innovations. This ended an era for Chris. But it provided the capital to scale the operation.

As he navigated this storm, Chris couldn't help but think of his family, the anchors in his life. He had married Patty, his college sweetheart, a woman who had always been his moral compass, guiding him through the roughest waters. Together, they had built a life, raised four children, and faced the world purposefully. But Chris hadn't always been the man he was now.

It was through Patty's Christian Walk that Chris found his faith. She had always been steadfast in her beliefs, a quiet but powerful force in his life. Slowly, Chris began to embrace that faith, finding a sense of peace and purpose that had been missing. It wasn't an overnight transformation but a gradual awakening to the idea that there was more to life than just the pursuit of success. Faith became a cornerstone of their life together. It was a foundation for their family and for facing life's challenges.

Their firstborn, Chris Jr., came into the world when they were still finding their way in Baltimore. Alyssa and Jessica followed, each bringing their own light into the family. However, the youngest, David, was born in Australia and faced the biggest challenge. From the start, David was different. He was slow to speak, struggled to connect with others, and often seemed lost in a world only he could see.

For a long time, Chris and Patty blamed themselves. They thought they had done something wrong and had somehow failed their son. Then, one day, Patty's brother sent her an article. Upon reading the article describing David's condition, Patty burst into tears, finally seeing the puzzle pieces fit together; David had Fragile X. Understanding what they were dealing with was a painful realization and a relief. It was a moment of clarity, bittersweet in its finality. They hadn't failed David; they just needed to learn a new way to support him, to help him navigate a world that wasn't built for him.

David's condition reshaped their lives, teaching them patience, resilience, and unconditional love. These lessons were more valuable than anything they had learned in their years of business. They grounded them, gave them perspective, and reminded them of what truly mattered. They learned to appreciate the small victories, to celebrate progress no matter how small, and to never give up. David's journey became their journey, and it profoundly influenced their approach to business and community initiatives.

Victory Innovations' success during the pandemic was overwhelming but came at a cost. The relentless work pace left little room for anything else. But Patty pulled him back, reminding him of the life they had built together, the life they were still building for their children.

As the world slowly emerged from the worst of the pandemic, Chris started to think about the future. Victory Innovations' success had been remarkable, but it wasn't enough. He wanted to do something more that would leave a lasting impact. That's when the H2 Trillium project came into focus. It aims to develop clean energy solutions while revitalizing areas like Appalachia.

For Chris, the project was more than just another business venture. It was a chance at redemption. Early in his career, he had been part of the wave that saw American jobs shipped overseas. This included his father's job when the factory in Buffalo shut down. Chris had been involved in closing the Hoover plant in Ohio, a decision that had weighed heavily on him for years. The H2 Trillium project was his chance to make amends. It could create jobs, help rebuild and replace those lost.

Chris's business skills and ability to navigate complex markets made him an asset to the project. He could scale operations, too. However, his journey, especially with David, gave him insight and empathy. It made the project truly impactful. He knew this wasn't just about creating jobs or developing clean energy. It was about building a future where everyone could thrive regardless of their circumstances.

As the plans for the Trillium H2 Power project took shape, Chris's thoughts turned to another project close to his heart, Hudson Community Living. Inspired by his experiences with David, Chris and Patty had long dreamed of creating a community where adults with special needs could live with dignity and independence. They had seen the challenges that families faced. They wanted to help.

Hudson Community Living was more than just a housing project; it was a vision for a better future. Chris and Patty worked tirelessly. They poured their hearts into every detail. This included securing funding, designing the layout, and selecting the staff. They aimed to create a place where people like David could thrive. They wanted him to experience life's milestones, like attending prom, working, and making friends, just like everyone else.

For Chris, Hudson Community Living was the culmination of everything he had worked for. It was a way to give back, make a difference in the world, and honor his journey. It was a place where he could see the future, not just for David but for all the families who had walked a similar path.

Chris stood at Hudson Community Living, watching the Ohio sunset, feeling deep peace. The road had been long and tricky. But it had led him here. He could now see the impact of his work and the difference he was making in the lives of others.

The Voltage Valley Revolution™ was more than a clean energy movement and advanced manufacturing. It was about people, about communities, and about creating a better future for everyone. Chris had played his part, and in doing so, he had found his place in that future. He had found a way to turn his challenges into something meaningful, something lasting. And in the end, that was what mattered most.

Chapter 29
Energy, Resilience, and the Power to Transform

Dr. William Paolillo w/ Charles Johnson

Sometimes, our paths don't just lead us forward—they lead us home.

Charles Johnson grew up in Upper Arlington, Ohio. It is a quiet suburb with clean streets and manicured lawns. The air was sweet with the smell of freshly cut grass and warm asphalt after summer rains. His father, Charles R. Johnson, was a driven, polished realtor. He worked in commercial real estate. His mother the matriarch of the family. On the surface, life seemed orderly and almost idyllic, but shadows lurked beneath.

In Charles's early years, his father's battle with alcoholism weighed on the family. By the time Charles entered middle school, his father was sober. This brought peace to their home and deepened their bond. This tough experience showed Charles that life can be fragile. It would shape his choices going forward.

Charles lived a comfortable life in the suburbs, but his family's roots ran deep in Appalachia. His grandfather, born in West Virginia, worked at GM after his time in the Navy. His grandmother, from Virginia, loved to reminisce. She grew up in the region's rolling hills. Charles's mother grew up moving between Virginia and North Carolina. Then, the family settled in Ohio. These family ties came alive during the family's frequent road trips through Appalachia. The winding roads of West Virginia, Virginia, and the Carolinas showed Charles a new world. Coal trains rumbled through the valleys. Tall smokestacks cast long shadows over the towns below.

Charles experienced these trips as a mix of adventure and monotony as a child. The long drives were filled with sibling squabbles and sticky heat. But, there were moments of quiet awe as the car wound through mountains and past rivers. At the time, he didn't fully grasp their significance. To him, these were just family vacations. A tradition, filled with laughter and the occasional roadside stop for snacks. But as he grew older, he began to understand the deeper purpose. These trips weren't just to visit family. They were to connect to a region that shaped his family's identity and a nation's industrial might.

In Upper Arlington, drinking was a rite of passage. "You played sports, drank beer, and partied," Charles recalls. By the time he left for Ohio University—a school infamous for its party culture. Ohio University was ranked as the number one-party school in the U.S. in 2015, around the time he attended. Charles had fully embraced the lifestyle. "I was good at drinking," Charles admits with characteristic candor. For a while, he thrived in it. But the late nights and hazy mornings caught up with him. He became directionless and questioned his path.

VOLTAGE VALLEY REVOLUTION™

After a tough year at Ohio University, his parents urged him to transfer to Ohio State University. The move brought him closer to home, but it didn't solve his deeper issues. By the age of 23, Charles found himself at a crossroads. Choosing sobriety was a pivotal moment in his life. It marked the start of a decade-long recovery journey. "Alcoholism isn't just a disease of substance, it's a disease of self," Charles reflects. His struggles gave him deep empathy for others facing similar battles. This was especially true in communities where poverty often fueled addiction. He began to see the link between opportunity and stability. Both were key to breaking those cycles.

Sobriety brought clarity, and with it came a hunger for purpose. But Charles' path was unconventional. He never graduated from college; instead, he chose to educate himself. He immersed himself in books and resources. He taught himself about energy markets, commodities, and power generation. It was a tough journey of self-education, fueled by relentless curiosity. Charles recognized that energy was a powerful force driving industries and transforming communities. "I didn't have a degree, but I had drive," he says. "If I didn't know something, I made it my mission to learn."

His work in energy connected him with high-power user' industries, like automotive and data centers. Data Centers power the digital economy, require vast electricity and reliable infrastructure. For Charles, it wasn't just about providing energy. It was a chance to bring change to struggling regions. In 2021, Charles attended a hydrogen conference in Columbus, Ohio. It was a modest event, with only about 50 attendees, as the world began emerging from the COVID-19 pandemic. Here, Charles met Wiley Rhodes, CEO of Trillium H2 Power. Rhodes spoke about turning old coal power plant sites into hubs for clean energy and advanced manufacturing. For Charles, it was a revelation.

These sites, equipped with transmission lines and substations, held untapped potential. Charles saw a broader opportunity—one that extended beyond energy production. He envisioned these sites as integrated manufacturing ecosystems. They would combine data centers, advanced factories, and small businesses. Based on his conversations with Wiley and further study, he saw real potential for Appalachia. These hubs would create jobs. They would restore pride and purpose to communities hollowed out by deindustrialization.

Charles' vision aligns with the Voltage Valley Revolution™. It aims to make Appalachia and the Midwest clean energy and manufacturing hubs. The initiative aims to revive regions that once fueled America's industrial economy. It will do this by using existing infrastructure. Key sites like Piketon, Ohio, and Paducah, Kentucky, are at the heart of this effort. These sites have capacities of up to 4 gigawatts; they are attracting the energy-hungry industries. But for Charles, the work goes far beyond technical achievements.

"This isn't just about power, it's about people," he says. He wants to help create self-sustaining ecosystems. They would help industries, small businesses, and local economies thrive together. Data centers and power plants would anchor efforts to rebuild jobs. The goal is to create vibrant, resilient communities. The Voltage Valley Revolution™ is about more than clean energy. It's about tackling issues like supply chain resilience and national security. The COVID-19 pandemic exposed flaws in global supply chains. It showed the need for more domestic manufacturing. The movement helps by bringing industries, like semiconductor production, back to America. It strengthens the country's independence and creates high-quality jobs.

Advanced manufacturing is another cornerstone of the revolution. Voltage Valley sets a new standard for sustainable production. It integrates digital, physical, and biological technologies. These innovations cut environmental harm. They also modernize and boost supply chains, making them more efficient and resilient. Charles sees the connection between economic opportunity and community stability clearly. He believes revitalizing these regions can also address societal issues like addiction. "Creating jobs might not solve everything," he says, "but it's a start. It gives people a reason to believe in the future.

Charles Johnson's story is one of transformation and resilience. His journey has been defined by resilience and reinvention. It took him from his suburban upbringing in Upper Arlington, through addiction, to a self-taught education in energy solutions. For Charles, this work is deeply personal. It honors his Appalachian roots - restores opportunity to struggling regions; and it creates a legacy that bridges the past and the future. "This isn't just about energy," he says. "It's about people. It's about community. And it's about ensuring no one gets left behind."

As the Voltage Valley Revolution™ gains steam, Charles stays focused on the road ahead. The challenges are immense. We must revitalize infrastructure, foster innovation, and address economic despair. A revitalized heartland, thriving towns, and a bright future make it a worthy mission. The road through Appalachia wasn't just a family tradition for Charles. It began a journey that would define his life and work. Sometimes, our paths don't just lead us forward—they lead us home.

Section – Forging A Path Forward

Chapter 30
A Mother's Vision, A Nation's Power

Dr. William Paolillo w/ Caroline Cochran PhD

"Great things are done by a series of small things brought together." – *Vincent van Gogh*

Caroline Cochran's journey began in Tulsa, Oklahoma, not far from the oil rigs that dot the prairies and form the industrial heart of the region. Yet Caroline wasn't raised in the rugged outdoors of Oklahoma. Instead, her parents, who were respected physicians, raised her in the city. From an early age, there was a subtle expectation of the future she would likely follow—a career in medicine, like her parents. But Caroline had different ideas that took her away from traditional paths.

In her childhood, Caroline was the type who watched and listened more than she spoke. She cared little for popularity. She preferred to remain quiet in classrooms. She could lose herself in math and science. In high school, her peers were busy with the usual activities. Caroline spent her time studying and working on projects, like the solar car team, and with a close circle of friends. Building and testing alternative energy sources sparked something in her. She became captivated by the challenges and potential of engineering.

With an engineering scholarship, Caroline entered college. But, she had no clear direction in the field of engineering. But everything changed when she discovered nuclear power. During a summer internship, she learned about atomic energy. It is a powerful, sustainable technology with great potential. Conversations with nuclear engineers about clean energy inspired her. This sparked her interest in using the atom as a future energy source.

After receiving her mechanical engineering degree, Caroliyne took a big leap. She applied to MIT to specialize in nuclear engineering. There, she was at the center of innovation. She worked on projects from medical imaging to fusion. Yet nuclear power for sustainable energy intrigued her the most. It was a challenge that required not only technical skills but also for a vision of the future of energy.

At MIT, Caroline met Jacob DeWitte, another student passionate about entrepreneurship. They shared ideas and, over time, refined a vision for a new type of nuclear reactor: smaller, safer, and more versatile than traditional models. Their shared vision became a company, Oklo, co-founded by Caroline and Jacob in 2013. They aimed to do more than just develop new technology. They wanted to change how people viewed nuclear energy. They aimed to show it as a clean, practical, and accessible power source.

Oklo's approach was nothing short of revolutionary. Their small modular reactors can produce 1.5 to 50 megawatts of electricity, capable of powering a small community or industrial facility.

This reactor could provide clean energy to remote areas. It could help end energy poverty where traditional solutions can't. Oklo wanted to change the story of atomic power. They sought to innovate, not compete with existing nuclear plants, in a world moving toward sustainable solutions.

Navigating this path was challenging. Nuclear power regulations were designed for massive, traditional reactors. They do not apply to small, advanced modular reactors or microreactors. Gaining approval from the U.S. Nuclear Regulatory Commission will take a lot of work and negotiations. It wasn't just Oklo's technology; they were challenging the rules that had shaped the nuclear power industry for decades.

By 2020, Oklo's journey took a significant leap forward with a groundbreaking project at the Idaho National Laboratory. Oklo was set to deploy its first nuclear reactor, fueled by recycled nuclear material from a research reactor. This move was monumental. Oklo aimed to show that nuclear waste could be repurposed as a valuable resource. This idea could redefine how society thinks about nuclear used fuel.

As Oklo grew, so did Carolinde's life outside of work. In the winter of 2023, she became a mother. Her son, Ellis, was born as Okolo's mission gained traction, adding a new layer of meaning to her work. Now, Caroline wasn't just leading a company; she was shaping a future for her child. I could hear Ellis cooing in the background. It gently reminded me of the balance she now keeps between building a new energy company and being a new mother.

For Caroline, becoming a mother added urgency to her mission. She always believed in nuclear power's potential. But now, the stakes were personal. Her vision for Oklo grew deeper. She wanted to create a world where her child could grow up in a cleaner, more sustainable place. Her work was no longer about pure innovation. It was about ensuring a future with clean, reliable, and accessible energy for all.

Caroline's work with Mothers for Nuclear, a pro-nuclear group, deepened. She had been a part of the organization before, but now she fully embodied its mission. The group's message—that a mother's love is a fierce commitment to her child's future—resonated more profoundly. Caroline saw the future of energy through a new lens. She focused not just on technology. She cared about her work's long-term impact on future generations.

Oklo's culture reflects Caroline's beliefs about ownership and shared responsibility. Early on, she and Jacab offered stock to all employees, from engineers to admin staff. This wasn't common in the energy sector, where equity is typically reserved for higher-ups. Oklo's team owns part of the company and its future. They share a commitment to a common purpose. Caroline's leadership is not just about vision. It's about building a team that believes in it as much as she does.

The company has a rare milestone. It is one of the few publicly recognized companies in the energy sector that was founded by women. Caroline noted in a recent interview that only 45 public companies in the U.S. were started by women. In a male-dominated industry, her presence is a symbol of change. Her leadership is a model for the future of energy. It should evolve with diverse voices and experiences guiding it.

Oklo's first small modular reactor is set to operate at Idaho National Laboratory. It's a pilot project that could change our views on nuclear waste and sustainable energy. Oklo is using recycled fuel. It is a big step to prove that atomic energy can be safe and eco-friendly. Yet, this project is only the beginning. The company plans to build larger reactors and nuclear powered microgrids. This will bring clean energy to data centers, remote communities, and power-dependent industries.

For Carolin, the journey has never been about conforming to what's expected. From her early days as a quiet student in Tulsa to her role as a leader in the nuclear industry, she has carved her own path. Her success isn't just about Oklo's achievements. It's about her commitment to the values that drive the company's mission. She believes that true innovation needs courage and resilience. It also requires a willingness to face challenges head-on.

Her lessons are woven into Oklo's DNA. They shape its unique culture and bold vision for the future. Oklo aims to do more than provide energy. It wants to lift communities, reduce emissions, and drive economic growth. It will do this by embodying environmental stewardship and social responsibility. This philosophy reflects the Voltage Valley Revolution's™ broader mission. It's a movement about more than just bringing new technologies to Appalachia. It aims to create a future. In it, prosperity and progress are shared.

The Voltage Valley, once reliant on coal, is shifting to clean energy and advanced manufacturing. Oklo's work aligns with this vision. Nuclear powered microgrids are localized systems. They can power themselves, without traditional infrastructure. They could greatly impact the region. Imagine microreactors powering communities in Appalachia. Clean, reliable energy could revive the economy.

Carolyn's journey and Oklo's mission are integral to this larger narrative. They represent the possibility of a future where clean energy is not just an ideal but a reality for communities nationwide. Her story shows that innovation doesn't require fitting in. It requires the courage to stand apart, take risks, and challenge what's possible.

In her quiet way, Caroline Cochran is helping to build a sustainable and resilient future. She is leading Oklo forward not only as an engineer and an entrepreneur but also as a mother. This journey is based on a belief. We must build a better world for tomorrow's generations. It will shape the future of the Voltage Valley Revolution™.

Chapter 31
Bridging Worlds:
The Diplomat and the Nuclear Fusion Scientist

Dr. William Paolillo w/Matthew Smith

"The best way to find yourself is to lose yourself in the service of others, embracing the interconnectedness of our world." – Inspired by Mahatma Gandhi

Stewart Smith's survival was in question from his very first moments outside the womb. His head was abnormally large at birth due to excess fluid. If he had been born a few years later, a shunt could have been placed in his head in utero. It would have preserved his brain's functions. But this was 1975, an awful year for the Smith Family. Cameron "Sonny" Smith, the family's breadwinner, could no longer work. He had early-onset Parkinson's Disease. Phoebe Smith was raising a seven-year-old and a two-year-old in Brooklyn, New York. She had just enough to keep a roof over their heads and food on the table. Later that year, the family would be evicted from their homes right before Christmas. Doctors debated with my parents whether Stewart should even be allowed to be born when he was born in August. The debate nearly destroyed Sonny and Phoebe's marriage. Doctors didn't expect him to survive his first year. Stewart did more than survive. To everyone's amazement, he laughed through 80 surgeries in his first three years of life. You see, the ability to cry was broken in Stewart's brain, along with the ability to see, sit up, and learn to speak. His ability to laugh was unbroken, though. He laughed as quickly as he breathed. This laughter comforted and inspired many. It helped medical professionals, parents of disabled children, and his family. Phoebe called Stewart her guardian angel. His smiles and laughter inspired his siblings. Stewart lived with a quiet, resilient joy that defied the odds for thirteen years.

Stewart passed away the summer between his oldest brother, Matt's freshman and sophomore year of college. Matt returned to school, and that first semester passed in a blur. However, as spring approached, grief caught up with him. For three weeks, he locked himself in his dorm room, sitting alone in the dark and barely eating as he thought about Stewart's life and what it all meant. Matt reached out for help at the college counseling center in his despair.

One day, as he waited for his session, he wandered to the career center. A brochure for the Foreign Service caught his eye. As he flipped through its pages, something stirred within him. The idea of building bridges between cultures and connecting with people across the globe resonated deeply. He decided immediately that a career in diplomacy was what he wanted to do with his life. The fog of grief lifted, and he talked his way back into his classes and the good graces of his professors. He applied himself to his studies like never before.

During his junior year at Hofstra University, Matt crossed paths with Susan. She was a unique individual; unlike anyone Matt had ever met. After transferring from SUNY Purchase, Susan had been a dance major at a top dance school. Her decision to focus on academics and earn a 4.0 GPA showed her quiet resilience and determination. Her perfect posture and inner light, reminiscent of Stewart's, captivated Matt. She was not just intelligent. She was strong and determined. A sense of humor drew people to her. Matt, now confident and driven, found himself pursuing someone for the first time. Their relationship developed slowly. Susan focused on her studies. Matt worked to prove himself worthy of her attention. After a year of persistence, Susan agreed to take a leap of faith with him. They married soon after graduation. Matt's mother initially opposed the young marriage.

Matt's journey to join the Foreign Service was not without its challenges. He failed the Foreign Service exam five times. Each failure was a bitter disappointment. After the fourth failure, they moved to rural Kakunodate, Japan. Matt took a job as an English teacher to improve his qualifications and be selected as a diplomat. Susan's support for Matt's dream was clear. She was willing to move with him and care for their two toddlers. She encouraged him to keep trying and reminded him of all he had overcome. Her belief in him was constant, and their marriage was built on this foundation of mutual support. Susan was not just a supportive partner in Matt's life. She was a driving force that pushed him to achieve his goals.

The move to Japan proved to be a turning point in Matt's career. His experience in Japan was vital. He learned to listen deeply, show true humility, and understand the Japanese concept of 'gaman'. It means to persevere without complaint. These skills, rooted in cultural understanding, would later prove to be invaluable in his diplomatic career.

Matt's first assignment was in Cameroon, a developing country in sub-Saharan Africa. They adopted the vibrant culture, warm people, and the challenges of a developing country. Matt dove into his work. He had to navigate the complexities of diplomacy in a country with strained U.S. relations due to human rights concerns. But Matt quickly built connection relationships grounded in empathy and humility. In Cameroon, Matt built a key relationship with Oumaru Chinmoun, a Foreign Affairs Ministry employee. Their friendship became a crucial asset, helping Matt navigate the local political landscape. Fifteen years later, Matt and Oumaru led their embassies in each other's countries as senior diplomats. Their relationship also built a cultural bridge for his family. It let them experience life in an African village. They saw the strong family ties that bring many Africans joy. Amelia and Avery, four and six, attended a small international school. It was a melting pot of cultures from fifty countries. This environment was transformative for them. They didn't see any people as different or "other"; instead, they saw a world full of friends, each with their own stories and ways of life.

After Cameroon, the family moved to Paris. Matt was sent to improve his French and build his diplomatic contacts. The move was hard for Amelia and Avery. They loved their small school and the warmth they had known in Japan and Cameroon. They attended a rigorous French school. Despite a daily grind of rote memorization and group punishments, both kids learned to speak

VOLTAGE VALLEY REVOLUTION™

French beautifully. They saw challenges as chances to grow. After Paris, the family briefly returned to Washington, D.C. Then, they were posted to Eritrea. It was one of Matt's toughest assignments. Eritrea is an isolated, authoritarian country where freedom is severely restricted. The environment was difficult, both professionally and personally. But it also offered unique opportunities for the children. With few distractions, Amelia and Avery focused on their studies. They learned the difference between a want and a need through their Eritrean classmates. They lived in cramped quarters and, in many cases, ate only one meal per day. Eritrea deepened their empathy and solidified their commitment to improving the world. They saw firsthand life under a repressive regime. This shaped their views on justice and human rights. For Amelia, it reinforced her desire to use her intellect to address global challenges. This drive would later lead her to focus on energy and nuclear fusion.

The family's next move was to Jordan, where Matt managed critical logistics for U.S. operations in Iraq. This was tough work for Matt. But, he stayed involved in his kids' lives. He never missed a play or a sporting event. He even coached their baseball team, which played on a dusty, pebble-strewn field in Amman. Avery played first base, and Amelia was the catcher. The diverse environment of their international school in Jordan broadened Amelia and Avery's view of the world. They made friends from across the Middle East and beyond. This reinforced their view of the world as a web of interdependent cultures, each with something valuable to contribute. Amelia skipped the eighth grade in Eritrea, and her academic brilliance continued to shine through in Jordan. Despite being two years younger than most of her classmates, she was the co-valedictorian of her high school class. Matt and Susan's home and her travels fueled Amelia's curiosity. This led to her acceptance into MIT at 15. She was the first student from the Amman Community School to be accepted to MIT in its sixty-year history.

After graduating from MIT, Amelia worked at Amazon on AI. Then, she moved to Navigant for energy consulting. But, she soon realized her true passion. It was to solve the biggest challenge of her generation: sustainable energy.

Amelia's choice to work on nuclear fusion stemmed from her childhood. She saw the effects of energy scarcity and environmental damage in the developing world. She got into the Technical University of Eindhoven's program in the Netherlands. Later, she worked in France on a 37-country effort to build a nuclear fusion reactor.

For Matt, watching Amelia's journey unfold is both humbling and fulfilling. As a diplomat, he wants to change the world for the better. He aims to connect cultures and promote peace and understanding. To see his daughter, take up a world-changing cause is the ultimate validation of the choices he and Susan made as parents.

Amelia's work in nuclear fusion stems from childhood grasping global unity. Her upbringing taught her to cherish diverse perspectives and individual contributions. These lessons drive her quest to improve the world.

VOLTAGE VALLEY REVOLUTION™

Watching Amelia's journey unfold is humble and deeply fulfilling for Matt. He aims to impact the world through his work as a diplomat. He wants to build bridges between cultures and promote peace. To see his daughter fight for a world-changing cause is the ultimate validation of the choices he and Susan made as parents.

Amelia's commitment to nuclear fusion and sustainable energy comes from her childhood. It was spent understanding the world's interconnectedness. Matt's values -empathy, resilience, and making a difference—shaped her. They came from his experiences as a diplomat and lessons from his family, including his late brother, Stewart. Stewart's quiet strength and joy amid troubles taught Matt to live with purpose and compassion. His lessons shaped Amelia's path.

Matt's career in diplomacy was more than a job. It was a legacy of building bridges between cultures and uniting communities. Now, that legacy lives on through Amelia. She is taking a leadership role in the Voltage Valley Revolution™. She leads the charge. Amelia will ensure the next generation of leaders creates a more connected, innovative, and resilient world. Matt's work as a parent and a diplomat laid the foundation for a new industrial revolution: The Voltage Valley Revolution™. We must approach it with the care and vision needed to succeed.

Chapter 32
Rooted to Rise: Microgreens, Medicine, and a New Appalachian Power

Dr. William Paolillo w/James Valencia

"The ultimate goal of farming is not the growing of crops, but the cultivation and perfection of human beings." - *Masanobu Fukuoka*, Japanese farmer and philosopher

The call came during high school. James' mom had multiple sclerosis. As a pediatrician and mother of three, she held the family together. She worked long hours, prepared meals, and managed everything. But eventually, something broke. Her body began to shut down—overworked, stressed, and depleted. At first, it didn't make sense, but over time, it became clear: the modern medical system to which she had devoted her life could only support her to a certain point. She underwent treatments involving pills, steroids, and chemotherapy, but the side effects piled up. Then came a car accident, a chemical reaction from the airbag, and a face full of lesions that refused to heal.

She stood for hours in front of the mirror every day, using tweezers to try to untwist her own skin. Even the dermatologists at Kaiser, one of the best systems in the country, didn't know what to do. It opened something in him. This gap between treatment and healing, care and cure, was clear. That was the moment things started shifting.

In a hot, echoing woodshop in suburban Los Angeles, a teenager ran a filthy old plank through a planer. The machine roared. A cloud of sawdust rose. And suddenly the air was thick with something unexpected: pine. Real pine. Not the warped, yellow boards from Home Depot. Instead, it was deep, resin-rich wood that smelled fresh, like the forest had just taken a deep breath. The shop teacher stopped mid-step. "This is the good stuff," he said. "That's probably seventy years old."

The kid stared at the board. Heavy, clean-grained, fragrant. He felt stunned. This was pine? It didn't look—or smell—like the lumber he'd known. That moment lodged itself in his brain. Not as a memory, but as a question: why did this feel so different?

Years later, that question would take James across the country to Appalachia. He traveled through engineering labs, hydroponic farms, old-growth forests, and basement grow rooms. The answer, he'd learn, was about time, ecosystems, how we treat the land, and what we ask it to give us back. He would begin to believe in something new. He became the quiet backbone of a revolution: food—grown right and differently—can heal.

Growing up in a mixed-race family in L.A.—Mexican and white, city and mountain—he saw two different relationships with food. His maternal side cooked to feed. Functional, quick meals. His mom was a pediatrician. She was always busy and caring. There was rarely time to connect over recipes. His dad's side had flavor, ritual, and culture. His grandmother flipped tortillas by hand on the comal. Used a molcajete passed down from her grandmother. But even there, the food didn't escape industrialization. His grandfather's advice, though unscientific, stuck: "When you need to poop, don't wait. Get the cancer out."

He thought about his grandfather again—about the old ways his family prepared food. In his grandmother's kitchen, beans were soaked overnight, sometimes twice, and rinsed until the bubbles stopped. Then they were simmered slowly with herbs, onions, or garlic. That wasn't just tradition—it was chemistry. Soaking removed antinutrients like lectins and phytic acid, which in excess can cause inflammation and prevent mineral absorption. Cooking for hours broke down hard fibers, making nutrients more bioavailable. The food wasn't just tasty—it was made safe. It was made healing.

When he joined an ancient philosophy class, he read a Pythagorean fragment: "Hand off beans." The echoes of ancestral food wisdom grew stronger. The warnings had always been there, coded into culture, handed down in kitchens. Now science was finally catching up.

After high school, he left the dry L.A. heat for Vanderbilt University in Tennessee. It was a sensory overload. Rain. Trees. Green like he'd never seen. He walked without a clear direction but discovered his way in environmental sociology, science, and tech communication. The more he studied, the more he noticed a problem. Public money funded research, but it was hidden behind paywalls and complex jargon. The solution, he thought, wasn't just better science. It was better storytelling.

That's when he picked up a microphone and started a podcast about old-growth forests. He talked to ecologists and loggers. He mapped the lifecycle of pine. Then he found out why that old board from his childhood smelled so different. It came from an old-growth tree that grew slowly and deeply. Today's pine is farmed fast and straight. Same name, different substance.

He thought he'd go into energy tech. Instead, he found himself in hydroponic farming without soil. His first project was a harvest cart designed for people. It was made for a farm near Mount Juliet, Tennessee. It blew his mind. Vegetables growing without dirt. Vertical systems. Controlled environments. He'd never even seen a farm growing up in L.A.

Then came microgreens. At a nonprofit maker space called The Forge in Nashville, he traded sweeping floors for membership. The space had woodshops, welders, artists, and engineers—a collision of creativity. He requested a 100-square-foot room to grow microgreens. He then sold them to local restaurants. Microgreens are tiny herbs and vegetables harvested young. They grow in inches of space and pack massive flavor and nutrition.

He handed out samples across the city but got no replies. Only later did he discover the email on his flyer was misspelled. A friend made the flyer, and no one could contact him. He registered the mistyped domain. Then came the email that changed everything.

Charlie had been growing microgreens in Nashville for 13 years. He saw the samples and reached out. They met. Charlie showed him a basement packed with racks of greens, grown under lights. There was no soil, no chemicals, just controlled environments and dedicated chefs.

Charlie's story had sharp edges. He bought that house to grow pot and used microgreens as a cover. He got caught and went to prison. When he got out, everything was gone—except a few lights. So he started over, one rack at a time. By the time they met, Charlie had 35 restaurant clients. He was consistent, loyal, and trusting—a rare thing in alternative agriculture.

Eventually, he took over Charlie's business, but he needed to scale. An abandoned greenhouse stood at the Nashville Farmer's Market. This is a city-owned spot right in the heart of the city. He asked to take it over. They said yes. To help fund the market he put in a green roof for a new hotel. The rest of the project was funded by a mix of loans, support from his sister, and help from the Forge community.

The business had two parts: selling to chefs and teaching consumers at the market. Chefs wanted flavor and consistency. Market-goers wanted story, sustainability, and health. He began focusing on "food as medicine."

Microgreens became the catalyst. One freezing night, the greenhouse barely held at 32 degrees. The next morning, pea shoots had turned deep blue. Cold shock had triggered the production of anthocyanins—powerful antioxidants found in blueberries. Accidentally, he'd unlocked an anti-cancer compound overnight. That changed everything.

He began experimenting. He added mushrooms like lion's mane for brain support. He grew lemon balm to help with anxiety and digestion. He sourced raw honey from the pristine Cherokee Mountains. He partnered with a local bakery to offer donuts—yes, donuts—using ancient grains, raw honey, and infused microgreens. Not just tasty, but functional.

The mission: create foods that help people heal.

He went looking for something older, something more profound. Not to replace medicine, but to complement it. To bridge the gap. That's where it began: with a plot of land he let go wild. Horsetail. Goldenrod. He started harvesting, steeping, and experimenting. Steeping is a culinary technique involving the soaking of solid ingredients in a liquid—typically water—to extract flavors, aromas, or nutrients. This method is commonly used in preparing beverages like tea and coffee, as well as in cooking processes such as making broths or infusions.

But even then, there were setbacks. After the accident, the chemicals in the airbag had triggered a traumatic reaction. Mom's face broke out in lesions. Deep, painful ones that refused to heal. She spent hours in front of the mirror each day, trying to untwist the skin with tweezers, desperate to find relief. The doctors were out of answers. James wasn't. He went back to the plants.

Applied compresses made from his herbal decoctions. Slowly, her face began to calm. Less tight. Less inflamed. The healing wasn't immediate, but it was progress and hope.

That experience deepened everything. It made the mission personal.

From then on, everything began to fit together, not by luck, but by alignment. A life once focused on engineering and sustainable tech shifted to food. Now, it's about food as intervention, culture, and medicine.

James's family always remained behind every breakthrough, every decision. His mom's illness was the spark, but it was his grandfather who lit the fire. James had watched him wither away in the hospital. Diabetes had ravaged his body. His limbs were swollen. His skin was gray. The doctors fed him apple juice and white rice—a cruel joke for someone whose blood sugar had already betrayed him. And yet, even then, he loved sweets. His favorite thing was donuts. He would sneak them into his hospital room when the nurses weren't looking.

James never forgot that. The way food, even terrible food, carries memory. Carried joy. Carried love. That's what drove him to create something better. Not to deny people their cravings, but to offer something new. Something just as delicious—but healing.

He began experimenting by using ancient grains instead of bleached flour. He chose raw honey from the Cherokee Mountains over refined sugar. He mixed his microgreens into delicious foods. These greens are packed with vitamins and anti-inflammatory compounds, so they taste great, not like medicine. He offered made baked goods, donuts— sourdough donuts and focaccia that could strengthen, nourish, and energize. They were donuts his grandfather would have enjoyed with pride. It wasn't about novelty. It was about dignity. James's sense of family and love drives him—and always has.

That's when Appalachia called.

Through AgLaunch, a network of sustainable farmers, he met David Wallace. David is a third-generation cattle rancher. He lives in Cleveland, Virginia, nestled in the Appalachian Mountains. David turned an old elementary school into a 65,000-square-foot space, meant for cannabis. Now, it stood empty.

The land around it—hilly, overgrown, and untamed—held echoes of the old-growth forests James had come to revere. There was a reverence in the soil, a kind of memory. Appalachian land still echoes with the history of vibrant ecosystems. These ecosystems once nourished generations through their rich biodiversity. For James, it wasn't just about farming, it was about honoring that legacy and discovering magic.

David began growing rare medicinal herbs, like stinging nettles. He also worked with the Appalachian Sustainable Development Council teaching. Together, they taught ethical foraging and aimed to create transparency in the black-market trade of wild herbs. He, like James, valued wildness, preservation, and respect for the land. He believed in dignity, health, and regeneration.

Together, they imagined a new operation: part herb farm, research lab, and apothecary. They'd grow nutrient-rich microgreens under lights, like nettle and lemon balm. Then, they'd bottle their extracts to infuse into kombucha and elixirs. So, they'd sell not just ingredients, but also health interventions.

The dream is bold: build a local supply chain for functional foods. It should be as convenient as pharmaceuticals. You can walk into a shop and get inflammation-fighting turmeric or stress-reducing lemon balm with the same ease as you buy Advil. They aim to make food the first medicine, not the last resort.

He views Appalachia as a final frontier. It's one of the few places in America where ancient wisdom thrives, found in both the land and its people. It's been industrialized and exploited. Still, there are untouched forests and heirloom knowledge. Now, a new industry focused on healing is emerging.

James is 25 years old, but his story covers centuries. It starts with his grandmother's molcajete and his mom's medical charts. It includes ancient pine and future foods. It moves from forgotten schools to underground farms. His journey takes him from L.A. to Nashville and deep into Appalachia.

Voltage Valley isn't just about energy. It's about growing a new kind of power that begins in the soil, the seed, and the stories we choose to feed.

Coming Soon January 2026

Voltage Valley Revolution™ : Tales from the Kitchen Table

Food as Medicine.

Conclusion

Success is the journey and what we learn along the way - Stephen Dean

You never know unless you try - Uncle Bill

My journey with the Voltage Valley Revolution™ didn't start with some grand idea. It started the way a lot of big changes do—with a loss.

I lost my job.

No big blow-up. No scandal. Just a quiet shift at the top of a Fortune 250 company. One day I was leading big energy projects and building partnerships. The next, I was out. Just like that.

At first, it felt like a punch to the gut. But looking back now, I see it for what it really was—a push. Maybe even a nudge from God. A chance to stop, listen, and ask myself: *What now? What matters most?* That still, quiet voice said, *Use what you've been given. Do something that counts.*

When things felt uncertain, I found myself thinking about my grandmother—**Carmela Paolillo**. She was the oldest of 21 kids, raised in a Brooklyn tenement. Life wasn't easy, but she learned how to keep going, how to adapt, how to carry others when she had nothing left herself.

My grandfather made his way delivering coal and ice in the city. From that hard-earned money, he bought a dairy farm down in Appalachia. That land became our family's foundation. My grandmother didn't just live there, she worked on that land right beside him. Milking cows. Raising kids. Holding everything together with quiet strength.

I worked on that farm during summer growing up. Learned how to shovel, sweat, fix things that broke, and finish the job even when you were tired. That place taught me what work really means. And every Thanksgiving, we'd pile in the car—my mom, dad, sisters and me—and head back to that land. "Over the river and through the woods to grandmother's house we go"—that wasn't a song lyric for us. It was real.

She was our anchor. Steady. Faithful. No big speeches. Just presence.

That farm wasn't fancy. But it stood for **care, resilience, sacrifice, hope**. The kind of values that stick with you. The kind that matter most when everything else falls away.

And I remember sitting with her as a kid, watching her knit. She'd pull out this big, tangled ball of yarn—looked like a mess to me. But slowly, stitch by stitch, she'd turn it into something useful. Something beautiful. Watching her, I learned something simple but true: **you don't fix the mess by yanking at it, you work it out with patience and care.**

That memory stuck with me. And when my own life got tangled, I thought about that yarn. I leaned on my community. I worked through the knots. I found strength and clarity, not all at once, but little by little.

That's what this book is about.

It's about turning struggle into a story. About honoring the people who came before us. About finding meaning in the mess and building something stronger on the other side.

In Appalachian and American folk tradition, yarn and quilts aren't just craft—they're stories. They hold memories, mark hardships, and tie generations together. Life, like a quilt, might be made from scraps—but when sewn with love, it becomes something whole.

That's the heart of the Voltage Valley Revolution™. Taking what's been handed down—good and bad—and making something new. Something useful. Something worth passing on.

The Voltage Valley Revolution™ emerged from this reflective period as a commitment—to recognize and amplify the extraordinary resilience and creativity found within communities.

Much of this work was shaped by the research methods I developed during my doctorate. But more than theory or method, the most important thing I learned came from my mentor, Dick Boland—who led doctoral programs at Case Western Reserve University and at Cambridge University in England. Dick didn't just teach scholarship; he taught the art of real conversation. The kind where people trust you with their hardest stories—of death, addiction, illness, and perseverance.

That kind of listening shaped my approach to this book. It grew from a wish to inspire others and to help spark a new kind of industrial revolution—one that values people and places as much as it values progress and performance.

Poverty still hangs heavy over many parts of Appalachia. Even after years of federal investment, it hasn't loosened its grip. Between 2000 and 2018, research shows that distressed ZIP codes—many of them right here—barely saw any progress. Wages stayed low, jobs didn't return, and too many buildings stayed boarded up. [See: *Clean Innovation Ecosystems: Lifting distressed communities in Appalachia with clean energy* in the appendix.]

The truth is, poverty isn't just about money. It's about being left out—again and again.

But something new is rising—not from the top down, but from the bottom up.

My Uncle Bill used to say, "You don't get through hard times by yourself." It takes neighbors, helping hands, and folks who don't quit on each other. That spirit lives on in people like **James Valencia**, a young leader trying to turn struggle into something better.

James didn't start with a big plan—he started with pain. When his mom got sick, it shook him. He began asking hard questions: What are we eating? How do we heal? How do we take care of each other when the system doesn't? That's when he turned to the land.

He didn't toss out tradition—he built on it. James is blending old-school Appalachian farming wisdom with a new kind of smart technology called **AI-powered Digital Spatial Intelligence (DSI).**

What does that mean in plain terms?

Think of it like giving a farm—or a factory or school—a brain. One that can **see what's happening in real time**, **learn from patterns**, and **make smarter decisions** over time.

For example, James uses DSI to monitor his different farm's soil, water, and plant health with sensors. The system helps him know exactly when to plant, how much to water, and how to keep the land healthy for future generations. It's like having an expert farm manager and a soil scientist, running 24/7—powered by AI.

And it doesn't stop at farms.

The same tools that help James are being used in factories to prevent equipment failures before they happen. In schools, they cut energy waste and make classrooms more comfortable. In clean energy hubs like solar or hydrogen, DSI keeps systems efficient and safe.

James also dreams of an app-based marketplace—like a local Amazon—where Appalachian farmers can sell directly to neighbors. Tech that **protects our land** and **keeps our dollars close to home**. [See AI Powered Digital Spatial Intelligence in Appendix]

This isn't science fiction. It's already happening—and it's helping Appalachia lead again.

With AI-powered DSI, we can make smarter farms, but also smarter factories, cleaner power plants, better schools, and stronger neighborhoods. In data centers, it cuts down energy use and keeps things running. In manufacturing, it avoids breakdowns before they happen. In clean energy hubs like hydrogen or solar, it makes the whole system run smoother and longer.

That's the real story of the **Voltage Valley Revolution™**: It's not just about new tools—it's about putting those tools in the hands of real people with real purpose.

At the center of this are **Clean Innovation Ecosystems (CIEs)**. These are groups of teachers, builders, corporate and government leaders, small business owners, farmers, students—coming together to fix what's broken, using tech that makes sense for where they live. They're already making a difference in places that were once left behind.

Malcolm Gladwell once said that *big change doesn't start with big moves—it starts with small, smart ones.*

And Appalachia is full of those.

One farmer. One factory. One small town with a big idea. That's how this new future begins—not all at once, but step by step, spark by spark.

The Voltage Valley Revolution™ is already in motion. It started right here, in the hills and hollers of Appalachia, but it's not stopping here. What we're building—smarter farms, stronger towns, better ways to live—it has the power to shape how the whole world thinks about food, land, and community.

Folks like **James Valencia** are showing us the way. He's mixing the old knowledge with new tools, proving that you don't have to pick between tradition and technology, you can knit them together, just like grandma's yarn, strand by strand. That's how we build something that lasts.

This calling? It wasn't mine alone.

Still, while we push forward with new tools and big ideas, we can't forget the pain that still lingers.

Matthew Desmond's Pulitzer Prize-winning Book *Evicted* showed us just how deep the roots of poverty go in this country. He didn't look away—he looked close. His work exposed the systems that fail people every day.

This book—*Voltage Valley Revolution*™—isn't meant to replace that kind of truth-telling. **It's meant to build on it.** Not with more analysis, but with action. Not by standing back, but by stepping in—hands first, heart open. This book is about ordinary people doing extraordinary things in the face of loss, change, and uncertainty.

If *Evicted* calls for justice through understanding, *Voltage Valley Revolution*™ calls for renewal through action.

For me, it came quietly—like a whisper I couldn't ignore. I believe God works that way sometimes. Steady. Silent. He speaks through memory, through people, through the pull to do something that matters.

For you, maybe it's not God. Maybe it's your gut. Your compass. A voice deep inside that says, *"You were made to help."*

Whatever you call it—it's there for a reason.

This book is my answer to my prayers and that voice. It's not perfect. It's not finished. It's a conversation. A patch in a much bigger quilt. A story shared in hopes that it'll spark something in you.

So, thank you—for picking this up, for reading it through, for staying with these stories.

I hope you walk away thinking not just about what you read, but what you might do next. Because here's the truth: **we need you.**

We're closing this chapter with hope. Like my grandmother Carmela's ball of yarn, we started tangled. But we kept going loop by loop, stitch by stitch. And now we're weaving something strong. Something whole.

When we bring together **technology, land, education, and care for each other**, we build systems that don't just run, they heal. They support. They last.

Still, let's not forget the pain that's still out there—**eviction, injustice, hunger, being left behind**. Desmond showed us how deep those wounds go. And **Gladwell** reminds us: it doesn't take a tidal wave to shift things. **Just the right ripple in the right place.**

This revolution is a ripple, a steady hand, a better way forward.

As we move toward regenerative farming, resilient communities, and a future worth staying for, we're not asking the world to watch it, we are asking you to join the revolution.

The journey's not over. Appalachia still has more to teach us.

If you've ever felt left out, counted out, or underestimated, then this revolution is for you. It's not just a story to read, it's a story to join.

What began in the hills and hollers of Appalachia won't end there. What we're building—smarter farms, advanced manufacturing, stronger towns, better ways to live, can reshape how the world thinks about food, work, and community.

And we're just getting started.

Final Reflection

Dr. William Paolillo

"Love the Lord your God with all your heart. Love your neighbor as yourself." (Matthew 22)
When we live this love, both people and communities flourish – even in difficult times.

Introduction

When I sat down to write this final reflection, I realized it wasn't just the end of a book, it was the weaving together of a lifetime. A child in a garage fight. An adult in a boardroom layoff. Summers on an Appalachian farm. The hum of factories. The quiet ache of job loss. The loud questions of technology, economy, and faith.

This reflection is not a theory. It's not a sermon. It is a story stitched together with Scripture, history, and scars. It's about what revolutions—industrial, digital, and personal—really ask of us.

It begins with whiskey and tariffs, wanders through Florence with the Medici, looks at Moore's Law under a microscope, and stands again in Appalachia where I found both loss and resurrection. Along the way, it measures Hemingway's vision of toughness against a deeper vision of integrity, and it dares to imagine a future where AI's power doesn't corrode us, but creates care, dignity, and renewal.

This is not just about economics or innovation. It's about identity. About what kind of people we will choose to become.

And so, I offer this reflection as both a testimony and a charge. My hope is that in these pages you hear not just my story, but the whisper of God—calling us to serve, to steward, to love, and to endure.

Every Revolution Asks Something of Us

Every revolution, in every age, asks something of us.
It does not simply ask for labor. It asks for more than our votes or our investments.

It asks for courage.
Not just political courage, but moral courage.
Not just economic courage, but spiritual courage.

The kind of courage that only emerges when you know—deeply and unshakably—who you are, and what you're for.

The Voltage Valley Revolution™ is not just another phase of progress. It's not merely a buzzword about batteries or AI. It's not confined to clean energy, semiconductors, or automation. And it's certainly not limited to tariffs, trade balances, or GDP projections.

It's something more. It's a test.

A test of whether people, companies and churches, families and communities, can lead not through dominance but through devotion.
Not by seeking conquest—but by living from a sense of calling.
Not to be praised—but to build a legacy that lasts.

What's on the line isn't just economic growth.
It's not just the health of supply chains or the hope of national renewal.
What's truly at stake is this: **the moral imagination of a people.**

Part I: Tariffs, Whiskey, and the Taxes That Bind a Nation

The power to tax isn't just a tool. It's a statement of values. That's why, from the very beginning, taxation in America was never only about revenue, it was about identity.

In 1791, the federal government levied its first domestic tax: an excise on whiskey. What followed was an explosion of resistance in western Pennsylvania. To those farmers, whiskey wasn't a luxury—it was currency. It was the most efficient way to move the fruits of their labor over the Appalachian Mountains.

The Whiskey Rebellion of 1794 wasn't just about liquor. It was about liberty. Armed farmers rose up, and President George Washington responded by sending 13,000 troops. The government prevailed, but the real legacy was a warning:

If taxes feel disconnected from the people's good, they breed rebellion, not cooperation.

Tariffs, in contrast, painted a different picture. For much of the 19th century, they funded nearly the entire federal government. Tariffs did more than raise money, they nurtured industries. They built steel. Textiles. Railroads. They acted as national investments in the work of the people.

As we move into the Voltage Valley Revolution™ era, we may need tariffs again—not as punishment, but as tools of stability and strategy. Done right, they can direct global capital toward rebuilding local supply chains—especially in clean energy and advanced manufacturing.

This isn't about isolationism. It's about shared strength.

"To whom much is given, much will be required." (Luke 12:48)

Part II: The Medici, the Black Plague, and Civilized Capitalism

The Black Plague devastated Europe, wiping out half its population. What followed, for many, was chaos: violence, blame, destruction.

But in Florence, the Medici family chose a different response.
They didn't retreat into wealth. They leaned into responsibility.

As bankers, they could have chosen safety. Instead, they funded churches, supported hospitals, and paid the priests who ministered to grieving families.

Their wealth became more than numbers on ledgers. It became culture.

They financed Michelangelo's Sistine Chapel. Brunelleschi's dome. Galileo's telescope. Their capital did not corrode—it civilized.

"The rich and poor meet together; the Lord is the maker of them all." (Proverbs 22:2)

Today, we face our own crisis: the collision of AI and clean energy. Left unchecked, AI could become a blade—cutting jobs, concentrating power, deepening divides.

But if we lead with compassion, AI could instead become a sanctuary: financing universal care, reviving forgotten towns, and opening new doors.

Part III: Moore's Law, Chips, and the Power of Less

In 1965, Gordon Moore observed a pattern: the number of transistors on a chip doubled every two years, while costs dropped. That became known as Moore's Law—and it unlocked exponential computing growth for decades.

But today, the miracle isn't just about more.
It's about less:

- Less energy per calculation
- Less waste across the digital world
- Less strain on creation itself

New AI chips, measured in nanometers, now perform billions of operations while consuming a fraction of the power.

Each step toward energy efficiency isn't just technological—it's theological.
Every saved watt is an act of obedience to God's call to care for His creation.

Part IV: The Integrity-Shaped Life in an Industrial Age

The Garage Fight: A Childhood Lesson in False Strength

At ten years old, I came home bruised. Blood on my face. Shame in my heart. I'd lost a fight in my neighbor's garage.

I wanted comfort. I got a lesson.

"You were fighting in his garage? Was there a wrench nearby? You never accept losing."

That was my dad. That day, I learned toughness—but also fear.
Fear of weakness.
Fear of vulnerability.
Fear of being seen as less.

My fists weren't the only things bruised. My spirit took the blow.

Years later, I heard a different voice. One that changed everything:

"You are my beloved son; with you I am well pleased." (Luke 3:22)

Not earned love. Not conditional approval. But grace. Belonging that doesn't have to be won.

Job Loss and Coming Home to Appalachia

Years later, I lost my job in a ten-minute restructuring meeting. Just like that - title gone. Income gone. Identity gone.

I walked out with a cardboard box and one haunting question: *Who am I now?*

At first, I thought it was the end. I had helped build major energy projects, forged partnerships, operated at the edge of tech and construction. I was in the middle of everything—until I wasn't.

I came back to Appalachia—not triumphant, but grieving. Not for a vacation. For a rebirth.

I remembered my grandfather, who delivered coal and ice in Brooklyn. He eventually saved enough to buy a farm in Delhi, New York. Summers on that farm shaped me—milking cows at dawn, baling hay, working land that gave and took.

My grandmother, Carmela, one of twenty-one children, taught me that reinvention is how we survive. Appalachia was in my blood long before I could name it. That heritage became my compass.

I began visiting union halls, factory towns, and job sites across the region. I saw people who had every reason to quit—but didn't.

I remembered what I'd once written to my kids: *Dream Big. Do Good.*
My daughter believed it so deeply; she tattooed it on her hip.

And there, among those who wouldn't quit, I began to believe again.
Appalachia whispered resurrection.

What I thought was an ending… was a beginning.

Hemingway's Lost Generation vs. A Life of Integrity

Hemingway was the literary voice of the coal and steel age. His short, sharp sentences echoed the machines of his time. His characters—men and women alike—were stoic, silent, strong.

But underneath that hardness was something broken.
Gertrude Stein called them *"a lost generation."* Scarred by war, burned by labor, hardened by loss.

Hemingway's myth of toughness was a mask—and his own tragic end proved it.

"Be watchful, stand firm in the faith, be strong. Let all that you do be done in love."
(1Corinthians 16:13–14)

Integrity offers another path.
Not silence, but service.
Not despair, but renewal.
Not hardness, but wholeness.

President Kennedy once said:
"The great industrial revolution, which has taken place in the United States, has brought wealth and strength, but it has also brought new challenges to those regions left behind." (1963)

Appalachia bore the cost. It must not be left behind again.

"The righteous walk in their integrity—blessed are their children after them." (Proverbs 20:7)

To redeem life, community, and economy—we must not walk ahead of truth in pride or behind it in fear. We must walk with integrity, in love and responsibility.

Part V: Clean-Innovation Ecosystems, Universal Income, and the Future of Care

Every past revolution has asked a core question: When productivity surges, who benefits?

Railroads didn't just bring freight—they brought schools and post offices.
Electrification didn't just bring power and light to farms and factories.
The Tennessee Valley Authority (TVA) didn't just build dams—it restored dignity to forgotten places.

In each case, abundance became civilization - because it was shared.

Now AI stands at the edge of another transformation. Productivity is rising fast, but if it lifts only a few, it won't be a blessing. It will be a curse. If we fail to distribute its fruits fairly, we risk creating a new elite coding aristocracy, disconnected from the rest of society.

During his 2020 presidential campaign, Andrew Yang proposed a Universal Basic Income (UBI): $1,000 per month for every American. Many dismissed it as utopian.

But look to history.
Tariffs once funded infrastructure.
Social Security transformed aging.
The GI Bill launched a middle class.

Each of those ideas was controversial—until it became foundational.

Today, a universal dividend could be the stabilizer families need in uncertain times. It could allow workers to participate in change without fear. It could give people room to breathe, dream, and act with dignity.

The machines were made to serve us—not the other way around.

And just as the Medici used their wealth to support art, hospitals, and churches, we too can direct today's wealth—generated by circuits and code—into housing, education, and health care.

Let AI's productivity power a new Renaissance.

"The worker deserves his wages." (1 Timothy 5:18)

Universal income is not charity. It's not a handout. It's a birthright in a just economy. It recognizes that abundance must belong to the people who help sustain the system itself.

If paired with innovation ecosystems—the kind emerging across Appalachia—UBI could become the foundation of a fair, sustainable, and resilient economy.

Part VI: Poverty, Orphans, and the Call of Community

I once wrote a research paper on how economic development lifts people from poverty. The truth it revealed was painful:

- Half of the children born into poverty will stay there for their entire childhood.
- Only about a third will escape poverty as adults. (Brookings)

At Church of the City, located in Franklin, Tennessee we're building a campus specifically for orphans. The need is urgent—and the stats are sobering.

When children age out of the foster system at 18:

- 60% of boys end up incarcerated
- 70% of girls become pregnant (National Foster Youth Institute)

Many of them land right back in the cycle—abandoned by systems that were supposed to protect them.

But when communities intervene intentionally - everything changes.

When we offer:

- Housing + mentoring
- Education + meaningful work
- Economic stability + spiritual care

We interrupt that cycle. We rewrite the story.

Combine these supports with universal income and local innovation ecosystems, and we don't just help individuals = begin to transform entire regions.

I'm currently pursuing permission to conduct a long-term study on our orphan campus. We want to track outcomes—not just in months, but over decades.

If this model proves successful, the results could rival the Medici's cultural impact or the TVA's regional transformation. Lasting. Measurable. Revolutionary.

Pulling It All Together: People, Technology and Renewal

From the garage fight to the boardroom layoff.
From tariffs to AI.
From the Medici family to Moore's Law.
From Hemingway's stoicism to Christ's sacrifice.
From my grandfather's dairy farm to today's conversations about universal dividends.

VOLTAGE VALLEY REVOLUTION™

We've covered technology, economy, faith, integrity, and memory.

And still, the world keeps shouting the same message:
Perform. Dominate. Consume. Despair.

But God whispers something better:
Serve. Steward. Love. Endure.

"Do not conform to the pattern of this world but be transformed by the renewing of your mind." (Romans 12:2)

The Voltage Valley Revolution™ is not merely an energy shift or an economic realignment.
It's a moment of identity.
A question of character.

What kind of people will we be?

We don't need more noise, we need clarity.
We don't need more brute strength, we need love.
We don't need more rugged individualism, we need resurrected community.
We don't need to walk alone.

We need to walk with each other, one step at a time, into the messy, holy work of renewal.

"For we are God's masterpiece, created anew to do the good things prepared for us long ago."

That's the voice I follow now.
That's the manhood I claim.
That's the revolution worth leading.

Epilogue
A Benediction for Appalachia and Beyond

May the fields of **Appalachia**—once carved up for coal and steel—now bloom with **clean energy**, **innovation**, and **underdog genius**.

May children born into poverty learn a **new story**: That their future is not fixed but filled with promise.
That they were made for more.

May the orphans aging out of foster care find not emptiness, but **family**. Not fear, but **hope**. Not systems, but **souls who stay**.

May fathers and sons, mothers and daughters, walk not in the silence of Hemingway's stoicism—but in the power and presence of **God's love**.

May we, together, walk into the next industrial revolution—not chasing **power**, but building **peace**.

Amen.

Let's build.

Appendix

Chapter 33
The Academic Article That Inspired This Book

Clean Innovation Ecosystems: Lifting Distressed Communities in Appalachia w/Clean Energy

The article Clean innovation ecosystems: Lifting distressed communities in Appalachia with clean energy was used to advise and inspire the writing of the book – Stories of the Voltage Valley Revolution™: The People of Appalachia: Saving the Planet & Restoring American Greatness through Clean Energy, Advanced Manufacturing, and Innovation. This academic article was originally published in July 2024 in F1000.

To cite the article: Paolillo W, Cross B, Zelek C, *et al*. clean innovation ecosystems: Lifting distressed communities in Appalachia with clean energy [version 1; peer review: 1 not approved]. F1000Research 2024, 13:808 (https://doi.org/10.12688/f1000research.150557.1)

Clean innovation ecosystems: Lifting distressed... | F1000Research

This is a summary of the original article.

Clean innovation ecosystems: Lifting distressed communities in Appalachia with clean energy

William Paolillo, Benjamin Cross, Zelek, Wingate et al.

1College of Engineering and Polymer Science, University of Akron, Akron, Ohio,

2Voinovich School of Leadership and Public Service, Ohio University, Athens, Ohio

Clean Innovation Ecosystems: Lifting Distressed Communities in Appalachia with Clean Energy

Abstract & Introduction (As Published original article)

The U.S. government has invested in distressed communities in the 21st century but with minimal effect. Regarding income, poverty, joblessness, and vacancy rates, the average distressed zip code in 2018 showed no improvement compared to its standing relative to the average prosperous zip code in 2000. We have discovered the formation of unique business clusters funded by public-private partnerships have the potential to make a difference in lifting distressed communities. Our research of literature and artifacts (photographs, videos, documents, digital media - websites or social media posts) suggests the discovery of a Clean Innovation Ecosystem (CIE). CIE refers to the network of social entrepreneurs, organizations, institutions, and individuals that work together to promote sustainable technologies and practices.

As of the 4th quarter of 2023, manufacturing annual run rate construction spending has skyrocketed to over $200 billion. There are another $600 billion of Voltage Valley projects announced that have not yet been built. Over the past two decades, private investment has been between $20 billion and $100 billion annually in U.S. manufacturing infrastructure. Governments are making unprecedented investments in clean energy - which include approximately $400 billion in funding from the Inflation Reduction Act (IRA), $8 billion to establish 6–10 regional Hydrogen Hubs in the U.S., investments in carbon capture, renewable energy technologies, and other investments in clean energy sectors and technologies. All these investments come with the condition that the investment lifts distressed communities.

This article explains why investing in Appalachia and geographic regions with similar characteristics will maximize the social benefit of public investment in a Clean Innovation Ecosystem. Our case study covers the Greater Central Appalachian Voltage Valley (GCAVV) – the states of Kentucky, West Virginia, Ohio, Upstate New York, and Michigan, as well as the Central Appalachian region as defined by 56 of the 85 distressed communities of Appalachia.

Introduction

Carbon dioxide, methane, and nitrous oxide levels in Earth's atmosphere have skyrocketed to a point unseen in the past 800,000 years. This rapid warming of our planet is triggering a series of catastrophic events, which are severe and often irreversible changes in the Earth's climate system. These events include rising sea levels, more frequent and intense heat waves, droughts, floods, and other extreme weather events. The world is at a tipping point, and we face urgent challenges requiring bold, innovative solutions. Governments are making unprecedented investments, which include approximately $400 billion in funding from the Inflation Reduction Act (IRA), $8 billion to establish 6–10 regional Hydrogen Hubs in the U.S., and additional investments in carbon capture, utilization, and sequestration, rare earth elements, renewable energy technologies, and a multitude of other investments in clean energy sectors and technologies.1 The Department of Energy defines a Hydrogen Hub as a hydrogen production, storage, and demand cluster.

The energy sector is a dynamic integrated system, with developments in one sector directly or indirectly impacting numerous others. This is particularly true for the low-carbon energy sector. Many of the technologies targeted have not been deployed at scale, lack the existing infrastructure to support their deployment, and lack established markets for low carbon products (electricity, low-carbon fuels, etc.) at levels that provide sufficient incentives to justify large-scale investment.2 Clean energy produced by renewable sources and/or employs technology to decarbonize industry and power production - as defined by the Department of Energy for the Hydrogen RFP. An example of decarbonization would be carbon sequestration. Carbon sequestration is a process that captures and stores carbon dioxide in specific geological formations.

These factors, combined with the historic investments of the IRA, have resulted in forming a unique configuration of stakeholders in which public-private partnerships have formed at a scale never seen. What we are witnessing is, in fact, the creation of a Clean Innovation Ecosystem (CIE). CIE is an extension, an evolution, of the concepts proposed by Michael Porter's seminal paper "Clusters and the New Economics of Competition," published in the Harvard Business Review in 1998.3 A thriving CIE will consist of and support a suite of business (industrial) clusters appropriate for a given geographic region, where its natural resources and collaborative efforts can provide a competitive advantage. Therefore, a CIE can be viewed as a collection of sustainable business clusters working together to promote economic development in a specific geographic region and focused on creating a competitive advantage.

Porter defines clusters as not just geographic concentrations of interconnected companies and institutions in a particular field, but as comprehensive ecosystems. These clusters encompass a wide range of linked industries and other entities crucial to competition. They include, for instance, suppliers of specialized inputs such as components, machinery, and services, and providers of specialized infrastructure. Clusters often extend downstream to supply channels and customers, laterally to manufacturers of complementary products, and to companies in industries related to skills, technologies, or standard inputs. Finally, many clusters incorporate governmental and other institutions—such as universities, standards setting agencies, think tanks, vocational training providers, and trade associations—that offer specialized training, education, information, research, and technical support.

Additionally, Porter points to the fact that clusters affect competition in three ways:

1. By increasing the efficacy of companies based in the area

2. By driving the direction and pace of innovation, which underpins future productivity growth

3. By stimulating the formation of new businesses, which expands and strengthens the cluster itself

A cluster allows each member to benefit as if it had a larger scale or had joined with others formally-without contractually requiring it to sacrifice its flexibility.

Lis explains that clusters are increasingly recognized as key coordinators within innovation ecosystems, facilitating comprehensive knowledge creation processes.4 The term ecosystem was originally an ecological metaphor used to describe system-level complexities and can be applied in various contexts. An innovation ecosystem is described as a network of interconnected organizations centered around a leading firm or platform, involving participants from both the production and usage sides, and focused on generating new value through innovation. A distinguishing feature of an innovation ecosystem is the significant role that universities or other research institutions play as primary sources of research outputs.4,5

In the Greater Central Appalachia region, the Voltage Valley business cluster currently being formed provides an excellent example of what can and needs to be done for a business cluster focused on hydrogen, as proposed by the DOE Hydrogen Hub Initiative.6 The region already has other industries that can become business clusters and join the Greater Central Appalachian CIE. Collectively, the business clusters can collaboratively create a thriving CIE that can ensure distressed communities are included. West Virginia, Ohio, Southwestern Pennsylvania, Eastern Kentucky, Western New York, and Michigan (not an Appalachian State but has close economic ties to Central Appalachia)-are experiencing a new industrial revolution centered around integrated circuits (IC), electrification, recycling, and the mining of information with artificial intelligence and machine learning as the region transforms into the GCAVV.6

These Clean Innovation Ecosystems are leading to the development of Voltage Valleys (Paolillo, 2022), where electric vehicle battery plants, data centers, microchip plants, recycling facilities, and other large power users affiliated with digital transformation or electrification are located. "An example of electrification is powering a car with electricity versus a carbon-based fuel like gasoline".7 Silicon Valley and electrification are the driving forces behind the construction of these advanced manufacturing facilities and the long-term jobs created by these factories. The Voltage Valley business cluster is different than our last significant business cluster formation.8

For many years, Silicon Valley on the West Coast of the United States was the epicenter of innovation and wealth creation. Silicon Valley produced groundbreaking solutions and entrepreneurial success stories. Silicon Valley is in the greater San Francisco Bay Area and ignited the growth of venture capital firms – 30% of U.S. venture investment flowed to the greater Silicon Valley in 2023.9 However, a significant part of the Silicon Valley success story involved outsourcing manufacturing to countries like China and Asia, which shifted the U.S. to a service-oriented economy. Unlike the Silicon Valley era, where most manufacturing jobs were outsourced, Voltage Valleys will generate employment opportunities during advanced manufacturing plants' construction and operation phases. This means jobs for hardworking constructors, makers, and doers who build and create the products that drive the digital age.9

Summary of the remaining article

The Tipping Point for Distressed Communities

Despite two decades of targeted federal support, the socioeconomic conditions in America's most distressed zip codes remain unchanged. Conventional programs haven't closed the gap. But a new approach—Clean Innovation Ecosystems (CIEs)—is taking shape in Appalachia. These ecosystems combine public-private investment, advanced energy technologies, regional business clusters, and social entrepreneurship into a coordinated model capable of delivering transformational change.

At the heart of this new approach is the concept of a *Clean Innovation Ecosystem*—a regionally rooted network of institutions, people, and technologies working in concert to build sustainable industries. Unlike past efforts that emphasized short-term aid, CIEs focus on developing advanced infrastructure, skilled labor pipelines, and environmentally conscious business practices that align with long-term economic and climate goals.

The study's central case: The Greater Central Appalachian Voltage Valley (GCAVV), a geography encompassing Kentucky, West Virginia, Ohio, Upstate New York, and Michigan. This area is home to 56 of Appalachia's 85 federally designated distressed counties. What is happening here could be a national model.

Understanding Clean Innovation Ecosystems

CIEs are the next step in the evolution of economic clustering. Building on Michael Porter's landmark theory of business clusters, which posits that geographically concentrated industries and supporting institutions generate competitive advantage, CIEs add an environmental and social dimension. In these modern ecosystems, universities, vocational programs, government entities, start-ups, and Fortune 500 companies coalesce around clean energy technologies and advanced manufacturing goals.

The Department of Energy's Hydrogen Hub initiative and the Inflation Reduction Act's $400 billion investment represent catalytic forces for these ecosystems. But the true engine of transformation lies in the regional configurations of actors—what the article refers to as *Regional Voltage Valley Business Clusters* (RVVBCs). These clusters are focused on electrification, data infrastructure, hydrogen energy, and recycling.

CIEs don't just innovate. They regenerate. The defining difference is in the outcomes they prioritize: a triple bottom line—profit, people, and planet.

The Socioeconomic Landscape

The article uses the Distressed Community Index (DCI) to frame the scale of the challenge. Seven indicators define distressed communities: low high school graduation rates, high housing vacancy, joblessness, poverty, stagnant or declining employment and business establishment numbers, and low median incomes. In regions like Central Appalachia, these indicators have been persistent. But the article argues that rather than being a barrier, this socioeconomic context makes the region an ideal candidate for investment.

The argument is both moral and strategic. Investment here will yield the greatest marginal benefit in terms of lifting people out of poverty, revitalizing local economies, and restoring dignity through meaningful work. By aligning infrastructure and industry development with educational pipelines, community engagement, and environmental restoration, CIEs offer a replicable model for inclusive prosperity.

Methods and Validation

The study employed a hybrid research design combining literature review with artifact analysis—photographs, videos, media posts, government documents, and interviews. This triangulation grounded the findings in both theory and real-world dynamics. Supplementary materials (17 curated sources) add additional credibility and context.

Results

Playbook for lifting distressed communities

What factors contribute to lifting distressed communities in a Clean Innovation Ecosystem and have their citizens to flourish? See Figure 2 for a graphic representation.

Hypotheses:

1. An established Community Advisory Board (CAB) in the geography funded by a PPP.
2. State and local government agencies work together to leverage federal and private funding.
3. A known and reliable regulatory structure for industrial development

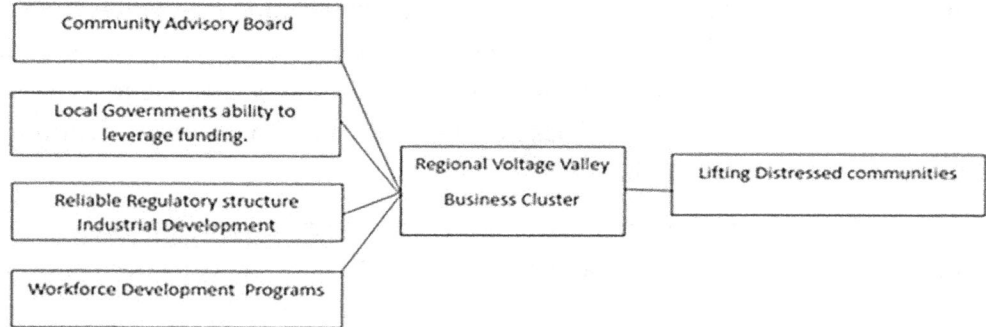

Figure 2. The factors that explain how to lift distressed communities with RVVBC as a moderator. Source: Created by the authors based on the research findings presented in the article, may be used without permission. - article citation of F1000 publication is all that is required for use work or paper.

1. Workforce development programs that are broadly supported in geography–to include K - 12 STEM programs, community colleges and technical schools, universities, and trade organizations.
2. Clean Innovation Ecosystem consisting of a diverse set of business clusters. For example: the formation of a Regional Voltage Valley Business Cluster growing and characterized by public companies and social entrepreneurship.

Our literature review shows that hypotheses 1–4 have a positive effect on lifting distressed communities. We extend the literature exploring hypothesis 5. The literature and artifacts explain our findings in Hypothesis 5.

The recent phenomenon of Regional Voltage Valley Business Clusters (RVVBC) will act as a moderator, amplifying the effects of Hypotheses 1-4.

To lift distressed communities, the following four items are recommended by literature and our research:

The establishment of Community Advisory Boards (CAB) within geographic regions funded by a Public Private Partnership (PPP).[14] Communities need to be fully engaged in the entire life cycle of an industrial development project to ensure the safety, security, and economic and environmental impacts are fully understood and the issues are fully addressed. This means the CAB needs to be fully aware of the environmental, social, and governance (ESG) issues related to industrial development in its geographic jurisdiction.[14]

State and local government agencies working together to leverage federal and private funding.[15] State and local government agencies must work with economic development organizations(EDOs)in the region to ensure all funding sources are being leveraged to the maximum extent possible. The Minority Business Development Agency (MBDA) is a federal agency that works to promote the growth and competitiveness of minority-owned businesses. By engaging with the MBDA, hydrogen hub developers in Appalachia can access resources and support to help promote diversity and inclusion in their projects, such as by partnering with minority-owned businesses or hiring a diverse workforce.[16]

The Appalachian Regional Commission (ARC) is a federal-state partnership. ARC actively works to promote economic development and enhance the quality of life in the Appalachian region. The ARC offers funding and technical assistance to projects that align with its strategic plan. This plan encompasses supporting social entrepreneurship, building community infrastructure, increasing economic opportunities, and fostering a culture of innovation. By teaming up with the ARC, investors in a hydrogen hub can ensure that their investments are in sync with the needs and priorities of the communities in the region. Moreover, the Arc funds projects prioritizing community benefit initiatives and supporting diversity and minority populations.[17]

A known and reliable regulatory structure for industrial development.[18] All legally required regulators must be identified and fully informed about industrial development activities. Agreements will need to be reached as to the roles and responsibilities of each regulator and how any overlap in responsibilities will be addressed. As part of the regulatory structure, each industrial development project must have a single point of contact/entity capable of responding to and addressing regulatory issues.[18]

Workforce development programs that are broadly supported in geography – to include K-12 STEM programs, community colleges and technical schools, universities, and trade organizations.[19] For each industrial development project, there needs to be a point of contact/entity to address workforce development issues; the entity should be able to coordinate with existing workforce development programs in the region and provide them a detailed description of their workforce needs, including required training and certification.[20] STEM (Science, Technology, Engineering, and Math) education is a critical foundation for workforce development, particularly for high-tech industries such as hydrogen production and fuel cell technology. K-12 STEM programs in Appalachia can provide students with early exposure to STEM fields, cultivate interest and enthusiasm, and help develop a skilled workforce for future high-tech industries.[20] Universities in Appalachia can play a vital role in advancing the development and implementation of hydrogen hub technology. By offering specialized education and training programs, universities can help to ensure that the region has a skilled workforce capable of supporting the growth of the hydrogen economy.[21] The presence of research institutions like the University of Kentucky's Center for Applied Energy Research (CAER) underscores the potential for collaboration between academia and industry in the development to hydrogen technology. CAER's work on hydrogen production and storage is a prime example of the kind of cutting-edge research that universities in the region can conduct to advance the field.[21] Moreover, universities can collaborate with industry partners to develop workforce training programs that are tailored to the specific needs of the hydrogen hub industry. By aligning their training programs with the requirements of the industry, universities can help to ensure that the region has a workforce that is well-prepared to meet the demands of the hydrogen economy. This kind of collaboration between industry and academia is key to the successful development and implementation of hydrogen technology.[21]

Universities, Trade Organizations, and Local Models

Institutions such as Ohio University, West Virginia University, Virginia Tech, and Marshall University are playing a pivotal role. Their research centers are focused on hydrogen energy, fuel cell development, and carbon capture. Programs like the Social Enterprise Ecosystem (SEE) and LIGHTS support small businesses, makerspaces, and incubators throughout Appalachia.

Trade groups like the Appalachian Hydrogen and Carbon Capture Center (AHCCC) and NETL are nurturing talent and collaboration. National organizations such as the Fuel Cell and Hydrogen Energy Association (FCHEA) provide training and certification frameworks.

These efforts align with a growing global focus on ESG metrics and net-zero carbon targets. As major manufacturers adopt sustainability mandates, regions like GCAVV gain new leverage as sites for production reshoring and circular economy innovations.

From Silicon Valley to Voltage Valley

One of the article's key narratives contrasts *Silicon Valley* with the emerging *Voltage Valleys* of Appalachia. While Silicon Valley offshore production and emphasized digital innovation, Voltage Valleys prioritize on shoring of clean industrial capabilities. They are building factories—battery plants, solar panel lines, semiconductor foundries—and hiring local workers to do it.

Notably, companies like GM, Ford, Honda, Intel, and Micron have announced or completed multibillion-dollar facilities in Lords town (OH), Glendale (KY), and Syracuse (NY). These investments are anchored by proximity to sustainable power sources, transmission lines, and a workforce steeped in industrial heritage.

Appalachia is not returning to coal; it is rising through clean hydrogen, advanced silicon production, and digitally enabled manufacturing.

The Piketon Project: A Case Study

One illustrative case is the Piketon Gaseous Diffusion Plant in Southern Ohio. Decommissioned in 2011, the site is now planned to be transformed by a Trillium H2 Power into a $1.5 billion clean hydrogen facility. The new plant will generate 500 metric tons of hydrogen daily, power a greenhouse farm, and use carbon capture to achieve near-zero emissions. What makes the project particularly innovative is its embrace of the *Mondragon Cooperative Model*, which prioritizes local ownership and profit-sharing.

This model—in which workers are co-owners, and a portion of profits goes to local nonprofits—is redefining what sustainable industry looks like in a post-coal economy. The digital twin modeling and human-machine collaboration embedded in the plant's design underscore the high-tech future now unfolding in Appalachia.

A New Industrial Identity

At its core, this article proposes a new narrative for industrial development in America: one rooted in justice, environmental stewardship, and collaborative innovation. In GCAVV, manufacturing construction spending has already surpassed $200 billion annually, with another $600 billion in projects announced. Every $1 billion adds an estimated 6,300 construction jobs, meaning Appalachia could add 63,000 jobs over the next five years in just one region.

This is not charity. This is strategy. With the right mix of policy, investment, and community empowerment, Appalachia is positioned to drive the clean energy economy—not as a bystander, but as a builder.

Conclusion

Clean Innovation Ecosystems are more than theory. In the Greater Central Appalachian Voltage Valley, they are becoming reality—powered by advanced manufacturing, inclusive investment, and collaborative governance. The formation of RVVBCs, the support of educational and trade institutions, and the emphasis on ESG principles are not only lifting communities but rewriting the playbook for American manufacturing.

The stakes are high. But so is the potential. Appalachia, long seen as left behind, is emerging as the proving ground for a new industrial age—one where sustainability, equity, and economic revitalization move forward together.

VOLTAGE VALLEY REVOLUTION™

Extended data

The supplementary materials provide comprehensive documentation of the sources, including hyperlinks to government reports, industry analyses, academic studies, and news articles relevant to the Clean Innovation Ecosystem in the Greater Appalachian Voltage Valley. These resources offer a diverse range of perspectives and up-to-date information on the subject matter. For additional details or specific data inquiries, readers are encouraged to consult the supplementary materials provided.

The artifacts used in the research can be found on the websites mentioned below:

Brookings Institution Report on Distressed Communities | Community Voice and Power Sharing Guidebook | Community Advisory Board Toolkit | Business Strategy and the Environment | Why State and Local Relationships Matter | Economic Policy Institute Report | Personal View: Ohio is Winner in Race to Create Voltage Valleys | A Typology of Social Entrepreneurs | Economic Impacts of Coal-Fired Power Plants | Houston Region Poised to Become Global Clean Hydrogen Hub | Innovation Ecosystems: A Conceptual Review | Flourishing: The New Spirit of Business Enterprise | Doing Interpretive Research | The Importance of Workforce Development | Working with Value: Industry-specific Approaches to Workforce Development | Center for Applied Energy Research (CAER) **National Research Center for Coal and Energy**

Acknowledgments

This article is informed by the past 13 years of ongoing work carried out by Ohio University's Voinovich School of Leadership and Public Service PORTS future Program. The program is planning for, developing, and pursuing the redevelopment of a federal facility in southern Ohio into a decarbonized energy production and sustainable manufacturing complex. This effort will bring economic stability and prosperity back to the communities in the region while also addressing many national priorities related to energy independence, reshoring of vital supply chains, advancing the clean energy economy, and combatting the climate crisis. PORTS future is carried out in partnership with local, regional, national, and federal entities, organized labor, private industry, and many other site stakeholders. Program activities include creating public-private partnerships, community outreach and engagement, data analyses and geographic information systems, economic impact analysis, workforce analysis, K-12 STEM education, and conducting applied environmental work, among other items. The PORTS future Program is funded by a grant from the US Department of Energy Office of Environmental Management Portsmouth/Paducah Project Office.

Chapter 34
AI-Powered Digital Spatial Intelligence: Empowering Asset Owners in Architecture, Engineering, and Construction to Maximize Operational Efficiency, Sustainability, and Lifecycle Value

Dr. William Paolillo *1, Phil Nagle*2, Dustin Lopez*3

Abstract

Digital Spatial Intelligence (DSI) combines BIM and IoT-driven analytics to transform static 3D models into dynamic operational insight across a building's lifecycle. This study uses a mixed-method approach, including interviews, materials analysis, and industry case studies. We look at how Digital Smart Infrastructure (DSI) helps connect Building Information Modeling (BIM), the Internet of Things (IoT), and operational performance. Qualitative findings indicate that DSI fosters proactive, data-driven workflows and improves collaboration, as real-time sensor integration keeps digital models up-to-date and actionable harmony-at.com. Quantitative results from case studies demonstrate significant performance gains. For example, smart building implementations achieved a 15% reduction in HVAC energy use desapex.com, and predictive maintenance strategies lowered maintenance costs by 18–25% com4.no. In the construction phase, DSI-enabled digital twin platforms have reduced project delays researchgate.net and cut change orders by 32% link.springer.com. These outcomes underscore DSI's value in converting one-off BIM datasets into "living" models for continuous monitoring and optimization, supporting predictive insights and lifecycle efficiency. In conclusion, DSI is a critical integrative framework that turns static spatial data into real-time Intelligence, enabling lifecycle optimization and effectively bridging BIM, IoT, and operational performance rics.org.

Keywords: Digital Spatial Intelligence; Building Information Modeling; Internet of Things; Digital Twin; Smart Buildings; Lifecycle Optimization; Architect, Engineering, Construction.

1. Introduction: The Dawn of Digital Spatial Intelligence in the Built Environment

1.1 The "Static Playbook" Analogy Revisited

The Architecture, Engineering, and Construction (AEC) industry is shifting from reliance on static two-dimensional drawings to interactive, data-rich three-dimensional models. Decades of practice based on paper or CAD blueprints have led to inefficiencies—projects remain prone to errors, delays, and cost overruns as information gets "lost" once construction ends. Recent technological advances offer a remedy: As one industry analysis noted, "3D modeling breathes life into flat 2D drawings and enhances construction projects through improved timelines, cost management, safety, and structural integrity" (Novatr, 2025). In other words, converting traditional blueprints into dynamic 3D digital models can significantly improve project outcomes.

However, even these enhanced models often fall short in practice. Like a football team would not rely solely on a static playbook without watching game footage and adjusting strategy during a live match, the AEC industry frequently underutilizes its digital playbooks after the design phase. Building Information Models (BIM) are created and shelved, rarely updated or leveraged during the operational "game." This disconnect represents a tremendous loss of what we define as operational Intelligence.

1.2 Why Digital Spatial Intelligence Now?

This paper defines Digital Spatial Intelligence (DSI) as an approach that treats spatial data as static design artifacts and living digital assets continuously enriched with real-time information. DSI integrates Building Information Models, digital twin technology, Internet of Things (IoT) sensor feeds, and analytical tools (e.g., AI/ML algorithms) into a unified system that provides ongoing insight, prediction, and decision support throughout an asset's lifecycle. Instead of remaining fixed after design, the digital representation of a facility evolves alongside the physical asset, enabling proactive management.

This concept builds upon the progression from BIM to digital twin: a BIM model captures design intent, whereas a digital twin "enables virtual interaction with [an] asset" across its lifecycle (Matterport, 2025). For instance, the WillowTwin platform used in the Dallas Smart District project demonstrates how real-time data integration allows facilities managers to monitor HVAC performance, optimize lighting, and improve energy use across multiple properties.

By leveraging IoT data and intelligent analytics, DSI transforms a one-time static model into a continuously updated source of operational insight. This transformation is now possible due to a convergence of enabling technologies—IoT, AI, semantic data frameworks, and real-time connectivity. The National University of Singapore's Smart Campus illustrates this by connecting over 5,000 sensors to digital twins that inform space utilization, energy consumption, and environmental comfort.

At the same time, buildings are becoming more complex, energy-intensive, and closely scrutinized for sustainability performance. These pressures demand more intelligent systems. Digital Spatial Intelligence responds by transforming static models into dynamic, predictive, and context-aware digital platforms that support operational excellence, cost control, sustainability goals, and human-centered outcomes.

Despite the promise of these innovations, implementation in practice is still nascent. Many organizations create detailed 3D models during design and construction, but those models often are not utilized after project handoff. The result is a wealth of spatial data that remains untapped for facilities management, safety monitoring, or strategic planning. This research addresses the gap between available digital data and its practical use in operations. We specifically investigate how 3D BIM data can be converted into actionable operational insight—identifying challenges, requirements, and best practices for achieving accurate digital spatial Intelligence in real-world settings.

The remainder of this paper is organized as follows: Section II reviews related work and industry trends in bridging design data to operations. Section III explains the mixed-methods research design, including interviews and artifact analysis. Section IV presents the findings, and Section V discusses their implications in the context of AI Powered DSI. Finally, Section VI concludes with recommendations and future research directions.

2. Literature Review and Epistemological Framework

Early efforts to enhance construction and asset management through digital technology have focused on Building Information Modeling (BIM). BIM provides a 3D digital representation of building components, improving visualization and coordination during design and construction. However, conventional BIM usage ends at project completion, capturing an "as-designed" snapshot. Based on our interviews, the BIM model is rarely updated over time. Unlike a static BIM model, a digital twin allows for real-time monitoring and simulations. It dynamically updates with maintenance logs, IOT sensor readings, and user inputs, enabling ongoing performance analysis. According to [Matterport's industry guide](), the BIM model is used for design visualization, whereas the digital twin "enables virtual interaction with [the] asset" during its operational phase. This key difference underpins the shift needed to achieve DSI: moving from static project files to interactive models linked with live data.

2.1 BIM as the Static Base

BIM sets the stage for digital models of buildings and structures. BIM offers rich geometric detail, embedded metadata, and multi-disciplinary coordination tools. BIM leads to improvements in clash detection, design collaboration, and the accuracy of documentation ([Novatr]()). However, BIM is primarily used during the design and construction phases. As-built conditions diverge from models over time, and the static nature of BIM creates a "digital cliff"—where high-value data is no longer maintained or usable in operations. The potential of BIM to inform long-term performance is unrealized, and its value to facilities managers remains limited unless connected to live data and dynamic updates ([Matterport]()).

2.2 Digital Twins for Synchronization

Digital Twins (DTs) emerged to bridge the gap between virtual design models and real-world operation. Defined as data-connected replicas of physical assets, Digital Twins synchronize real-time conditions such as equipment status, temperature, and occupancy (Matterport). However, many Digital Twins operate as visual monitoring tools rather than cognitive engines. They mirror reality but rarely interpret it. Without embedded Intelligence, semantic relationships, or predictive logic, most Digital Twins function more like advanced dashboards than autonomous systems. The next step—Digital Spatial Intelligence—builds on this by embedding context, prediction, and actionability into the digital-physical feedback loop.

2.3 Semantic Technologies for Context

Semantic technologies are software systems and data frameworks that allow machines to understand and reason about data based on its meaning, not just its format. Currently, databases in the AEC industry store data in rows and columns without context; semantic technologies add relationships and structure, enabling machines to interpret how different pieces of information connect.

At the heart of semantic technologies are ontologies—standardized vocabularies that define objects, properties, and their relationships. For example:

- Room A is part of Floor 2
- Thermostat 12 controls Room A
- AHU-3 serves Zone 4

These relationships allow systems to interpret data spatially and functionally.

Key semantic frameworks include:

- BRICK Schema: Represents building systems in a consistent, machine-readable way.
- IFC (Industry Foundation Classes): Platform-neutral schema for exchanging data across BIM and facility management tools.
- SIMLAB: Integrates simulation and live data into a cohesive operational system for multi-domain reasoning.

These frameworks create digital representations of building systems and their interactions. These systems facilitate real-time optimization and cognitive automation.

2.4 AI and Machine Learning for Cognition

AI and ML transform Digital Twins from reactive systems to intelligent infrastructures. AI enables predictive maintenance, real-time optimization, and adaptive behavior. For instance:

- ML algorithms forecast equipment failure.
- AI-driven HVAC adjusts based on occupancy forecasts.
- Optimization engines balance energy, comfort, and cost.

AI closes the loop between sensing, reasoning, and acting, transforming static models into adaptive systems ([Hexagon](#)).

2.5 IoT and the Cost Collapse of Digitization

The proliferation of IoT devices and affordable 3D scanning has democratized access to spatial Intelligence. Sensors now offer real-time data on environmental and operational variables, while reality capture technologies like LiDAR make spatial modeling faster and cheaper. These advances make it possible for schools, small businesses, and towns to deploy DSI affordably, accelerating adoption at scale ([Forbes](#)).

2.6 Industry Trends and Practical Barriers

So, how do we operationalize digital twins? Companies like Hexagon have created platforms to help manage and simulate real-time industrial operations. Companies like Hexagon have created platforms to help manage and simulate real-time industrial operations. Using advanced technology in operations has many advantages. It improves situational awareness, allowing teams to respond to changes quickly. This enables predictive maintenance to spot equipment problems before they lead to failures, reducing downtime. However, there are still challenges:

1. Siloed Data: A gap between design and operations creates fragmented data, which is difficult to analyze and make decisions.
2. Skills Gaps: A lack of trained staff limits companies' use of advanced technologies and analytics.

Overcoming these challenges is crucial for organizations to harness advanced operational technologies' potential fully.

Literature indicates few strategies for updating BIM post-construction or quantifying digital twin ROI. Our research addresses this by analyzing project artifacts and interviewing professionals to explore how to transform static data into dynamic Intelligence.

2.7 DSI for the Triple Bottom Line

DSI unites BIM, Digital Twins, semantic modeling, AI, IoT, and 3D scanning into a cognitive framework. It repositions buildings as adaptive learning systems that manage complexity over time and support the Triple Bottom Line:

- **People**: Enhanced comfort and experience
- **Planet**: Resource efficiency and sustainability
- **Profit**: Reduced costs and performance-based contracting

DSI is no longer aspirational. Enabled by affordable tech and proven use cases, it is now an essential infrastructure for modern facilities ([Novatr](#)).

3. Methodology

We adopted a **mixed-methods research design** combining qualitative interviews, data sources, and the literature to explore the research questions. The study consisted of two main components: semi-structured interviews and artifact analysis.

A. Interviews: We conducted 30 semi-structured interviews with stakeholders involved in the Voltage Valley Revolution™. Dr. Paolillo describes the Voltage Valley Revolution™ as a transformative movement to revitalize distressed communities in Appalachia and similar regions through developing a Clean Innovation Ecosystem (CIE). This ecosystem encompasses public-private partnerships focused on sustainable technologies, including clean energy, advanced manufacturing, and digital innovation (Crain's Business 2022). Participants included diverse perspectives – engineers, developers, operators, labor, and workforce advocates – and commented on how they encountered technology. Each interview lasted approximately 60 minutes and focused on the participants' journey in the new industrial revolution. These transcripts are available upon request. The qualitative data from these interviews form a narrative of current practices and mindsets regarding technology in the AEC industry today and the future.

B. Artifact Analysis: In addition to interviews, we analyzed relevant artifacts to provide contextual and quantitative evidence. These artifacts included project documents such as BIM models, as-built drawings, maintenance logs, and digital twin dashboards from selected case projects. We utilized previously completed construction projects where BIM was implemented, and the facilities included at least pilot digital twin systems.

By triangulating insights from interviews with hard evidence from project artifacts, our methodology increases the validity of findings. The combination of methods allows us to report what practitioners are saying about technology and compare it against what is *happening* in their projects and lived experiences. This approach helps to identify discrepancies between perception and practice and to ground recommendations in observed reality.

4. Findings and Analysis

Bridging the Gap Between Promise and Practice

AI Powered Digital Spatial Intelligence (DSI) holds significant promise for transforming facility operations, yet its practical adoption remains limited. Drawing on thirty semi-structured interviews and artifact analysis, this section categorizes key insights into three thematic areas: (1) Current Use of 3D Data in Operations, (2) Barriers to Effective Implementation, and (3) Opportunities and Benefits of DSI.

4.1 Current Use of 3D Data in Operations

Most organizations still treat Building Information Models (BIM) and 3D data as design deliverables rather than operational tools. Interviews revealed that while nearly all respondents create detailed BIM models during design and construction, only a minority continue using them during operations.

A case study at Mount Sinai West Hospital in New York City revealed that despite several renovations and mechanical upgrades, the BIM models used during construction remained outdated for over two years after occupancy. This revealed a significant gap between design modeling and actual use.

However, forward-thinking organizations are breaking this trend. The University of British Columbia's Smart Campus project uses live 3D digital twins for space utilization, emergency simulations, and HVAC optimization. Their real-time dashboards integrate IoT feeds and predictive analytics to reduce energy costs and improve occupant comfort. These pilots illustrate that dynamic, real-time usage is feasible and impactful.

4.2 Barriers to Effective Implementation

Implementation challenges fall into five key categories:

- **Organizational Silos**: BIM is typically managed by design and construction teams, while operations staff lack ownership or familiarity. This "over-the-wall" handoff leads to neglect post-construction (Gallaher et al., 2020).

- **Skills and Training Gaps**: Many facilities teams are unfamiliar with 3D software or semantic modeling. Without proper training, they cannot leverage complex models in daily operations (Lin & Lucas, 2023).

- **Integration Difficulties**: At the Federal Ministry of the Interior building in Frankfurt, a smart building pilot under the EU Smart Spaces Initiative encountered delays due to software incompatibility between legacy HVAC systems and its 3D dashboard interface. These issues extended the project timeline by 18 months.

- **Cost and ROI Uncertainty**: Management is reluctant to invest in DSI without a short-term return. High upfront software, sensors, and integration costs make the business case difficult without benchmarks (FM Benchmarking Report, 2024).

- **Cultural Resistance**: Some professionals still prefer analog methods. Skepticism toward digital workflows persists, mainly due to past failures or inadequate onboarding.

4.3 Opportunities and Benefits of DSI

- **Predictive Maintenance**: At an ST Telemedia Global Data Centre in Singapore, a 3D-integrated IoT dashboard detected abnormal vibrations in a chiller pump. The issue was resolved proactively, preventing a $250,000 failure. Predictive DSI maintenance can reduce downtime by 20–30% and maintenance costs by up to 25% (Siemens, 2023).

- **Optimized Space Utilization**: The City of Helsinki conducted a pilot combining sensor data with 3D models across six municipal buildings, achieving a 12% improvement in space use by reallocating underutilized areas.

- **Enhanced Communication**: In the Dudley Council school district (UK), DSI-enabled dashboards made complex building data accessible to administrators. This saved an estimated 120 staff hours annually and improved decision-making transparency (Smart Building Alliance UK).

- **Lifecycle Efficiency**: Smart buildings using BrainBox AI and Siemens Smart Infrastructure report 15–25% energy savings and 30–40% HVAC efficiency gains. Respondents also noted longer equipment life and fewer failures.

- **Strategic Differentiation**: Global design firm IBI Group (now part of Arcadis) reported a 12% increase in bid success rate after demonstrating real-time asset monitoring using ArcGIS and BIM 360.

4.4 Case Study: McCormick Place Convention Center, Chicago

McCormick Place, one of North America's largest convention centers, offers a strong example of Digital Smart Infrastructure (DSI). Historically dependent on static BIM files and fragmented FM systems, it implemented a semantic digital twin powered by AI and IoT. The result: a 32% drop in energy costs and a 40% improvement in maintenance response time over three years—saving $1.2 million in operational expenses (Hexagon, 2025).

4.5 Summary

The findings show a sector in transition. While DSI tools are available, adoption remains inconsistent. Legacy habits, skill gaps, and uncertainty about benefits hinder progress. However, adopters report real outcomes: 25% maintenance cost savings, 40% energy efficiency gains, and stronger internal communication. As access to real-time feedback grows, the focus is no longer *on whether* DSI will be used but *on how* it will be scaled to drive lifecycle value, resilience, and equity.

5. Discussion: Operationalizing Digital Spatial Intelligence (DSI)

Our results show that using Digital Spatial Intelligence (DSI) in the built environment can bring positive changes, but there are challenges. The conversation around DSI must go beyond technological capabilities to consider its systemic, business, ethical, and social implications. This section explains our findings about the overall vision for DSI. We also discuss the implications for business strategy, product lifecycle, and changes in the industry.

5.1 From Technology to Organizational Transformation

Our study confirms that the availability of advanced tools alone does not ensure their practical use. BIM models, laser scans, and IoT sensor networks frequently go underutilized. The organizational barriers—status quo workflows, limited training, and resistance to change—are as critical as the technologies themselves. Interviewees repeatedly referenced this disconnect, describing BIM models that remain untouched post-handover. This underutilization echoes

Lopez's observation that much of the built environment's digital data is "used once... and forgotten."

A cultural and organizational shift is required. Roles like "Digital Facility Manager" can help ensure that models evolve alongside the assets they represent. Some organizations have begun embedding digital twin responsibilities into core operations, fostering accountability and continuous engagement with live data systems. Technology alone is not sufficient. A powerful BIM or digital twin model often goes dormant post-construction due to a lack of ownership, training, and workflows prioritizing static deliverables over dynamic engagement. As a part of the construction and operation plan for the asset, we need to establish a digital continuity plan. Assigning responsibility for model maintenance and system updates—is a practical first step toward making DSI a core operational tool.

5.2 Integration and Interoperability

Technical integration challenges persist despite the promise of platforms like Hexagon. Participants voiced frustrations with middleware requirements, incompatible standards, and siloed systems. This highlights the need for clearer implementation frameworks—such as ISO 19650 for BIM data governance—and sector-wide alignment around open APIs and semantic data models.

Integrating AI and real-time data into legacy systems remains complex. Even with open protocols, IT infrastructure and facilities teams often operate in silos, making holistic transformation difficult. Best-practice playbooks that outline DSI implementation in stages—starting with pilot programs, quantifying early ROI, and scaling based on lessons learned—can help build momentum. Demonstrating ROI through these small-scale implementations—such as the 10% space utilization gain we documented—builds internal credibility for larger DSI investments.

5.3 Business and Lifecycle Implications

Strategic Benefits

DSI represents a shift from static, schedule-based facilities management to continuous, data-informed optimization. Real-time feedback loops—powered by IoT sensors, AI models, and semantic frameworks—enable buildings to learn, adapt, and perform autonomously. This design translates into longer asset life, improved energy efficiency, and heightened occupant satisfaction.

DSI supports the triple bottom line:

- **Profit** through reduced lifecycle costs, predictive maintenance, and better capital planning.
- **People** through improved air quality, comfort, and user experiences;
- **Planet** through real-time emissions tracking, energy optimization, and regulatory compliance.

Organizations under pressure to meet Environmental, Social, and Governance (ESG) metrics can leverage DSI for transparent reporting and third-party validation. Facilities can show real-time

IAQ (indoor air quality), emissions trends, and occupancy wellness data, enhancing trust with regulators and investors.

New Business Models

DSI enables new models such as **"Building-as-a-Service,"** where performance, comfort, and uptime can be sold as recurring services. This supports outcome-based contracts, and a building owner can shift risk and accountability to service providers (JLL, technologies 2023).

Vendors can provide regular updates for digital twins, ongoing commissioning, and analytics subscriptions. These services align with investors' growing demand for long-term operational insights over one-time design outputs. Smart contracts tied to performance guarantees—like energy savings or equipment uptime—become viable with continuous verification enabled by DSI (IEE 2025).

These shifts redefine economic relationships in the built environment, turning infrastructure into platforms for ongoing value delivery and continuous optimization.

Portfolio Optimization

DSI offers profound portfolio-level advantages. When applied at scale, cross-site analytics support benchmarking, risk prediction, and capital planning. For example, a large university or hospital system can prioritize retrofits based on energy performance trends or track equipment longevity across sites.

Smart command centers and cloud-based twin platforms allow a few operators to manage dozens of buildings with synchronized insights. Reducing operating costs boosts resilience and improves data-driven growth plans. It also helps cut carbon emissions and update systems. DS provides the efficiency and quick responses needed as operations become more complex because of energy price changes and labor shortages.

5.4 Ethics and Human-Centered Design

AI Powered DSI systems must ensure privacy, transparency, and explainability. Tenants should know what data is collected, why, and how it will be used. They should also be able to opt into controls and receive meaningful feedback about how their environment responds.

Explainable AI is critical. Systems that adjust lighting, access, or HVAC in response to predictive logic must remain auditable. Reliance on black-box systems risks undermining trust. Privacy-by-design principles—such as user consent, data minimization, and granular controls—must be embedded in all DSI implementations.

Interfaces should support users with different levels of digital skills, physical abilities, and cognitive needs. It is also crucial to prioritize cybersecurity to protect systems that ensure safety and manage the environment. In human-centered design, we focus not only on function but also on making things accessible, empowering users, and engaging ethically.

5.5 Alignment with Industry 4.0

AI Powered DSI aligns directly with Industry 4.0 principles—automation, digitization, and self-learning systems. While the factory floor has adopted cyber-physical systems, most buildings have not. SI brings that logic to schools, hospitals, offices, and cities.

Feedback loops, real-time sensing, and digital control layers mean buildings can now participate in adaptive networks. For example, transportation systems can respond to occupancy in nearby buildings, or municipal planners can coordinate services based on digital twin models of public infrastructure. Integration across sectors—including energy, logistics, and public services—positions DSI as a key building block for smart cities.

Parametric and generative design, augmented by live performance data, also supports faster iteration and optimization in design and operations. This mirrors the advances seen in advanced manufacturing, digital fabrication, modular retrofits, and robotics. This is now becoming a reality in the built environment.

5.6 Social Equity Potential

Finally, DSI can help address the equity gaps in building quality and environmental health. Intelligent systems have mainly been used in high-end properties. AI Powered DSI provides affordable ways to bring these benefits to schools, hospitals, public housing, and community centers. Here are some examples:

- **Schools** that adjust lighting and air quality based on occupancy to enhance learning outcomes.
- **Affordable housing** that uses automation to lower utility costs and increase resident control.
- **Public buildings** that leverage DSI for disaster response, air quality alerts, and energy resilience.

The key is intentional design. Regulatory standards, public-private partnerships, and outcome-based funding models will be essential. Quality must be embedded in the design and distribution of AI Powered DSI technologies if we are to realize their full societal benefit. In the modern era, access to smart buildings must become as fundamental as access to clean water or electricity.

The future of intelligent infrastructure is not just about smarter buildings but about building a smarter, more inclusive, and more sustainable society.

6. Conclusion

AI-Powered Digital Spatial Intelligence (DSI) will reshape how we design, operate, and extract value from the built environment. AI Powered DSI transforms buildings from static structures into dynamic, responsive systems by integrating Building Information Modeling (BIM), Digital Twins, Artificial Intelligence (AI), semantic data, and real-time IOT sensing. AI Powered DSI is both a technological system and a strategic asset—capable of driving down operational costs, maximizing asset lifespan, and enabling better decisions across the architecture, engineering, and construction (AEC) lifecycle.

The implications are profound for asset owners. AI Powered DSI delivers measurable gains in energy efficiency, predictive maintenance, space utilization, and lifecycle ROI. It also positions owners to meet evolving ESG goals and regulatory standards through transparent, data-driven operations. The value extends beyond performance—it enables differentiation in a competitive marketplace where intelligent infrastructure is increasingly expected.

AI-Powered DSI reimagines buildings as continuously evolving platforms capable of learning from occupants, adapting to external conditions, and aligning with organizational priorities. This represents a shift from time-bound project thinking to an era of adaptive infrastructure, where every facility becomes a source of strategic Intelligence.

This vision will depend on more than technology. It requires a culture shift across disciplines - designers, engineers, operators, and executives. They will need to working through shared digital models and unified goals. It also demands ethical governance, inclusive design, and investment in skills that bridge the digital and physical worlds.

As the AEC industry faces mounting pressures - from climate risk and energy volatility to demographic change and digital disruption. AI-Powered DSI emerges not just as a tool but as a foundational capability. The next industrial revolution in the built environment is underway. It begins by turning static blueprints into living, thinking systems that serve people and the planet and profit equally.

Future Research Directions

To fully realize the potential of AI-powered Digital Spatial Intelligence, several research priorities must be addressed:

- **AI Explainability in Operational Contexts**: Investigating how AI decisions, especially those affecting energy use, safety, and comfort, can be made transparent and auditable in real-time environments.

- **DSI for Small-Scale and Public Infrastructure**: Expanding use cases beyond commercial real estate to schools, public housing, and municipalities, ensuring equity in digital infrastructure.

- **Cross-Disciplinary Skill Development**: Establishing new educational models and certifications that prepare professionals to manage, interpret, and design with DSI.

- **Longitudinal Impact Studies**: Measuring the long-term financial, environmental, and social returns of DSI deployments across diverse building types and geographic contexts.

Future research must bridge the technical, social, and policy dimensions of AI Powered DSI to guide responsible adoption and ensure the technology delivers on its transformative promise.

Chapter 35
Unlocking the Future of Clean Energy: DOE Programs

All projects must meet financial requirements - "The real value of an investment is seen in the lives it transforms and the futures it secures." **Inspired by Michael Peck**

The road to a sustainable future is paved with innovation, collaboration, and strategic investment. In the heart of Appalachia and the U.S., the Voltage Valley Revolution™ is a mix of advanced manufacturing, clean energy, and revitalized communities. At the core of this change are programs led by the U.S. Department of Energy's (DOE) Loan Programs Office (LPO). The Inflation Reduction Act (IRA) bolstered these programs. They fund projects that aim to reshape American industry. The links and writing is by no means a complete list but will get you started in the right direction.

The Loan Programs Office: Financing the Next Industrial Revolution

The DOE's LPO plays a crucial role in financing innovative projects that bring clean Energy and advanced technology to the forefront of American industry. Through its Title 17 Clean Energy Financing Program, the LPO offers loan guarantees to projects that reduce greenhouse gas emissions and substantially benefit the environment and economy. These initiatives align perfectly with the objectives of the Voltage Valley Revolution™, which seeks to re-establish America's industrial prowess through sustainable practices.

The LPO's **Title 17 Project Readiness Checklist** outlines eight critical readiness criteria that projects must meet to qualify for financing. A requirement includes

- demonstrating technical and financial viability,
- having a well-defined project plan and
- ensuring compliance with environmental regulations like the National Environmental Policy Act (NEPA).

The readiness checklist serves as a roadmap for applicants, guiding them through the rigorous requirements that ensure only the most promising and impactful projects receive support.

Among the detailed resources available is the **LPO Financing Overview**, a 24-page presentation that comprehensively examines how the LPO structures its loans, evaluates projects, and manages risks. This document is indispensable for potential applicants seeking to understand the complexities of the financing process and the strategic benefits of LPO involvement, igniting their motivation to explore these opportunities further.

For state-level initiatives, the LPO also offers the **State Energy Financing Institution (SEFI) Introduction**, a 12-slide overview that explains how states can craft eligible financing institutions and access federal support. This program is particularly relevant for regions like Appalachia, where state energy offices and local governments are pivotal in fostering clean energy development and economic growth.

Here are some valuable materials for those interested in exploring these opportunities further:

- Handout-title-17-guidance-overview (energy.gov)
- *(Link: https://www.energy.gov/sites/default/files/2023-03/handout-title-17-guidance-overview.pdf)*
- Title 17 Lending Reference Guide
- *(Link: https://www.energy.gov/sites/default/files/2023-03/title-17-lending-reference-guide.pdf)*
- *The Title 17 Lending Reference Guide provides an in-depth look at the loan structuring process, offering detailed insights into how loans are arranged, the conditions under which they are granted, and the specific financial terms that apply. This guide is essential for anyone looking to navigate the complexities of the Title 17 program and secure financing for clean energy projects.*
- Title 17, Energy Infrastructure Reinvestment, aka 1706
- *(Link: https://www.energy.gov/sites/default/files/2023-03/t17-downloadable-handout-eir-projects.pdf)*
- Top 10 Questions for Prospective Applicants, as of December 21, 2023
- *(Link: https://www.energy.gov/lpo/articles/top-10-questions-all-applicants-should-ask-applying-lpo)*
- *This document addresses the most common concerns and inquiries from potential applicants. It offers valuable advice on the application process, eligibility criteria, and what applicants can expect as they seek LPO financing.*
- Frequently Asked Questions (FAQ)
- *(Link: https://www.energy.gov/lpo/title-17-frequently-asked-questions)*
- *The FAQ document provides clear and concise answers to frequently asked questions about the Title 17 program, including eligibility, application steps, and the types of projects that qualify. It is an essential resource for applicants to ensure they meet all requirements.*
- Narrative of Loan Process and Details on Third-Party Advisors

- *(Link: https://www.energy.gov/lpo/articles/pricing-lpo-financing-program)*

The Impact of the Inflation Reduction Act

The Inflation Reduction Act (IRA) passage has significantly expanded the scope and reach of LPO programs. The IRA provides substantial funding and incentives to reduce carbon emissions, enhance energy efficiency, and promote the deployment of renewable energy technologies. These incentives are designed to catalyze private sector investment and ensure that America remains at the forefront of the global clean energy transition. The IRA's role in providing financial support and incentives for clean energy projects, particularly in regions like Appalachia, is crucial and should be thoroughly understood by potential applicants.

One of the most significant aspects of the IRA is its focus on community benefits, particularly in economically distressed areas. The **Community Benefits Plan** is a critical component of any application to the LPO, requiring projects to demonstrate how they will create jobs, promote environmental justice, and contribute to local economic development. A projects community benefits plan aligns with the goals of the Voltage Valley Revolution™, which seeks to uplift Appalachian communities through sustainable industrial growth.

The LPO's commitment to transparency and accountability is further underscored by its obligations under the Freedom of Information Act (FOIA). While navigating these legal requirements can be complex, the LPO provides clear guidelines and recommends that applicants seek experienced FOIA legal counsel to ensure compliance.

Navigating the Application Process

The journey to secure LPO financing is rigorous but rewarding. Applicants begin by familiarizing themselves with the **Title 17 Lending Reference Guide**, which details the loan structuring process and provides insights into the financial terms and conditions. This is followed by a thorough review of the **Top 10 Questions for Prospective Applicants** and the **Frequently Asked Questions (FAQ)** documents, which address common concerns and provide practical advice for crafting a strong application.

A key consideration for applicants is the cost structure associated with LPO loans. The LPO outlines specific fees, including external advisor fees, facility fees due at financial close, and annual maintenance fees. These costs, though substantial, are offset by the long-term economic and environmental benefits of the projects they support. The LPO's **Interest Rate Spread** guidance explains how loan interest rates are calculated, ensuring that applicants understand the financial commitments involved.

For projects led by Native American communities or involving tribal lands, the LPO offers specialized financing options through the **LPO Tribal Energy Financing** program. This initiative supports the development of clean energy projects that benefit Native American communities, providing both economic opportunities and environmental benefits.

The Road Ahead: Building the Future with LPO and IRA

The synergy between the LPO's financing programs and the IRA's incentives creates an unprecedented opportunity for American industry to lead the global transition to a sustainable future. In the context of the Voltage Valley Revolution™, these programs are not just financial tools but catalysts for change. They empower innovators, constructors, and operators to bring their visions to life, transforming the landscape of American manufacturing and setting the stage for a new era of industrial growth.

As we move forward, the resources and support offered by the DOE and the LPO will be instrumental in realizing the full potential of the Voltage Valley. These programs are designed to ensure that the clean energy transition benefits all Americans, particularly those in regions like Appalachia that have been historically underserved.

The Voltage Valley Revolution™ is more than a movement, it is a blueprint for the future. By leveraging the financial and regulatory support provided by the LPO and the IRA, we can build a sustainable, prosperous, and resilient American industry that serves as a model for the world. The journey will be challenging, but with the right tools and resources, we can create a better sustainable future for America.

The Department of Energy's (DOE) **Loan Programs Office** (LPO) provides access to debt capital for high-impact energy and manufacturing projects. Over more than a decade, LPO has developed a strong understanding of what makes a project more likely to advance through LPO's **processes**, as well as the areas that commonly slow down or stop projects in the process. The following tips suggest best practices for considering whether LPO **financing** could be the right choice and what to include or what to avoid when applying to work with LPO.

For additional details about these areas and many others, please refer to the **Getting to Know LPO** blog series. You may also want to learn more about the types of projects in LPO's **portfolio**, as well as the types of projects that are in LPO's **pipeline**. If you believe your project could be the right fit for a DOE loan or loan guarantee, submit an online request for a **pre-application consultation**.

Click here to learn more about how to get started on your CBP. To view all LPO projects, visit the **project map**.

www.ingramcontent.com/pod-product-compliance
Lightning Source LLC
Chambersburg PA
CBHW080438110426
42743CB00016B/3209